ISBN 978-1-3999-9024-0

Dedicated in loving memory to my Mum and Dad; one a Liverpudlian, one an Evertonian

In 1985, legendary Bayern Munich coach Udo Lattek described Howard Kendall's team as the best in Europe and, through no fault of their own, they didn't get the chance to prove it. Even before then, Everton's history was as illustrious as any in world football.

Sky Sports and the Premier League would have us believe that football began in 1992. Since then, the FA Cup success in 1995 apart, Everton have generally been also-rans, making up the fixtures and watching the 'bigger' clubs collect the trophies.

This book is for any Blues' fan who has grown up during the last thirty years and had to endure mostly on-field and off-field mediocrity. Read these pages, re-live the memories of Goodison Park and elsewhere, then look forward to the glory days returning to the club once more, only this time on the banks of the Royal Blue Mersey.

THE 80s TEAM

CONTENTS

"If you don't know history, then you don't know anything.
You are a leaf that doesn't know it is part of a tree."
Michael Crichton

Introduction

The BBC's teletext service Ceefax and its commercial equivalent, Oracle, first appeared on TV screens in the 1970s and they became the primary source of information for millions of people from the early 1980s onwards.

Some of you may not remember Oracle and be more familiar with its successor as, in 1992, the franchise to provide ITV's service was awarded to Teletext Limited and Oracle became, confusingly, Teletext, the same name as the medium itself.

Both services gave viewers free and immediate access to the very latest information in a pre-internet era where the only alternative was to wait for the next television or radio bulletin or buy a newspaper.

For those unfamiliar with the technology, the services worked by pressing in three numbers on your TV remote corresponding to the page you wanted to bring onto the screen. For example, on Oracle, the Football Index was page 140 and the top football story was on page 141.

The banners at the bottom of the page were generally used for advertising on Oracle and to promote other sections of the service on the non-commercial Ceefax service.

The Retrotext designs in this book are my tribute to teletext and similar ones featured in Rob Sloman's brilliant documentary about the Blues in the 1980s, *Everton, Howard's Way.*

You will see P141 in the top left-hand corner of all the pages, while the banners on the ones featuring Everton's League games show how the Blues were progressing during the season with details of games played, won drawn or lost, goals for and against, points tally and position in the table (P W D L F A Pts Pos).

The four coloured words/phrases at the very bottom of each page were known as fastext links and gave the viewer quicker access to that information than would be the case when keying in the relevant three-digit page number.

The beauty of Ceefax and Oracle was that while you were reading a match report about Everton beating Bayern Munich or winning the FA Cup against Watford, you could still hear the programme being broadcast on BBC or ITV - whether it was Only Fools And Horses or Coronation Street - and could switch back to whatever you had been watching immediately at the push of a button.

During the halcyon days of the mid-1980s, Evertonians, like all football fans, relied on Ceefax and Oracle for the latest football scores and breaking news, with many a transfer rumour quashed with the words, "Well, there's nothing about it on teletext." Though the one about Gary Lineker proved to be right!

As teletext pages were updated almost continuously each day, the content wasn't saved but there are enthusiasts able to retrieve them from the videotape used to record TV programmes so that future generations can view them.

The two pages above and those featured on other pages were recovered in this way.

ITV's Teletext, the successor to Oracle, ceased broadcasting in 2009 and BBC's Ceefax in 2012, though there are still some active and popular teletext services in Europe even to this day.

The book's title derives from the hugely popular TV show *The A Team* broadcast between 1983 and 1987. Everton and teletext have both played a big part in my life and it has been enjoyable to have the opportunity to bring the two of them together.

One: 1983-1984
EVERTON FC*

HOWARD KENDALL - MANAGER

COLIN HARVEY - COACH

MICK HEATON - COACH

JOHN CLINKARD - PHYSIO

ADRIAN HEATH

ALAN IRVINE

ALAN HARPER

ANDY GRAY

ANDY KING

DAVID JOHNSON

DEREK MOUNTFIELD

GARY STEVENS

GRAEME SHARP

JIM ARNOLD

JOHN BAILEY

KEVIN RATCLIFFE

KEVIN RICHARDSON

KEVIN SHEEDY

MARK HIGGINS

NEVILLE SOUTHALL

PETER REID

TREVOR STEVEN

*as at the start of the season plus Andy Gray who joined in November

August to December 1983

At the end of the 1981-82 campaign, the club had finished in a modest eighth place in the League, were beaten in the fourth round of the League Cup by Ipswich Town and went out in the third round of the FA Cup to West Ham.

The lowest point of the following 1982-83 season was the infamous 5-0 hammering by Liverpool at Goodison Park with Ian Rush scoring four and on-loan defender Glen Keeley being sent off after twenty minutes, in his first and only game for the Blues.

Everton did recover to finish in seventh spot but there was disappointment in the FA Cup as Kendall's side lost in the quarter-final of the FA Cup to an 89th minute winner from Manchester United's Frank Stapleton at Old Trafford.

One of the brightest spots during that campaign was the form of Kevin Sheedy in his first season at the club after signing from Liverpool. Sheedy scored thirteen goals for the Blues earning him the Supporters' Club Player Of The Year Award.

As the 1983-84 season approached, only two of 'The Magnificent Seven' players brought in by Kendall when he first took over were still at the club, goalkeepers Jim Arnold and Neville Southall. Among the new faces were Trevor Steven and Alan Harper.

Howard Kendall signed Steven from newly-relegated Burnley for £300,000, while local lad Alan Harper moved from Liverpool for an initial fee of £30,000 plus a further £30,000 after 30 first-team appearances.

But the campaign began poorly with the Blues finding goals hard to come by and on November 6th the team suffered another hammering by League leaders Liverpool, this time 3-0 at Anfield.

Kendall's side languished in seventeenth spot in the table on fifteen points from twelve games and having scored just seven goals.

A member of Everton's famed 'Holy Trinity' of Ball Harvey Kendall which had won the League title in style in season 1969-70, Howard Kendall was appointed Everton player-manager in May 1981, succeeding Gordon Lee, and tasked with bringing the glory days back to the club.

Kendall set about transforming the squad and signed no less than seven players during that summer:

Strikers Mick Ferguson from Coventry City and Alan Biley from Derby County, midfielders Alan Ainscow from Birmingham City and Mickey Thomas from Manchester United (with John Gidman moving to Old Trafford), defender Mike Walsh from Bolton Wanderers, goalkeepers Jim Arnold from Blackburn and Neville Southall from Bury.

On Saturday 29th August 1981, the Kendall era began with a 3-1 home success against Birmingham City with goals from Ainscow, Peter Eastoe and Biley.

It's A Grand Old Team To Play For

Howard Kendall was signed by Everton boss Harry Catterick for a fee of £80,000 in March 1967, much to the dismay of Liverpool manager Bill Shankly who had been a long-term admirer.

He joined the club the day before the famous FA Cup tie with Liverpool which was watched by 64,851 fans at Goodison and another 40,149 via CCTV at Anfield, but was ineligible to play and made his debut a week later against Southampton.

Howard was a key member of the team which won the Division One League title in 1969-70 and was part of the revered midfield trio of Ball Harvey Kendall. He was transferred to Birmingham in 1974 as part of the deal which brought Bob Latchford to Goodison Park.

August to December 1983

Three days later, on Wednesday 9th November, it was confirmed that Colin Harvey was being promoted to first team coach as a result of the hugely impressive start to the season by his reserves side which had won all eight games, scoring twenty-one goals without reply.

That evening, the Blues enjoyed a come from behind victory over Coventry City in a League Cup tie, inspired by the introduction of Peter Reid as a sixty-ninth minute substitute, with Adrian Heath equalising and Graeme Sharp scoring a last gasp winner.

The following day brought more positive headlines, with news that Everton were seeking to sign Andy Gray from Wolves to bolster the club's attacking options.

The Scottish striker had been the most expensive player in English football in 1979 when he joined Wolves from Aston Villa for £1.5 million but he had endured injury problems and Howard Kendall was able to secure his services for a bargain £250,000.

It was a similar scenario with Peter Reid, who previous Blues boss Gordon Lee had tried to sign from Bolton Wanderers for £600,000 in 1980 but who Kendall brought to the club a week before Christmas in 1982 for £60,000.

Reid and Gray were both in the side which beat Nottingham Forest at Goodison Park that weekend, Adrian Heath with the solitary goal, but this was followed by an away defeat at Arsenal and a home loss to Norwich City.

On the last day of November, Kendall's side drew 2-2 at Upton Park in a fourth round League Cup tie, winning the replay a week later on home soil thanks to extra-time goals from Andy King and Kevin Sheedy.

Sandwiched between those two matches was an impressive 1-0 League win at Old Trafford, Sheedy again on target, but this upturn in results was short-lived.

A home draw with Aston Villa was followed by a 2-0 defeat at QPR and entering the Christmas period – when the team faced three games in six days – Everton were a lowly sixteenth in the table.

On Boxing Day, the Blues drew 0-0 with Sunderland at Goodison but the following day saw a crushing 3-0 defeat away at bottom club Wolves.

On December 31st, 13,659 fans watched as Everton played out a dismal 0-0 draw with Coventry City to increase the pressure still further on the manager.

Club Chairman Philip Carter was forced to quash rumours that Kendall was to be replaced - the Wales manager Mike England was one of the names being mentioned.

So, as 1983 gave way to 1984, the manager's future and that of his players was shrouded in uncertainty and it was imperative that they got the New Year off to a winning start.

It's A Grand Old Team To Play For

In September 1963, Colin Harvey famously made his debut for Everton in the European Cup at the San Siro stadium in Milan against Internazionale, aged just 18. He earned plaudits for his mature performance but, after a 0-0 draw in the first leg at Goodison, the Blues lost 1-0 to the Italian side on the night.

Colin only made two further appearances in the first team that season but he then became a regular. Though never a prolific goalscorer, he hit the winner for Everton in the 1966 FA Cup semi-final against Manchester United and was also on target when the Blues clinched the 1969-70 Division One title, rifling the ball home from 25 yards.

He joined Sheffield Wednesday in 1974 but returned to the club in a coaching capacity two years later.

January 1984

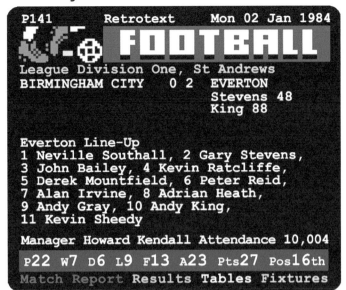

```
P141      Retrotext      Mon 02 Jan 1984
        FOOTBALL
League Division One, St Andrews
BIRMINGHAM CITY     0 2    EVERTON
                           Stevens 48
                           King 88

Everton Line-Up
1 Neville Southall, 2 Gary Stevens,
3 John Bailey, 4 Kevin Ratcliffe,
5 Derek Mountfield, 6 Peter Reid,
7 Alan Irvine, 8 Adrian Heath,
9 Andy Gray, 10 Andy King,
11 Kevin Sheedy

Manager Howard Kendall Attendance 10,004
P22 W7 D6 L9 F13 A23 Pts27 Pos16th
Match Report Results Tables Fixtures
```

```
P141      Retrotext      Sat 07 Jan 1984
        FOOTBALL
FA Cup 3rd Round, Victoria Ground
STOKE CITY          0 2    EVERTON
                           Gray 66
                           Irvine 84

Everton Line-Up
1 Neville Southall, 2 Gary Stevens,
3 John Bailey, 4 Kevin Ratcliffe,
5 Derek Mountfield, 6 Peter Reid,
7 Alan Irvine, 8 Adrian Heath,
9 Graeme Sharp, 10 Andy Gray,
11 Kevin Sheedy

Manager Howard Kendall Attendance 16,462
      Nil Satis Nisi Optimum
Match Report Results Tables Fixtures
```

These two teams were the lowest scorers in the entire division, with Birmingham on seventeen goals and Everton a woeful eleven in twenty-one games.

In dreadful conditions, the Blues managed to start 1984 on the front foot with a victory at St Andrews, scoring two goals in a League game for only the second time that season.

Gary Stevens and Andy King were the ones on the score-sheet but the Blues were also thankful for a string of fine saves at crucial moments in the game by Neville Southall.

Southall had started the campaign as second choice goalkeeper with Jim Arnold, who Kendall had signed from his previous club Blackburn, preferred for the first seven games.

But the big Welshman's reputation was growing and his form led Arnold to lodge a transfer request a couple of days before the FA Cup third round clash with Stoke City which Kendall rejected.

Pat van den Hauwe was in the Birmingham team this day and obviously created a strong impression as the Blues signed the left-full back at the start of the following season.

The victory eased some of the pressure which had been building up on Kendall ahead of a tricky FA Cup tie.

Andy Gray and Graeme Sharp had played only one game together since Gray's transfer, the impressive League win at Old Trafford at the end of November.

Kendall was delighted that Sharp had recovered from an ankle injury which had kept him out for six games so he could reunite the duo for this third round tie at Stoke City, who had recently sacked their manager Richie Barker.

Like Everton, Stoke were struggling for goals and their caretaker boss Bill Asprey had been weighing up a move for ex-Blue Bob Latchford as a possible solution but ultimately a deal didn't happen.

Andy Gray broke the deadlock with a superb flying header on sixty-six minutes and the Blues booked their place in the fourth round with an Alan Irvine goal six minutes from the end.

After the match, Howard Kendall paid tribute to the travelling Everton fans, saying: "As we sat in the dressing room before the game, I opened the window. The noise which came in was deafening. It was far more inspirational than any team talk I could have given.""

The only sour note to the victory was an injury to Gary Stevens which threatened his participation in the League Cup quarter-final against Oxford United the following week.

If You Know Your History

This was Everton's first game in the newly-formed Football League, which originally consisted of six clubs from Lancashire (Preston North End, Accrington, Blackburn Rovers, Burnley, Bolton Wanderers and Everton) and six from the Midlands (Aston Villa, Derby County, Notts County, Stoke, West Bromwich Albion and Wolverhampton Wanderers).

At the end of this campaign, Preston were the first winners of the League championship, finishing eleven points ahead of Aston Villa with Everton in eighth place. The following season, Preston won the title again with Everton in second spot just two points behind and in 1890-91 the Blues would be crowned champions for the first time.

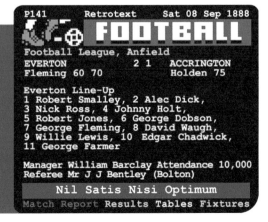

```
P141      Retrotext      Sat 08 Sep 1888
        FOOTBALL
Football League, Anfield
EVERTON           2 1    ACCRINGTON
Fleming 60 70            Holden 75

Everton Line-Up
1 Robert Smalley, 2 Alec Dick,
3 Nick Ross, 4 Johnny Holt,
5 Robert Jones, 6 George Dobson,
7 George Fleming, 8 David Waugh,
9 Willie Lewis, 10 Edgar Chadwick,
11 George Farmer

Manager William Barclay Attendance 10,000
Referee Mr J J Bentley (Bolton)
      Nil Satis Nisi Optimum
Match Report Results Tables Fixtures
```

January 1984

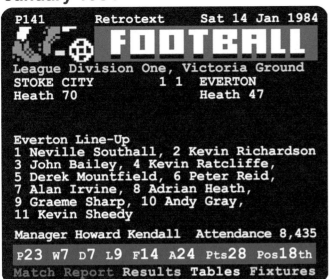

```
P141      Retrotext      Sat 14 Jan 1984
       FOOTBALL
League Division One, Victoria Ground
STOKE CITY          1  1     EVERTON
Heath 70                     Heath 47


Everton Line-Up
1 Neville Southall, 2 Kevin Richardson
3 John Bailey, 4 Kevin Ratcliffe,
5 Derek Mountfield, 6 Peter Reid,
7 Alan Irvine, 8 Adrian Heath,
9 Graeme Sharp, 10 Andy Gray,
11 Kevin Sheedy
Manager Howard Kendall  Attendance 8,435
P23 W7 D7 L9 F14 A24 Pts28 Pos18th
Match Report Results Tables Fixtures
```

```
P141      Retrotext      Wed 18 Jan 1984
       FOOTBALL
League Cup Quarter-Final,Manor Ground
OXFORD UNITED       1  1     EVERTON
McDonald 47                  Heath 81


Everton Line-Up
1 Neville Southall, 2 Gary Stevens,
3 Alan Harper, 4 Kevin Ratcliffe,
5 Derek Mountfield, 6 Peter Reid,
7 Alan Irvine, 8 Adrian Heath,
9 Graeme Sharp, 10 David Johnson
(Kevin Richardson), 11 Kevin Sheedy
Manager Howard Kendall Attendance 14,333
Nil Satis Nisi Optimum
Match Report Results Tables Fixtures
```

In the draw for the fourth round of the FA Cup, Everton were paired with third division Gillingham who had beaten Brentford 5-3 in their tie after having seemed on the verge of elimination from the competition when trailing 1-3 with just fourteen minutes left.

On the run-up to a return to the Potteries in a League game, there was encouraging news on the injury front with Terry Curran able to return to light training after a four-month absence due to a thigh problem.

Signed for £90,000 from Sheffield Utd in September (having been on loan with the Blues for a month the season before), Curran suffered the injury against West Brom the same month.

As expected, Gary Stevens was not in the starting line-up and his place was taken by Kevin Richardson, with Andy King on the bench.

Former Stoke star Adrian Heath put the Blues ahead, but it was another Heath, the home side's Phil, who levelled things up with his first goal for the club.

There was a health scare for 'Inchy' ahead of the midweek League Cup clash with Oxford United when he was sent home from training after complaining of a sore throat.

Oxford United had smashed their gate receipts record in the previous round of the League Cup against Manchester United, a tie they won 2-1 after extra time in a second replay, having already beaten Newcastle and Leeds.

Another cash bonanza for the third division giantkillers loomed as a full house of almost 15,000 was expected for this quarter-final clash.

Controversially, the club, then chaired by media magnate Robert Maxwell, had raised their ticket prices from £3 for the United game to £4 for a terrace place for this one but 2,900 Evertonians were undeterred.

Oxford went ahead through Bobby McDonald, the same player having scored twice to knock the Blues out of the FA Cup at the quarter-final stage in 1981 when at Manchester City.

The Blues took off David Johnson and replaced him with Kevin Richardson, allowing Adrian Heath to push further forward.

It was Inchy who carved his name into Everton folklore with nine minutes left as he pounced on Kevin Brock's back pass, rounded the keeper and curled the ball home to earn a replay for the visitors at Goodison Park the following week.

If You Know Your History

Everton had the opportunity to clinch their first League title as early as January 10th in their penultimate match of the season against defending champions Preston at Anfield, but the visitors won 1-0. Due to bad weather, Everton didn't play their final game until March.

Preston were on course to win their third League title until a 6-2 loss at Burnley a week before this game. This meant they could now only match Everton's tally of 29 points and the destination of the title could be decided on goal average. However, Preston were unable to take advantage of Everton's defeat as they lost 3-0 at Sunderland. The famous League Championship trophy was presented to the champions for the first time and Everton were the proud recipients.

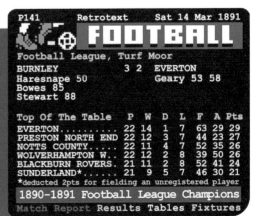

```
P141      Retrotext      Sat 14 Mar 1891
       FOOTBALL
Football League, Turf Moor
BURNLEY             3  2     EVERTON
Haresnape 50                 Geary 53 58
Bowes 85
Stewart 88

Top Of The Table    P  W  D  L  F  A Pts
EVERTON.......... 22 14  1  7 63 29 29
PRESTON NORTH END 22 12  3  7 44 23 27
NOTTS COUNTY..... 22 11  4  7 52 35 26
WOLVERHAMPTON W.. 22 12  2  8 39 50 26
BLACKBURN ROVERS. 21 11  2  8 52 41 24
SUNDERLAND*...... 22  9  5  7 46 30 21
*deducted 2pts for fielding an unregistered player
1890-1891 Football League Champions
Match Report Results Tables Fixtures
```

January 1984

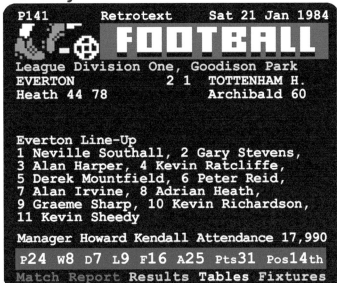

```
P141      Retrotext      Sat 21 Jan 1984
       FOOTBALL
League Division One, Goodison Park
EVERTON         2 1    TOTTENHAM H.
Heath 44 78            Archibald 60

Everton Line-Up
1 Neville Southall, 2 Gary Stevens,
3 Alan Harper, 4 Kevin Ratcliffe,
5 Derek Mountfield, 6 Peter Reid,
7 Alan Irvine, 8 Adrian Heath,
9 Graeme Sharp, 10 Kevin Richardson,
11 Kevin Sheedy
Manager Howard Kendall Attendance 17,990
P24 W8 D7 L9 F16 A25 Pts31 Pos14th
Match Report Results Tables Fixtures
```

```
P141    Retrotext.uk  Tue 24 Jan 1984
       FOOTBALL
League Cup Quarter-Final Replay,
Goodison Park
EVERTON            4 1   OXFORD UNITED
Richardson 7             Hinshelwood 89
Sheedy 34
Heath 52
Sharp 90
Everton Line-Up
1 Neville Southall, 2 Gary Stevens,
3 Alan Harper, 4 Kevin Ratcliffe,
5 Derek Mountfield, 6 Peter Reid,
7 Alan Irvine, 8 Adrian Heath,
9 Graeme Sharp, 10 Kevin Richardson,
11 Kevin Sheedy Manager Howard Kendall
         Nil Satis Nisi Optimum
Match Report Results Tables Fixtures
```

After the League Cup semi-final draw was made, the dream of a first-ever all-Merseyside Final at Wembley was still alive.

Having drawn 2-2 at Hillsborough, Liverpool would have to beat Sheffield Wednesday in a replay to face Walsall while the Blues would play Aston Villa if they overcame Oxford.

Cup-tied for the Oxford game, Andy Gray had been expected to return to the starting eleven in place of David Johnson, but the Scottish striker succumbed late on to a viral infection.

The Blues had beaten Tottenham 2-1 earlier in the season at White Hart Lane and they picked up all three points in this match after coming out on top by the same scoreline.

Adrian Heath was again the hero with a couple of goals and Neville Southall once more excelled between the posts with a string of great saves.

There were clear signs that Inchy was throwing off the burden of being the club's record signing and, after the match, manager Howard Kendall said:

"I am absolutely delighted for him. I think that everyone has always agreed that he is a very good player and now they are seeing the best of him. He is playing with confidence and looking sharp."

Following Adrian Heath's dramatic equaliser the week before, Everton finished off giant-killers Oxford United in blizzard conditions at Goodison Park.

The visitors were never really in this replay after Kevin Richardson put the Blues 1-0 up early on and it was 2-0 just after the half-hour mark when Peter Reid set up Kevin Sheedy.

In the second half, Inchy was on target again to record his fifth goal in four games and after Paul Hinshelwood thundered home from 20 yards, Graeme Sharp lobbed the keeper to make the final score 4-1.

The victory set up a two-legged semi-final clash with Aston Villa, bringing back memories of the epic 1977 League Cup Final between the clubs.

After a 0-0 draw at Wembley and another stalemate at Hillsborough when Bob Latchford levelled Roger Kenyon's own goal in the dying seconds, the match was settled in Villa's favour in agonising fashion at Old Trafford following a five-goal thriller.

As Howard Kendall prepared his side for a fourth round FA Cup tie with Gillingham at the weekend, there was good news on the injury front, with Terry Curran back in full training and lined up for a reserve team outing the following week.

If You Know Your History

Having left Anfield, Everton celebrated the opening of their new ground at Goodison Park with a 4-2 friendly win over Bolton Wanderers the day before this first competitive match of the season in the newly-expanded first division of the Football League.

The match report in the Liverpool Mercury newspaper said: "It is as certain as light succeeds darkness that Goodison Park has 'caught on' and is as popular as ever the old battle ground at Anfield Road was in its halcyon days. Yes, Everton is now more than ever the town's club, despite all attempts at its dethronement."

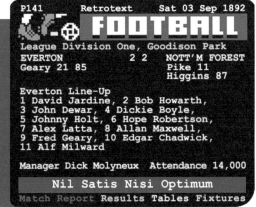

```
P141     Retrotext     Sat 03 Sep 1892
       FOOTBALL
League Division One, Goodison Park
EVERTON         2 2    NOTT'M FOREST
Geary 21 85            Pike 11
                       Higgins 87
Everton Line-Up
1 David Jardine, 2 Bob Howarth,
3 John Dewar, 4 Dickie Boyle,
5 Johnny Holt, 6 Hope Robertson,
7 Alex Latta, 8 Allan Maxwell,
9 Fred Geary, 10 Edgar Chadwick,
11 Alf Milward

Manager Dick Molyneux  Attendance 14,000
         Nil Satis Nisi Optimum
Match Report Results Tables Fixtures
```

February 1984

```
P141      Retrotext      Sat 04 Feb 1984
        FOOTBALL
League Division One, Goodison Park
EVERTON           4  1  NOTTS COUNTY
Heath 26 38 68            McParland 8(pen)
Sheedy 28(pen)

Everton Line-Up
1 Neville Southall, 2 Gary Stevens,
3 John Bailey, 4 Kevin Ratcliffe,
5 Derek Mountfield, 6 Peter Reid,
7 Alan Irvine, 8 Adrian Heath,
9 Andy Gray, 10 Kevin Richardson
11 Kevin Sheedy

Manager Howard Kendall Attendance 13,191
P25 W9 D7 L9 F20 A26 Pts34 Pos14th
Match Report Results Tables Fixtures
```

```
P141      Retrotext      Mon 06 Feb 1984
        FOOTBALL
FA Cup 4th Round 2nd Replay,
Priestfield Stadium
GILLINGHAM        0  3  EVERTON
                        Sheedy 27 38
                        Heath 33

Everton Line-Up
1 Neville Southall, 2 Gary Stevens,
3 John Bailey, 4 Kevin Ratcliffe,
5 Derek Mountfield, 6 Peter Reid,
7 Alan Irvine, 8 Adrian Heath,
9 Andy Gray, 10 Kevin Richardson,
11 Kevin Sheedy

Manager Howard Kendall Attendance 17,817
         Nil Satis Nisi Optimum
Match Report Results Tables Fixtures
```

Having been on the bench for the midweek FA Cup replay at Gillingham, Andy Gray was restored to the starting line-up for this Division One clash with Notts County.

But it was his strike partner Adrian Heath who won the plaudits again with the first hat-trick of his career that took his goals tally to eight in seven games, though in front of the lowest League gate of the season at Goodison.

The victory stretched Everton's unbeaten run to ten matches, having last lost on December 27th to bottom club Wolverhampton Wanderers.

Belief was growing in the team and Inchy said after the game "We got two goals against Spurs, four against Oxford and another four goals against County so maybe we have turned the corner."

The increasing confidence also fed through to the fans with the chants on the terraces ringing out of...

"Tell me Ma, me Ma, I don't want no tea, no tea, We're going to Wem-be-lee, tell me Ma, me Ma"

and the equally enchanting...

"Tell me Ma, me Ma, to put the champagne on ice, We're going to Wembley twice, tell me Ma, me Ma"

On the face of it, the FA Cup fourth round draw had been kind to the Blues with a home tie on the 28th January against Gillingham, two divisions below them.

Though the Blues largely dominated that match, the visitors did have chances but ultimately it ended 0-0, forcing a replay at the Priestfield Stadium three days later in front of a packed house.

Not for the first or last time, Neville Southall was the Blues hero in the first replay, producing a string of top saves to earn Kendall's men another attempt to see off their rivals.

Everton chairman Philip Carter lost the toss for choice of venue and so the Blues were away from home in the second replay the following week.

In stormy conditions, the Blues finally showed the gulf in class between the two sides in this match with three first-half goals in a devastating ten-minute period, two from Kevin Sheedy and yet another from Adrian Heath, taking his total to nine in eight games.

In the fifth round draw, Howard Kendall's side had been paired with second division Shrewsbury, but after the struggle to get the better of Gillingham, there would certainly be no complacency from him or the players.

If You Know Your History

This was an historic day as it saw the first-ever Merseyside derby and such was the interest amongst the local population that a new gate receipt record of £1,026 was set. The Liverpool Mercury newspaper speculated that for a sum like that to have been achieved the attendance must have been around 40,000.

The first goal was headed in by Tom McInnes but his day would be cut short as he would have to leave the field with an injury later in the half. The home side went 2-0 up after Alex Latta converted a cross from Jack Bell and it was Bell himself who rounded off the win when he found the back of the net two minutes from time.

```
P141      Retrotext      Sat 13 Oct 1894
        FOOTBALL
League Division One, Goodison Park
EVERTON           3  0  LIVERPOOL
McInnes 10
Latta 60
Bell 88

Everton Line-Up
1 Tom Cain, 2 Jimmy Adams, 3 Charlie
Parry, 4 Dickie Boyle, 5 Johnny Holt,
6 Billy Stewart, 7 Alex Latta, 8 Tom
McInnes, 9 Jack Southworth,
10 Abe Hartley, 11 Jack Bell

Manager Dick Molyneux Attendance 40,000
         Nil Satis Nisi Optimum
Match Report Results Tables Fixtures
```

February 1984

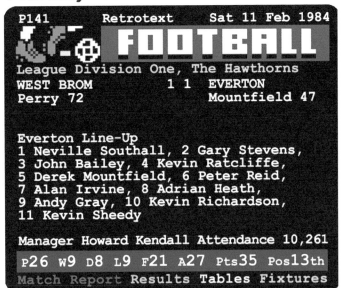

```
P141        Retrotext      Sat 11 Feb 1984
    FOOTBALL
League Division One, The Hawthorns
WEST BROM         1  1    EVERTON
Perry 72                  Mountfield 47


Everton Line-Up
1 Neville Southall, 2 Gary Stevens,
3 John Bailey, 4 Kevin Ratcliffe,
5 Derek Mountfield, 6 Peter Reid,
7 Alan Irvine, 8 Adrian Heath,
9 Andy Gray, 10 Kevin Richardson,
11 Kevin Sheedy

Manager Howard Kendall Attendance 10,261
P26 W9 D8 L9 F21 A27 Pts35 Pos13th
Match Report Results Tables Fixtures
```

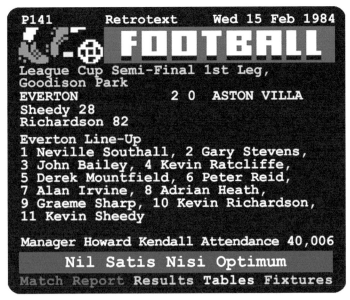

```
P141        Retrotext      Wed 15 Feb 1984
    FOOTBALL
League Cup Semi-Final 1st Leg,
Goodison Park
EVERTON           2  0    ASTON VILLA
Sheedy 28
Richardson 82
Everton Line-Up
1 Neville Southall, 2 Gary Stevens,
3 John Bailey, 4 Kevin Ratcliffe,
5 Derek Mountfield, 6 Peter Reid,
7 Alan Irvine, 8 Adrian Heath,
9 Graeme Sharp, 10 Kevin Richardson,
11 Kevin Sheedy

Manager Howard Kendall Attendance 40,006
Nil Satis Nisi Optimum
Match Report Results Tables Fixtures
```

West Brom had been beaten 5-0 by Nottingham Forest in midweek and lost both strikers Cyrille Regis and Gary Thompson to injury, but they proved tough opponents for the Blues who nevertheless extended their unbeaten run to twelve.

The match is perhaps most notable for the fact that Derek Mountfield scored his first goal for the club, not surprisingly a powerful header from a pin-point Kevin Sheedy cross just after half-time. To their credit, the home side responded well to going behind to force an equaliser.

Ahead of a big week of Cup football for the Blues, there were no new injury scares with the same starting eleven expected to face Aston Villa in the midweek League Cup semi-final, apart from Graeme Sharp replacing the ineligible Andy Gray.

With that match in mind, Howard Kendall named Trevor Steven instead of Sharp as the substitute against West Brom to ensure his young striker would be available to start.

With a large crowd expected, Kendall said: "It will be a tremendous night. The fans can play a big part in this first leg. We need to be patient but everyone is aware of the rewards. The lads are determined to give the supporters that long-awaited success."

This first leg tie had been delayed by a week due to Everton's second replay in the FA Cup against Gillingham and the Blues knew who waited them in the Final – local rivals Liverpool who beat Walsall.

Centre-forward for the visitors was scouser Peter Withe, a lifelong Evertonian who almost signed for the Blues in 1980 when Gordon Lee was manager. He chose Villa as he felt they had a better chance of winning trophies and his decision was vindicated as the club won the League title in 1981 then the European Cup, Withe scoring the winning goal.

On twenty-minutes, Aston Villa goalkeeper Nigel Spink was caught out by a cross from Kevin Sheedy which took a slight deflection and somehow ended up in his net to give the Blues the lead.

Eight minutes from time Kevin Richardson grabbed a valuable second goal when he drove the ball into the net despite having played for more than half the game with what turned out to be a fractured and dislocated wrist.

Richardson was also involved in late drama when Villa players claimed they should have been awarded a penalty after he handled a shot from Gary Shaw on the line. But the referee disagreed and the visitors didn't get the chance to narrow Everton's advantage ahead of the second leg.

If You Know Your History

Everton had lost two previous FA Cup Finals, in 1893 to Wolves and 1897 to Aston Villa, so it was third time lucky in 1906.

On the road to the Final, the Blues had beaten Liverpool 2-0 in the semi-final at Villa Park, courtesy of two goals in two minutes midway through the second half from Walter Abbott and Harold Hardman. Sandy Young had already had a goal ruled out for offside in this match but struck again fifteen minutes from time.

The President of the FA, Lord Kinnaird, presented the trophy to captain Jack Taylor and also offered his condolences to the people of San Francisco after the devastating earthquake a few days before.

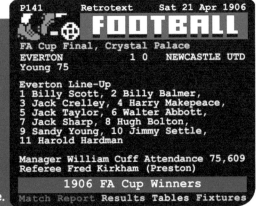

```
P141        Retrotext      Sat 21 Apr 1906
    FOOTBALL
FA Cup Final, Crystal Palace
EVERTON           1  0    NEWCASTLE UTD
Young 75

Everton Line-Up
1 Billy Scott, 2 Billy Balmer,
3 Jack Crelley, 4 Harry Makepeace,
5 Jack Taylor, 6 Walter Abbott,
7 Jack Sharp, 8 Hugh Bolton,
9 Sandy Young, 10 Jimmy Settle,
11 Harold Hardman

Manager William Cuff Attendance 75,609
Referee Fred Kirkham (Preston)
1906 FA Cup Winners
Match Report Results Tables Fixtures
```

February 1984

```
P141        Retrotext     Sat 18 Feb 1984
█▛◉ FOOTBALL
FA Cup 5th Round, Goodison Park
EVERTON            3 0  SHREWSBURY TOWN
Irvine 29
Reid 61
Griffin 85(og)

Everton Line-Up
1 Neville Southall, 2 Gary Stevens,
3 John Bailey, 4 Kevin Ratcliffe,
5 Derek Mountfield, 6 Peter Reid,
7 Alan Irvine, 8 Adrian Heath (Graeme
Sharp), 9 Andy Gray, 10 Andy King,
11 Kevin Sheedy

Manager Howard Kendall Attendance 27,106
        Nil Satis Nisi Optimum
Match Report Results Tables Fixtures
```

```
P141        Retrotext     Wed 22 Feb 1984
█▛◉ FOOTBALL
League Cup Semi-Final 2nd Leg,
Villa Park
ASTON VILLA         1 0   EVERTON
Rideout 62         (1 2)

Everton Line-Up
1 Neville Southall, 2 Gary Stevens,
3 John Bailey, 4 Kevin Ratcliffe,
5 Derek Mountfield, 6 Peter Reid,
7 Alan Irvine, 8 Adrian Heath,
9 Graeme Sharp, 10 Andy King,
11 Kevin Sheedy

Manager Howard Kendall Attendance 42,426
        Nil Satis Nisi Optimum
Match Report Results Tables Fixtures
```

Second division Shrewsbury Town had caused a shock in the fourth round by knocking out Bobby Robson's Ipswich Town 2-0 at Gay Meadow.

But having struggled to beat third division Gillingham in the previous round, Howard Kendall's men made no mistake in this one.

Transfer-listed Andy King replaced the injured Kevin Richardson and Andy Gray started in place of Graeme Sharp.

Alan Irvine gave the home side a 1-0 half-time lead and it was his pass which allowed Peter Reid to double the advantage on the hour mark, while an own goal five minutes from time ensured the Blues would be in the draw for the sixth round.

As usual at the time, the draw took place on Monday afternoon, with Everton drawn away at Notts County, a team they had already beaten twice this season, 1-0 at Meadow Lane and 4-1 at Goodison just a couple of weeks earlier.

High-flying Southampton had been installed by bookmakers as favourites to lift the trophy in May at odds of 11/4, with Everton available at 4/1 together with Watford, Sheffield Wednesday 11/2, Birmingham City 6/1, Notts County 8/1, Derby County 20/1 and Plymouth Argyle 33/1.

Everton had sold their full allocation of tickets for the second leg of the League Cup semi-final which could see the first-ever all-Merseyside Cup Final.

Kevin Richardson was ruled out due to his wrist injury on medical advice while the cup-tied Andy Gray (he had played 90 minutes for Wolves back in October) was replaced by Graeme Sharp.

As expected, it was a hard-fought second leg which could have been made easier had first half strikes from Adrian Heath and Graeme Sharp not hit the woodwork.

Transfer-listed Andy King, the only member of the team to have played in the 1977 League Cup Final against Villa, was restored to the line-up.

Paul Rideout, who would later join the Blues and is fondly remembered for his winning goal in the 1995 FA Cup Final against Manchester United, was introduced as a second half substitute by Villa boss Tony Barton.

He latched on to the unfortunate King's attempted backpass to pull a goal back just minutes after coming on and ensure a nervy finale.

But the Blues deservedly held on to set up the dream Final at Wembley, even though this was their first loss of the year.

If You Know Your History

Despite the country being at war with Germany from August, the 1914-15 football season was played out in full. The argument in favour of carrying on was that it would keep up morale as well as provide opportunities for recruitment and fund-raising, but many critics were appalled at the continuation while soldiers were dying.

With three games of the campaign left, Oldham topped the table three points ahead of Everton. But a draw and two successive home defeats (one to Liverpool) coupled with back-to-back wins for the Blues, swung the pendulum in Everton's favour and this draw with Chelsea confirmed the club as champions for the second time, having also won the title in season 1890-91.

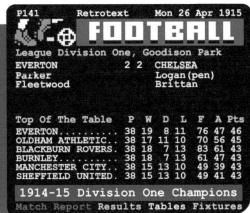

```
P141        Retrotext     Mon 26 Apr 1915
█▛◉ FOOTBALL
League Division One, Goodison Park
EVERTON            2 2  CHELSEA
Parker                  Logan(pen)
Fleetwood               Brittan

Top Of The Table    P  W  D  L  F  A Pts
EVERTON..........  38 19  8 11 76 47 46
OLDHAM ATHLETIC..  38 17 11 10 70 56 45
BLACKBURN ROVERS.  38 18  7 13 83 61 43
BURNLEY..........  38 18  7 13 61 47 43
MANCHESTER CITY..  38 15 13 10 49 39 43
SHEFFIELD UNITED.  38 15 13 10 49 41 43
    1914-15 Division One Champions
Match Report Results Tables Fixtures
```

February 1984

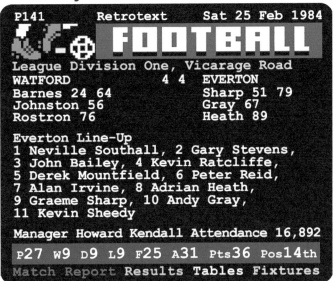

```
P141      Retrotext       Sat 25 Feb 1984
              FOOTBALL
League Division One, Vicarage Road
WATFORD            4  4  EVERTON
Barnes 24 64           Sharp 51 79
Johnston 56            Gray 67
Rostron 76             Heath 89

Everton Line-Up
1 Neville Southall, 2 Gary Stevens,
3 John Bailey, 4 Kevin Ratcliffe,
5 Derek Mountfield, 6 Peter Reid,
7 Alan Irvine, 8 Adrian Heath,
9 Graeme Sharp, 10 Andy Gray,
11 Kevin Sheedy

Manager Howard Kendall Attendance 16,892

P27 W9 D9 L9 F25 A31 Pts36 Pos14th
Match Report Results Tables Fixtures
```

```
P133 CEEFAX 133  Sat 30 Aug  23 19/04
BBC
SPORTS   Football
NEWS....
      FIRST DIVISION TABLE (top half)

                   Home       Away
               P W D L F A W D L F A Pts
Manchester U.  4 2 1 0 6 2 2 0 0 4 2  7
West Ham       4 2 0 0 4 2 1 1 0 4 3  7
Coventry       4 1 1 0 3 1 1 1 0 5 2  6
QPR            4 1 1 0 30 1 1 0 7 3  6
Newcastle      4 1 1 0 4 1 1 0 1 5 3  5
Middlesbrough  4 2 0 0 3 0 0 1 1 2 5  5
Arsenal        4 1 0 1 2 2 1 1 0 3 1  5
Liverpool      4 1 1 0 5 4 1 0 1 3 2  5
Everton        4 1 0 1 4 4 1 1 0 2 1  5
Leeds          4 1 0 0 1 3 1 1 0 3 1  5
Stoke          4 0 1 1 3 4 1 1 0 2 1  4

(not including today'sgames)    A B C D
```

The only injury doubt coming into this match was Neville Southall, who had injured his eye in an accidental clash with Villa's centre-forward Peter Withe during the week, but he was passed fit.

Everton had been in tremendous form in 1984 with the reverse at Villa their only loss, but their opponents on this day were also flying.

Graham Taylor's men had won ten of their last twelve games and seven on the bounce at Vicarage Road. Like the Blues, they had also reached the FA Cup quarter-finals, beating Liverpool's conquerors Brighton along the way.

Though he had played well in midweek against Aston Villa, apart from his errant backpass which led to the Villa goal, Andy King was left out of the side by Howard Kendall so Andy Gray could return.

In-form Watford led 1-0 at the break thanks to a John Barnes goal and though Graeme Sharp equalised, the Blues soon found themselves 3-1 down after Mo Johnston and Barnes again struck.

Andy Gray made it 3-2 mid-way through the second half but Wilf Rostron looked to have secured the points fourteen minutes from the end only for Sharp to notch his second and Adrian Heath to grab a last-gasp equaliser.

This is an original Ceefax page recovered from an old VHS recording. The corruption is caused by the retrieval process.

It is the oldest Everton-related page in The Teletext Archive, dating back to 1975. Everton's first four games of the 1975-76 season had produced five points, after a 4-1 defeat by Coventry City at Goodison on the opening day followed by a 1-1 draw with Burnley, a 1-0 win at Birmingham City and a 3-0 home win over Sheffield United.

On this day, the Blues beat reigning champions Derby County 2-0 at Goodison, thanks to second-half goals by Mike Lyons and Bob Latchford, a victory which moved them up to fourth place in the table.

It's A Grand Old Team To Play For

William Ralph 'Dixie' Dean joined Everton from Tranmere Rovers in March 1925 and in his first full season at the club he scored 33 goals in 40 appearances. During the summer of 1926, he fractured his skull in a motorcycling accident and didn't play his first game of the 1926-27 season until October but ended the campaign with 24 goals.

In the title-winning season of 1927-28, he notched 60 League goals and 3 in the FA Cup. A slump in the club's fortunes saw the Blues relegated in 1929-30 but in Division Two he scored 48 goals in total as the team earned immediate promotion as champions.

Everton won the Division One title again in 1931-32 when Dixie struck 46 times and he was on target 29 times during the FA Cup winning campaign of 1932-33, including in the Final. In total, he scored 383 goals in 433 appearances for the club.

March 1984

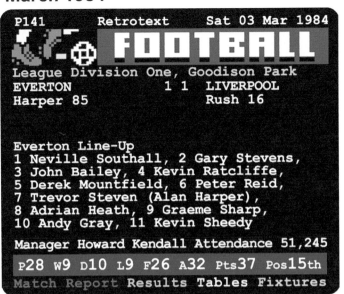

```
P141      Retrotext      Sat 03 Mar 1984
      FOOTBALL
League Division One, Goodison Park
EVERTON          1 1  LIVERPOOL
Harper 85             Rush 16


Everton Line-Up
1 Neville Southall, 2 Gary Stevens,
3 John Bailey, 4 Kevin Ratcliffe,
5 Derek Mountfield, 6 Peter Reid,
7 Trevor Steven (Alan Harper),
8 Adrian Heath, 9 Graeme Sharp,
10 Andy Gray, 11 Kevin Sheedy
Manager Howard Kendall Attendance 51,245
P28 W9 D10 L9 F26 A32 Pts37 Pos15th
Match Report  Results Tables Fixtures
```

```
P141      Retrotext      Sat 10 Mar 1984
      FOOTBALL
FA Cup 6th Round, Meadow Lane
NOTTS COUNTY     1 2  EVERTON
Chiedozie 18          Richardson 6
                      Gray 47

Everton Line-Up
1 Neville Southall, 2 Gary Stevens,
3 John Bailey, 4 Kevin Ratcliffe,
5 Derek Mountfield, 6 Peter Reid,
7 Alan Irvine, 8 Kevin Richardson,
9 Graeme Sharp, 10 Andy Gray,
11 Kevin Sheedy (Alan Harper)
Manager Howard Kendall Attendance 19,534
     Nil Satis Nisi Optimum
Match Report  Results Tables Fixtures
```

It had been announced during the week that Kevin Ratcliffe had been appointed captain of Wales, having been made skipper at Everton back In December due to Mark Higgins' injury issues.

Before this match, Howard Kendall received the Bell's Manager Of The Month award for February in recognition of his side's exploits in two Cup competitions and the unbeaten League run in 1984.

Everton's line-up against Liverpool included three players who had never featured in a Merseyside derby previously – Derek Mountfield, Peter Reid and Andy Gray.

Trevor Steven returned to the Blues' starting eleven for the first time since the Anfield derby back in November, replacing the injured Alan Irvine, but he only lasted twenty minutes before an achilles tendon injury saw him replaced by Alan Harper.

This was the 130th League derby between the sides and the prolific Ian Rush gave the visitors an early lead when he headed home Craig Johnston's cross on seventeen minutes, his 33rd goal of the season.

In the second half, Graeme Sharp's penalty was saved by Liverpool goalkeeper Bruce Grobbelaar but substitute Alan Harper ensured the spoils were shared against his former club.

Adrian Heath had scored a hat-trick against County a few weeks earlier but he was ruled out with an ankle injury and Trevor Steven hadn't recovered from the achilles injury suffered against Liverpool so Alan Irvine came in.

Though barred from playing for the reserves at the start of the week due to the plaster cast on his wrist, Kevin Richardson was cleared to play in another reserve game on Friday evening.

Given seventy-five minutes by Kendall in that one, he was back in the first team on Saturday afternoon after the referee gave his cast the all-clear.

The travelling fans were delighted he did, as he opened the scoring after just six minutes though the home side soon levelled things up.

Immediately after the half-time interval, Andy Gray put the Blues ahead again, scoring with a diving header from just a few inches off the ground, and this time there was to be no equaliser for the home team.

In the semi-final, Everton were drawn against Southampton or Sheffield Wednesday whose game at Hillsborough finished 0-0. Lawrie McMenemy's Saints hammered Howard Wilkinson's Wednesday 5-1 at The Dell to set up a clash with the Blues.

It's A Grand Old Team To Support

For William Ralph Dean, joining Everton had been the thrilling fulfillment of a dream and the realisation of a vow he made to himself when he had been taken to Goodison by his father as an 8-year-old.

"I didn't feel really terribly sad about leaving Tranmere because I did always want to get away and get to the one and only club... Everton. That's been my club since I was a kid. So that's it. I'd have played for nothing there.

I just knew I'd come off at Everton. It had been there since I was a child. I just seemed to know that I could do something and, of course, it didn't take me long to prove it."

From Dixie Dean: The Inside Story Of A Football Icon by John Keith

EVERTON
NIL SATIS
NISI OPTIMUM
GOODISON
PARK L4

March 1984

Terry Curran continued his attempted comeback from injury by playing in a reserve match at Ewood Park, together with club captain Mark Higgins and wantaway star Andy King.

The first team, meanwhile, fresh from their Cup success over County, travelled back to Nottingham for a clash with Brian Clough's Forest.

Top scorers Adrian Heath and Kevin Sheedy missed out with ankle injuries and the Blues lost their unbeaten League record in 1984 to a Steve Hodge volley forty-five seconds from the end.

It was a disappointing result for the Blues but was only their first League defeat since the poor 3-0 loss to bottom club Wolves just after Christmas and only their second defeat in nineteen games overall.

Three players picked up knocks at the City Ground but manager Howard Kendall expected Alan Irvine, Gary Stevens and Peter Reid to be fit to face Ipswich Town at the weekend, as well as Heath and Sheedy.

It wasn't a good night for Everton as the reserves also lost at Blackburn, 2-1, but on the positive side Curran was able to be play the full ninety minutes with no ill-effects. However, Mark Higgins was still no closer to a return to first-team action.

Bobby Ferguson had replaced Bobby Robson as manager after the latter was appointed England boss and his Ipswich side had beaten the Blues comprehensively at Portman Road earlier in the season and sat second in the table at the time.

But a disastrous recent run, coupled with the loss of top scorer Paul Mariner to Arsenal, saw them mired in relegation trouble, third from bottom of the First Division.

John Bailey missed the match due to suspension, with Alan Harper covering for him, as did Kevin Sheedy who was replaced by Kevin Richardson. On the plus side, Adrian Heath was back in the starting line-up.

The visitors were aiming to stave off a seventh consecutive loss but got off to the worst possible start when Derek Mountfield put the Blues ahead after just four minutes but that was as bad as it got for the Tractor Boys.

The big worry for Howard Kendall was that Graeme Sharp limped off with a knee injury to be replaced by Trevor Steven, just a week before the Milk Cup final clash with Liverpool, and he was rated very doubtful for the midweek game against Leicester City.

If You Know Your History

The 1927-28 season saw Everton become Division One champions for the third time and the legendary William Ralph 'Dixie' Dean achieve his amazing total of sixty League goals in a single campaign, completed with this hat-trick on the final day.

Though the official attendance was less, the match report in that evening's Liverpool Football Echo said around 60,000 fans were inside Goodison Park to witness history being made and that the crowd didn't stop cheering for eight solid minutes after Dixie's third goal went in. Afterwards, Everton chairman W. C. Cuff congratulated the team on their achievement in what he described as "the most wonderful season the game of football has ever known."

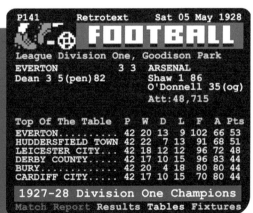

March 1984

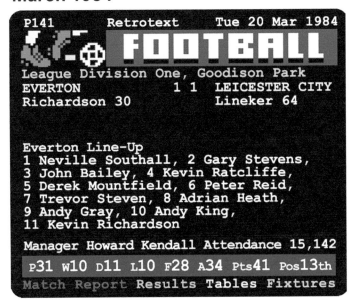

```
P141      Retrotext      Tue 20 Mar 1984
[LOGO] FOOTBALL
League Division One, Goodison Park
EVERTON              1 1   LEICESTER CITY
Richardson 30              Lineker 64


Everton Line-Up
1 Neville Southall, 2 Gary Stevens,
3 John Bailey, 4 Kevin Ratcliffe,
5 Derek Mountfield, 6 Peter Reid,
7 Trevor Steven, 8 Adrian Heath,
9 Andy Gray, 10 Andy King,
11 Kevin Richardson

Manager Howard Kendall Attendance 15,142
P31 W10 D11 L10 F28 A34 Pts41 Pos13th
Match Report Results Tables Fixtures
```

```
P141      Retrotext      Sun 25 Mar 1984
[LOGO] FOOTBALL
League Cup Final, Wembley Stadium
EVERTON              0 0   LIVERPOOL



Everton Line-Up
1 Neville Southall, 2 Gary Stevens,
3 John Bailey, 4 Kevin Ratcliffe,
5 Derek Mountfield, 6 Peter Reid,
7 Alan Irvine, 8 Adrian Heath,
9 Graeme Sharp, 10 Kevin Richardson,
11 Kevin Sheedy (Alan Harper)

Manager Howard Kendall Attendance 100,000
Nil Satis Nisi Optimum
Match Report Results Tables Fixtures
```

John Bailey returned to the team after suspension but, as expected, Graeme Sharp's injury kept him out and Andy King made a rare start.

Kevin Richardson put the Blues ahead in the first half but Gary Lineker equalised mid-way through the second period for the visitors.

The transfer-listed King had the chance to put the Blues back in front almost immediately but his penalty kick was saved by Leicester keeper, Mark Wallington.

As the first all-Merseyside League Cup Final became ever nearer, there was bad news for Everton's club captain Mark Higgins who had been told by his specialist that further rest was the only way to try and combat his groin injury, effectively ruling him out for the rest of the season.

The other Blues player with a long-standing injury to overcome, Terry Curran, continued his recovery with a reserve team outing at Burnley.

David Johnson, meanwhile, ended his second spell at Goodison when he joined Manchester City on a free transfer. He had rejoined the Blues in August 1982 but had been unable to nail down a regular place in Howard Kendall's team, making only eight appearances during this season.

At the end of 120 minutes of a pulsating Final, the two Merseyside rivals could not be separated.

The biggest talking point of the game came as early as the sixth minute when Adrian Heath dispossessed Bruce Grobbelaar in the Liverpool goal and shot towards an empty net only for Alan Hansen to get in the way with a combination of his knee and his hand.

Controversially, referee Alan Robinson did not point to the penalty spot and instead the game continued and the same referee would be involved in another contentious incident during the 1986 FA Cup Final.

There was one big winner on the day, though, and that was the hordes of Scousers who travelled down to London, often sharing the same mode of transport.

After being presented to the Queen Mother, Everton and Liverpool did a joint lap of honour around Wembley as both sets of fans sang in unison "Merseyside, Merseyside, Merseyside".

The man in charge of Wembley security said: "From how the fans behaved on Sunday, I would have them back at any time. No one was arrested inside the ground and only one person had to be ejected. It was as I had hoped and a great family occasion."

If You Know Your History

As reigning champions, Everton made a decent start to the 1928-29 campaign but the side's form dipped alarmingly as the season went on, so much so that the team ended up in eighteenth spot after losing eight of the last nine games.

It was a sign of the things to come in the following 1929-30 season, as the Blues finished bottom of the table and were relegated.

With Dixie Dean loyally staying with the club, immediate promotion from Division Two as champions followed after the 1930-31 campaign and the rollercoaster ride was completed in 1931-32 as Everton were crowned Division One League champions once again.

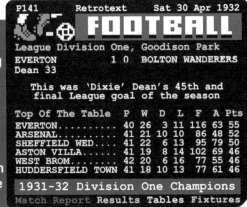

```
P141      Retrotext      Sat 30 Apr 1932
[LOGO] FOOTBALL
League Division One, Goodison Park
EVERTON              1 0   BOLTON WANDERERS
Dean 33

This was 'Dixie' Dean's 45th and
final League goal of the season

Top Of The Table   P  W  D  L   F   A Pts
EVERTON.......... 40 26  3 11 116  63  55
ARSENAL.......... 41 21 10 10  86  48  52
SHEFFIELD WED.... 41 22  6 13  95  79  50
ASTON VILLA...... 41 19  8 14 102  69  46
WEST BROM........ 42 20  6 16  77  55  46
HUDDERSFIELD TOWN 41 18 10 13  77  61  46
1931-32 Division One Champions
Match Report Results Tables Fixtures
```

March 1984

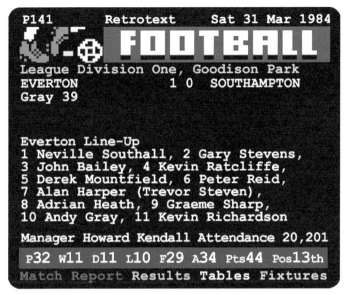

Having replaced the injured Kevin Sheedy in the first game, Alan Harper was given a starting berth in the replay at Manchester City's ground.

Andy King, the only Everton survivor from the club's last appearance in the League Cup final back in 1977 against Aston Villa, was on the substitute's bench.

As with the Wembley game, there was very little between the two sides but ultimately it was Graeme Souness's sublime strike on twenty-one minutes which proved the difference and secured Joe Fagan his first trophy as Liverpool boss since taking over from Bob Paisley.

Though there were tears in the Everton dressing room after going toe-to-toe with Liverpool over two games and only narrowly coming up short, there was also a growing confidence as to what this team could achieve and there was still an opportunity to win some silverware before the season was out.

To compound the disappointment, Howard Kendall revealed that Kevin Sheedy would miss the rest of the season after having an operation on the ankle injury he sustained at Wembley, a major blow for the side ahead of the impending FA Cup semi-final match with Southampton.

It was Grand National day so this game kicked off early to avoid a clash with the world famous steeplechase.

Ahead of the FA Cup semi-final rehearsal against Lawrie McMenemy's Southampton, Howard Kendall confirmed that Andy Gray would return to the starting line-up after being cup-tied for the League Cup Final and that Trevor Steven would replace Andy King on the subs' bench.

It was Gray who grabbed the only goal of the game five minutes before half-time latching on to a pinpoint cross from John Bailey to see off their rivals who had been in fourth spot in the table coming into the game.

Trevor Steven did his chances of a semi-final starting place no harm with a solid performance off the bench with Alan Harper injured.

Terry Curran was also pushing his claims to be involved in the semi-final after playing in a Liverpool Senior Cup quarter-final against Marine which an Everton XI won 4-1, Andy King grabbing two goals.

For the record, the Grand National result was:
1st Hallo Dandy 13/1
2nd Greasepaint 9/1F
3rd Corbiere 16/1
4th Lucky Vane 12/1

It's A Grand Old Team To Support

Joe Mercer has travelled far in the world of football but when you mention the name 'Everton' the corners of his twinkling eyes crease into a nostalgic smile and he says:

"Sixteen years at one of the greatest clubs in the country - if not the world - are not easily forgotten, and I wouldn't want it any other way."

It was in 1930 that Mercer went to Goodison as a 16-year-old and like any other youngster as football daft as he was, the magnificence of it all overwhelmed him. "What a ground! What an atmosphere! What a team! I soon learned the meaning of their tradition that 'The Best Is Good Enough'.

Joe Mercer in *The Everton Football Book* Edited by Derek Hodgson

April 1984

Everton were without Kevin Ratcliffe, who was serving a one match suspension, and Andy Gray who had picked up an injury in training. Alan Harper played at right back with Gary Stevens replacing Ratcliffe and Peter Reid was captain.

Terry Curran had featured in four reserve games to build his fitness back up following his thigh muscle injury back in September and he was given a starting berth by Howard Kendall.

On fifty minutes, Luton went down to ten men after Mal Donaghy was dismissed for a foul on Adrian Heath and from that point the visitors took full advantage of their numerical superiority.

Derek Mountfield grabbed his third goal of the season on sixty-three minutes, Adrian Heath added a second and doubled up from the penalty spot with two minutes left.

It was Everton's fifth away win of a campaign which had improved significantly since January with the trials and tribulations of early season now consigned to history.

Curran came through the game with no ill-effects and was in line for another place in the starting line-up for the re-arranged match with Arsenal on Monday evening.

Just forty-eight hours after his comeback match, Terry Curran was given another chance to prove his fitness and form ahead of the upcoming FA Cup semi-final against Southampton, his former club.

Curran scored the winning goal for the Saints in the 1979 League Cup semi-final against Leeds and played in the Final - alongside ex-Everton hero Alan Ball - but lost 3-2 to Brian Clough's Nottingham Forest.

Kevin Ratcliffe and Andy Gray returned to the starting line-up but the game ended in in a hard-fought stalemate.

Crucially, none of the players suffered any serious injury with boss Howard Kendall saying he was happy with Curran's performance and later in the week confirming he would be in the starting line-up against Southampton.

Kendall told the Liverpool Daily Post: "Terry has the right sort of temperament for this game. He has the ability to raise his performance on big occasions."

When asked which of his two old teams would go through, Alan Ball said he favoured Southampton because they had more match winners, singling out Steve Moran, Danny Wallace and Steve Williams.

It's A Grand Old Team To Support

I'll never forget my first sight of Liverpool when I got off the train at Lime Street (in 1930). Those wonderful imposing buildings like St George's Hall had me staring for a long time. And I was practically speechless when I saw Goodison Park. I remember thinking 'why, the front door comes right onto the pavement'.

Everton were not just a football club; they were a way of life to players, directors and fans alike. To be part of a set-up such as they had was an experience no player could ever forget. If you played for them you had to play it their way. The result was a brand of football that became part and parcel of their tradition. In my view, Everton were undoubtedly the finest club in England.

Cliff Britton in *The Everton Football Book* Edited by Derek Hodgson

EVERTON
NIL SATIS
NISI OPTIMUM
GOODISON
PARK L4

April 1984

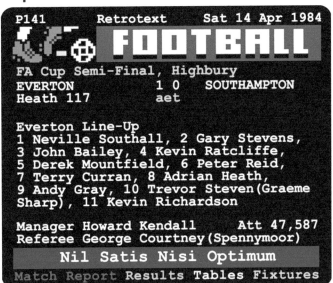

```
P141      Retrotext    Sat 14 Apr 1984
         FOOTBALL
FA Cup Semi-Final, Highbury
EVERTON          1  0    SOUTHAMPTON
Heath 117            aet

Everton Line-Up
1 Neville Southall, 2 Gary Stevens,
3 John Bailey, 4 Kevin Ratcliffe,
5 Derek Mountfield, 6 Peter Reid,
7 Terry Curran, 8 Adrian Heath,
9 Andy Gray, 10 Trevor Steven(Graeme
Sharp), 11 Kevin Richardson

Manager Howard Kendall    Att 47,587
Referee George Courtney(Spennymoor)
      Nil Satis Nisi Optimum
Match Report Results Tables Fixtures
```

```
P141      Retrotext    Tue 17 Apr 1984
         FOOTBALL
League Division One, The Dell
SOUTHAMPTON      3  1    EVERTON
Armstrong 46 79         Richardson 56
Moran 80

Everton Line-Up
1 Neville Southall, 2 Gary Stevens,
3 Alan Harper, 4 Kevin Ratcliffe,
5 Derek Mountfield, 6 Peter Reid,
7 Terry Curran, 8 Adrian Heath,
9 Andy Gray, 10 Trevor Steven,
11 Kevin Richardson

Manager Howard Kendall Attendance 16,978
P35 W12 D12 L11 F33 A37 Pts48 Pos11th
Match Report Results Tables Fixtures
```

Southampton were having a terrific season and would ultimately finish second in the Division One table just three points behind champions Liverpool, so going into this match - a record-equalling nineteenth FA Cup semi-final for the Blues - Howard Kendall's side were undoubtedly the underdogs.

As expected, Terry Curran was included in the starting eleven at Highbury with Graeme Sharp the man to miss out and Adrian Heath pushed forward to play alongside Andy Gray.

It was a tense battle with Saints fielding a full strength team unlike for the League outing a couple of weeks earlier when four senior players were rested to avoid possible suspensions.

As the game went into extra time with a replay looking likely, Everton were awarded a free kick.

Peter Reid floated the ball into the area where Derek Mountfield headed it on and Adrian Heath nodded it into the net to send an estimated 22,000 Everton fans in the ground wild.

It was his fifteenth goal of the season and he could claim to have been the catalyst for the Blues' Cup success in 1983-84 with his goals against Coventry and Oxford in the League Cup, plus this one, to take the club back to Wembley.

On the run-up to a third clash with Southampton in less than three weeks, there was concern that Kevin Sheedy may have played his last game for the club.

The Republic of Ireland international had been ruled out of the rest of the season due to an ankle injury and his contract was due to run out in the summer but he had refused to sign a new one.

John Bailey was ruled out of the clash at the Dell due to an injury he picked up in the semi-final with utility player Alan Harper replacing him.

Trevor Steven was to play in Sheedy's position on the left, with Andy Gray and Inchy continuing up front with Graeme Sharp on the bench.

It was a bad-tempered affair with tackles flying in from both sides and seven players booked. Steve Moran missed an eighth minute penalty and the first half ended goalless.

A minute into the second period the home side went ahead through David Armstrong but Kevin Richardson soon equalised.

Terry Curran and Andy Gray both had efforts disallowed before two goals in two minutes turned the match in the Saints' favour, Armstrong with his second of the night and Moran atoning for his earlier miss from the spot.

If You Know Your History

Everton's road to Wembley and a second FA Cup Final success saw victories over Leicester (2-3), Bury (3-1), Leeds United (2-0) and Luton Town 6-0 with a 2-1 semi-final win against West Ham.

This was the first occasion when shirt-numbering was used with the Everton players 1 to 11 and Manchester City 22 (for the goalkeeper) to 12, thus 'Dixie' Dean became the Blues' first-ever Number 9.

The Everton entourage arrived at Lime Street on Monday evening and were taken in a horse-drawn carriage, a replica of the one used to welcome the team back in 1906 and driven by the same man, to a reception at the Town Hall with huge crowds cheering all the way.

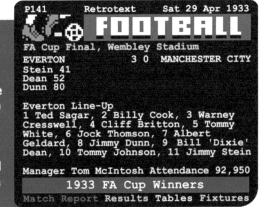

```
P141      Retrotext    Sat 29 Apr 1933
         FOOTBALL
FA Cup Final, Wembley Stadium
EVERTON          3  0    MANCHESTER CITY
Stein 41
Dean 52
Dunn 80

Everton Line-Up
1 Ted Sagar, 2 Billy Cook, 3 Warney
Cresswell, 4 Cliff Britton, 5 Tommy
White, 6 Jock Thomson, 7 Albert
Geldard, 8 Jimmy Dunn, 9 Bill 'Dixie'
Dean, 10 Tommy Johnson, 11 Jimmy Stein

Manager Tom McIntosh Attendance 92,950
      1933 FA Cup Winners
Match Report Results Tables Fixtures
```

April 1984

```
P141      Retrotext      Sat 21 Apr 1984
FOOTBALL
League Division One, Roker Park
SUNDERLAND          2 1   EVERTON
Robson 15                 Heath 44
West 66


Everton Line-Up
1 Neville Southall, 2 Gary Stevens,
3 John Bailey, 4 Kevin Ratcliffe,
5 Derek Mountfield, 6 Peter Reid
(Alan Harper), 7 Terry Curran,
8 Adrian Heath, 9 Graeme Sharp,
10 Trevor Steven, 11 Kevin Richardson

Manager Howard Kendall Attendance 15,876
P36 W12 D12 L12 F34 A39 Pts48 Pos14th
Match Report  Results Tables Fixtures
```

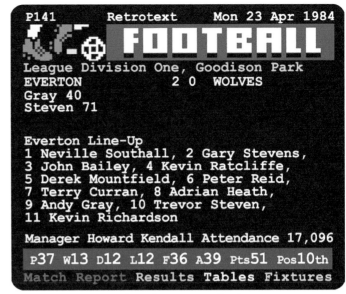

```
P141      Retrotext      Mon 23 Apr 1984
FOOTBALL
League Division One, Goodison Park
EVERTON             2 0   WOLVES
Gray 40
Steven 71


Everton Line-Up
1 Neville Southall, 2 Gary Stevens,
3 John Bailey, 4 Kevin Ratcliffe,
5 Derek Mountfield, 6 Peter Reid,
7 Terry Curran, 8 Adrian Heath,
9 Andy Gray, 10 Trevor Steven,
11 Kevin Richardson

Manager Howard Kendall Attendance 17,096
P37 W13 D12 L12 F36 A39 Pts51 Pos10th
Match Report  Results Tables Fixtures
```

John Bailey returned to the starting eleven at Roker Park after missing out through injury at the Dell during the week.

The Blues went behind after fifteen minutes when Sunderland's 38-year-old player/first team coach Bryan 'Pop' Robson scored the 301st goal of his remarkable career, having made his League debut for Newcastle way back in 1964.

Though top scorer Adrian Heath equalised a minute before half-time, his sixteenth goal of the season, Colin West secured the points for Len Ashurst's side midway through the second period.

It was a very physical match and Peter Reid was booked for a heavy tackle on Sunderland's Paul Bracewell before being substituted having been on the receiving end of a number of robust challenges himself. He had picked up a knock but was expected to shake it off before the game against Wolves on Monday.

Bracewell would sign for the Blues at the end of the season while centre-half Ian Atkins would be another Howard Kendall signing in November.

This was the second defeat for Everton in five days but the FA Cup Finalists rallied to stay unbeaten from here on in, winning five of their remaining seven matches.

After the recent FA Cup semi-final success over Southampton, Howard Kendall reflected on the remarkable turnaround in the club's fortunes and cited the 3-0 defeat to bottom club Wolves on December 27th as the lowest point of Everton's season.

It was only Wolves second League win in nineteen matches and sandwiched between 0-0 home draws against Sunderland and Coventry, it was a very bleak Christmas period for Evertonians.

The Midlands side had continued to struggle and were coming into this match well adrift at the bottom of the table. A 3-0 home defeat by Ipswich on the Saturday meant relegation would be confirmed if they were beaten at Goodison Park.

Commenting on that likelihood for his former club in the match programme, Andy Gray said: "I'd rather it didn't happen here. It's important that we should win today, but I'd take no joy from pushing Wolves out the First Division."

As fate would have it, Gray scored the opener for the home side five minutes before the interval. Trevor Steven's deflected shot on seventy-one minutes finally made the game safe and doomed the visitors to the drop after just one season back in the top flight.

It's A Grand Old Team To Play For

Before signing for Everton, Ted Sagar was playing for Thorne Colliery in the Doncaster Senior League. He made his first team debut in January 1930 and kept a clean sheet as the Blues beat Derby County 4-0.

Before World War Two, he won two League titles with the club, in seasons 1931-32 and 1938-39, as well as the FA Cup in 1933. During the conflict, Sagar served with the Royal Signals and when top flight football began again in 1946, he resumed his career with the Blues.

His last appearance for the club was in the Liverpool Senior Cup Final in May, 1953, against Tranmere Rovers. Sagar was made captain for the day as Everton ran out comfortable 4-1 winners in front of a bumper crowd of 27,090.

April 1984

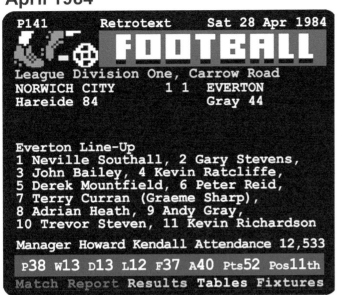

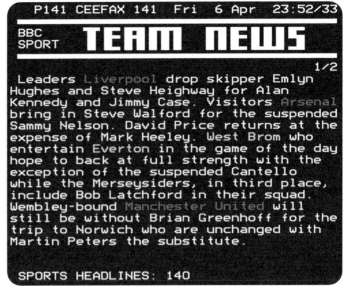

With the first team away at Norwich on the Saturday, over 9,000 Everton fans turned up at Goodison Park on Thursday evening to cheer on the youngsters in the first leg of the FA Youth Cup Final.

The Blues had last won the trophy in 1965, and first half goals from Rob Wakenshaw and Neil Rimmer gave them a 2-0 lead at half-time. But Stoke bounced back in the second period to leave the match on a knife-edge at 2-2 ahead of the second leg.

At Carrow Road, Everton were unchanged from the side that had beaten Wolves but after just ten minutes Terry Curran had to come off with a hamstring injury to be replaced by Graeme Sharp.

The visitors had a goal from Kevin Richardson ruled out midway through the first half for offside but Andy Gray finally put them ahead just before the interval, heading home Adrian Heath's cross for his seventh goal since joining in November.

Late pressure from the home side saw Aag Hareide grab an equaliser.

John Bailey picked up a booking which would lead to a two-game suspension but, thankfully, he would be available for selection in the Cup Final.

This is an original Ceefax page recovered from an old VHS recording.

The page features a roundup of team news from April, 1979. West Brom and Everton stood second and third in the table on 44 points, four behind leaders Liverpool, but the Blues had played five more games than the Baggies.

A goal from Ally Brown six minutes from time at the Hawthorns earned the home side both points to keep the pressure on Bob Paisley's team who beat Arsenal 3-0.

It's A Grand Old Team To Support

Although born in Yorkshire, Ted Sagar had been an Everton fan from childhood and the chance to play alongside his boyhood hero in March 1929 sealed a relationship with the club that would last decades.

He said: "I got a trial with two leading clubs, Sheffield Wednesday and Everton, but I only bothered going to one. I think it was a photograph of the Everton team with Dixie Dean that swayed me."

Upon his retirement in 1953, aged 43, he commented: "I have enjoyed every minute of my time here. I came here to do a job and I hope I have made a success of it. If I had a chance to do my footballing again I would choose Everton. There is no better club in the world."

From the Liverpool Echo, February 1999

May 1984

```
P141        Retrotext        Sat 05 May 1984
        FOOTBALL
League Division One, Goodison Park
EVERTON            1 1   MANCHESTER UTD
Wakenshaw 58             Stapleton 72


Everton Line-Up
1 Neville Southall, 2 Gary Stevens,
3 John Bailey, 4 Alan Harper,
5 Derek Mountfield, 6 Peter Reid,
7 Robbie Wakenshaw (Ian Bishop 76),
8 Andy King, 9 Graeme Sharp,
10 Trevor Steven, 11 Kevin Richardson

Manager Howard Kendall Attendance 28,802
P39 W13 D14 L12 F38 A41 Pts53 Pos11th
Match Report  Results  Tables  Fixtures
```

```
P141        Retrotext        Mon 07 May 1984
        FOOTBALL
League Division One, Villa Park
ASTON VILLA        0 2   EVERTON
                        Richardson 67
                        Sharp 72

Everton Line-Up
1 Neville Southall, 2 Gary Stevens,
3 John Bailey, 4 Kevin Ratcliffe,
5 Derek Mountfield, 6 Peter Reid,
7 Andy King, 8 Adrian Heath,
9 Graeme Sharp, 10 Trevor Steven,
11 Kevin Richardson

Manager Howard Kendall Attendance 16,792
P40 W14 D14 L12 F40 A41 Pts56 Pos10th
Match Report  Results  Tables  Fixtures
```

Ahead of this League game with Manchester United, Everton's problems were adding up.

Adrian Heath was serving a one-match ban while hamstring injuries ruled out Terry Curran and Peter Reid. To add to manager Kendall's woes, Kevin Ratcliffe and Neville Southall both picked up knocks during the midweek international between England and Wales at the Racecourse Ground.

In the end, Ratcliffe, Curran and Andy Gray missed out against United so 18-year-old striker Rob Wakenshaw made his debut alongside Graeme Sharp, with another youth team product Ian Bishop on the bench. Andy King returned to the starting eleven for the first time since March.

United were pushing Liverpool hard for the Division One title and stood just two points behind Joe Fagan's side with four games each left to play.

But Everton's depleted side went ahead through the debutante Wakenshaw just before the hour mark, slamming the ball home after a goal-mouth scramble. The youngster was later forced to leave the field suffering from cramp.

The visitors equalised on seventy-two minutes through Frank Stapleton but it was a solid point for the battling Blues.

The games were coming thick and fast and two days later Everton travelled down the M6 to face Aston Villa. Tony Barton's side were seeking to avenge their League Cup semi-final defeat by the Blues back in February.

Kevin Richardson scored the opener with a great twenty-five yard shot and six minutes later Graeme Sharp – without a goal in eleven matches – finally found the back of the net again.

The following day, ahead of the first team's appearance at Wembley, Everton's youngsters secured the first piece of silverware for the trophy cabinet by beating Stoke City 2-0 in the second leg of the FA Youth Cup Final, for a 4-2 aggregate success.

A superb individual goal by full-back Darren Hughes gave the Blues the lead just after the hour mark and Rob Wakenshaw, fresh from his debut goal for the first team against Manchester United on Saturday, doubled the advantage fourteen minutes from the end, enabling skipper Ian Marshall to lift the trophy.

It was the first time since 1965 that the youth team had won the trophy and they were able to do a lap of honour at the home match with QPR a few days later.

If You Know Your History

Everton secured their fifth Division One title having not been out of the first two in the table all season and, under manager Theo Kelly, the team also established a club record for points won.

With Dixie Dean having joined Notts County the previous season, Tommy Lawton took on the goal-scoring responsibility and in 38 League games during this title-winning campaign he notched up 34, having recorded 28 in 39 appearances the season before.

The 1939-40 season began on time but after three games it was abandoned following the outbreak of World War Two and League football would not re-start again until August, 1946.

```
P141        Retrotext        Sat 06 May 1939
        FOOTBALL
Top                     P  W  D  L  F  A Pts
EVERTON..........      42 27  5 10 88 52 59
WOLVERHAMPTON W..      42 22 11  9 88 39 55
CHARLTON ATHLETIC      42 22  6 14 75 59 50
MIDDLESBROUGH....      42 20  9 13 93 74 49
ARSENAL..........      42 19  9 14 55 41 47
DERBY COUNTY.....      42 19  8 15 66 55 46
STOKE CITY.......      42 17 12 13 71 58 46
BOLTON WANDERERS.      42 15 15 12 67 58 45
PRESTON NORTH END      42 16 12 14 63 59 44
GRIMSBY TOWN.....      42 16 11 15 61 69 43
LIVERPOOL........      42 14 14 14 62 63 42
ASTON VILLA......      42 16  9 17 71 60 41
1938-39 Division One Champions
Match Report  Results  Tables  Fixtures
```

May 1984

P141   Retrotext   Sat 12 May 1984

FOOTBALL

League Division One, Goodison Park
EVERTON   3 1   QPR
Heath 38   Micklewhite 58
Sharp 78 81

Everton Line-Up
1 Neville Southall, 2 Gary Stevens,
3 Alan Harper, 4 Kevin Ratcliffe,
5 Derek Mountfield, 6 Peter Reid,
7 Trevor Steven, 8 Adrian Heath,
9 Graeme Sharp, 10 Andy Gray,
11 Kevin Richardson

Manager Howard Kendall Attendance 20,712

P41 W15 D14 L12 F43 A42 Pts59 Pos10th

Match Report Results Tables Fixtures

P141   Retrotext   Mon 14 May 1984

FOOTBALL

League Division One, Upton Park
WEST HAM UNITED   0 1   EVERTON
                         Richardson 14

Everton Line-Up
1 Neville Southall, 2 Gary Stevens,
3 Alan Harper, 4 Kevin Ratcliffe,
5 Derek Mountfield, 6 Peter Reid,
7 Trevor Steven, 8 Adrian Heath,
9 Graeme Sharp, 10 Andy King,
11 Kevin Richardson

Manager Howard Kendall Attendance 25,452

P42 W16 D14 L12 F44 A42 Pts62 Pos7th

Match Report Results Tables Fixtures

Everton returned to Goodison for the final home game of the season with the successful FA Youth Cup winners parading the trophy.

John Bailey watched from the stands as he began his two-match suspension. As expected, Alan Harper replaced him at left-back with Andy Gray coming back into the side and Adrian Heath dropping into midfield.

Terry Curran had pulled up again in training, ruling him out for the rest of the season along with Mark Higgins, Kevin Sheedy and Alan Irvine, who had recently had a knee operation.

It was Heath who put the Blues ahead before half-time with his eighteenth goal of the campaign, but their high flying opponents - who had lost only once in ten games and stood third in the table – equalised just before the hour mark.

Graeme Sharp had found his scoring boots in midweek against Villa and he did his prospects of booking a place in the side at Wembley no harm with two late goals to give Kendall's men all the points.

After the game, impressed QPR midfielder Ian Stewart said: "One thing is certain, Everton will win the FA Cup and Graeme Sharp and Andy Gray will win it for them."

That left just one more League game to play before the FA Cup Final and the Blues travelled down to West Ham to complete the 1983-84 campaign.

The main transfer news ahead of the Final involved Paul Bracewell who had been voted Sunderland's Player Of The Year. Howard Kendall remained confident of securing the deal despite speculation that Aston Villa were looking to hijack the move.

With one eye on the Final, Andy Gray was rested and Andy King came into the side for his last game in a Blue shirt as he would be moving on during the summer.

Another player making his final appearance was West Ham legend Trevor Brooking, who retired after this game.

John Bailey served the second of his two match ban but was due to play for the reserves in the Central League ahead of the Wembley showpiece.

Kevin Richardson scored the only goal of the match, emphasising his importance to the side.

The victory made it six League games unbeaten for the Blues and secured seventh spot in the table for the second successive season, a highly respectable position given how poor the first half of the campaign had been.

It's A Grand Old Team To Play For

Everton signed Tommy Lawton on New Year's Eve 1936 for a fee of £6,500. Lawton had made his first appearance for Burnley in March of that year, with the Turf Moor club signing him on as a professional when he turned seventeen in October and he marked the occasion by scoring a hat-trick against Tottenham.

During the 1937-38 campaign, Lawton was increasingly the first-choice number nine, as 'Dixie' Dean's relationship with club secretary Theo Kelly deteriorated to the point he felt he was being pushed out of the club. He scored twenty-eight goals that season as the Blues finished in mid-table and 'Dixie' moved on to Notts County.

Lawton notched another thirty-four goals the following season as Everton secured the Division One title for the fifth time in the club's history.

May 1984

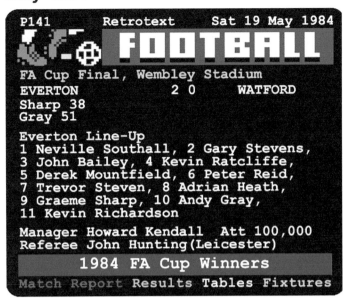

```
P141      Retrotext     Sat 19 May 1984
FOOTBALL
FA Cup Final, Wembley Stadium
EVERTON         2  0      WATFORD
Sharp 38
Gray 51

Everton Line-Up
1 Neville Southall, 2 Gary Stevens,
3 John Bailey, 4 Kevin Ratcliffe,
5 Derek Mountfield, 6 Peter Reid,
7 Trevor Steven, 8 Adrian Heath,
9 Graeme Sharp, 10 Andy Gray,
11 Kevin Richardson

Manager Howard Kendall  Att 100,000
Referee John Hunting(Leicester)
      1984 FA Cup Winners
Match Report Results Tables Fixtures
```

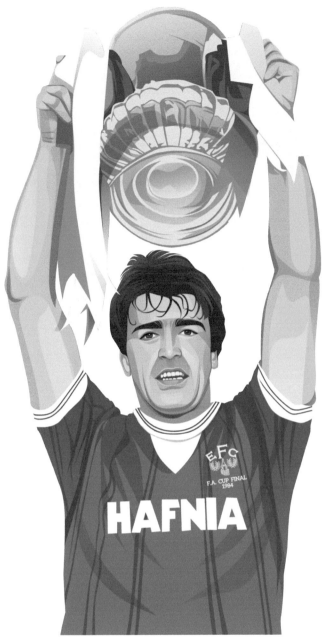

Ahead of the Final, it was announced that Howard Kendall and first-team coaches Mick Heaton and Colin Harvey had all signed new four-year contracts.

Having lost the 1964 Final with Preston and the 1968 Final with Everton, Howard was keen to avoid a hat-trick of defeats at Wembley in this competition.

He said before the team travelled to London, "We're going there not just to play our part but to bring the Cup home."

The Blues took the lead thanks to a neat finish from Graeme Sharp and doubled it when Andy Gray headed the ball into the net after the Watford goalkeeper had looked favourite to claim it. Everton saw the game out to win the FA Cup for the first time since 1966.

Midfield dynamo Peter Reid looked back on the difference a few months had made to the team's fortunes, saying:

"We're not that different a team now to early in the season. What we had around January was a change in confidence not in attitude or style. A good team playing without confidence can look a bad side even though they're not."

It had been a remarkable turnaround for Kendall and his team; from being booed off the Goodison Park pitch on New Year's Eve to running round Wembley with the Cup just five months later. Now the manager's thoughts turned to planning for the 1984-85 season which would prove to be the greatest in the club's illustrious history.

It's A Grand Old Team To Play For

Thomas George 'TG' Jones was signed by Everton in March 1936 from Wrexham for a fee of £3,000 when he was just 18-years-old. He established himself as automatic choice at centre half during the 1937-38 season and was a key member of the great side which won the Division One title prior to the outbreak of war in 1939.

He resumed his career with the club after World War Two with his talent recognised far and wide. Italian side Roma tried to sign him in 1947 for £15,000 but the deal fell through due to foreign exchange problems. He was briefly made club captain in 1949 but fell out with the board and left to join small Welsh club Pwllheli in 1950.

Described by 'Dixie' Dean as "the greatest all-round footballer I ever saw", TG made 175 appearances in total for the Blues, scoring five goals.

Two: 1984-1985
EVERTON FC*

HOWARD KENDALL - MANAGER

COLIN HARVEY - COACH

MICK HEATON - COACH

JOHN CLINKARD - PHYSIO

ADRIAN HEATH

ALAN HARPER

ANDY GRAY

DEREK MOUNTFIELD

GARY STEVENS

GRAEME SHARP

JIM ARNOLD

JOHN BAILEY

KEVIN RATCLIFFE

KEVIN RICHARDSON

KEVIN SHEEDY

MARK HIGGINS

NEVILLE SOUTHALL

PAT VAN DEN HAUWE

PAUL BRACEWELL

PETER REID

TERRY CURRAN

TREVOR STEVEN

*as at the start of the season plus Pat van den Hauwe who joined in September

August 1984

```
P141      Retrotext      Sat 18 Aug 1984
FOOTBALL
FA Charity Shield, Wembley Stadium
EVERTON          1 0   LIVERPOOL
Grobbelaar 56(og)


Everton Line-Up
1 Neville Southall, 2 Gary Stevens,
3 John Bailey, 4 Kevin Ratcliffe,
5 Derek Mountfield, 6 Peter Reid,
7 Trevor Steven, 8 Adrian Heath,
9 Graeme Sharp, 10 Paul Bracewell,
11 Kevin Richardson

Manager Howard Kendall Attendance 100,000
         Nil Satis Nisi Optimum
Match Report Results Tables Fixtures
```

```
P141      Retrotext      Sat 25 Aug 1984
FOOTBALL
League Division One, Goodison Park
EVERTON          1 4   TOTTENHAM H.
Heath 16(pen)          Falco 39
                       Allen 43 56
                       Chiedozie 52

Everton Line-Up
1 Neville Southall, 2 Gary Stevens,
3 John Bailey, 4 Kevin Ratcliffe,
5 Derek Mountfield, 6 Peter Reid,
7 Trevor Steven, 8 Adrian Heath,
9 Graeme Sharp, 10 Paul Bracewell,
11 Kevin Richardson (Andy Gray)

Manager Howard Kendall Attendance 35,596
 P1 W0 D0 L1 F1 A4 Pts0 Pos22nd
Match Report Results Tables Fixtures
```

As the build-up to the season-opening Charity Shield match against Liverpool began, Howard Kendall took his squad to Switzerland and Greece for a short tour.

Although Andy King had left the club for a second time during the summer, there was good news on the contract front with both Kevin Richardson and Kevin Sheedy finally putting pen to paper.

Alan Irvine would sign for Steve Coppell's Crystal Palace before the new season began for a fee of £50,000, leaving only the future of goalkeeper Jim Arnold to be resolved.

The Blues began in Switzerland with a 5-3 success on penalties over Servette, with Neville Southall saving a couple of the Swiss side's spot kicks.

A 1-0 loss to Brazilian side Botafogo followed, despite Kendall's men looking the better side, and then there was a 1-0 win over St Gallen. The final leg of the tour was in Athens, where the Blues beat Olympiakos in impressive fashion by three goals to nil.

At Wembley, the match was settled by a bizarre Bruce Grobbelaar own goal which gave Everton only their third victory over Liverpool since 1972, sending out a signal that the Blues would be a force to be reckoned with in the coming season.

Opponents Tottenham arrived at Goodison having won the UEFA Cup back in May but with a new manager, Peter Shreeves having replaced Keith Burkinshaw.

Strikers Steve Archibald and Alan Brazil had left to join Terry Venables at Barcelona and Ron Atkinson at Manchester United respectively, but they had invested in new blood in the shape of John Chiedozie from Notts County and Clive Allen, a £700,000 purchase from QPR.

Kevin Sheedy had been ruled out of the Everton team after picking up an injury in training during the week, but Andy Gray was deemed fit enough for a place on the bench after a pre-season of niggling injuries had limited his game time.

Ahead of the game, the FA Cup, FA Youth Cup and Charity Shield trophies were paraded around the ground. The feelgood factor for fans continued when Adrian Heath put the home side ahead early on but Mark Falco and new boy Clive Allen gave the visitors a half-time lead.

Chiedozie and Allen again then piled on the misery for the home team in the second half with two quick-fire strikes and the supporters left Goodison Park in a state of shock after all the pre-match optimism.

If You Know Your History

Everton had struggled to recapture former glories after the end of World War Two, finishing tenth in the table after the 1946-47 season and fourteenth in 1947-48. Coming into this derby, the Blues were rock bottom with only one win in eight games, though they put on a spirited performance before a record Goodison Park crowd.

In October, Cliff Britton, a member of Everton's 1933 FA Cup winning side, was appointed manager and at the end of the campaign the team finished eighteenth, as it did in 1949-50. On the final day of the 1950-51 season, the Blues needed just a point at bottom club Sheffield Wednesday to avoid relegation but they were hammered 6-0 and so dropped down to Division Two.

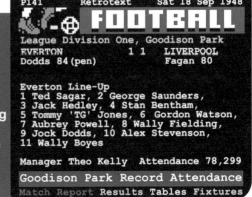

```
P141      Retrotext      Sat 18 Sep 1948
FOOTBALL
League Division One, Goodison Park
EVERTON          1 1   LIVERPOOL
Dodds 84(pen)          Fagan 80


Everton Line-Up
1 Ted Sagar, 2 George Saunders,
3 Jack Hedley, 4 Stan Bentham,
5 Tommy 'TG' Jones, 6 Gordon Watson,
7 Aubrey Powell, 8 Wally Fielding,
9 Jock Dodds, 10 Alex Stevenson,
11 Wally Boyes

Manager Theo Kelly  Attendance 78,299
Goodison Park Record Attendance
Match Report Results Tables Fixtures
```

August 1984

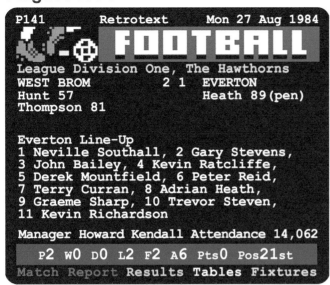

```
P141      Retrotext      Mon 27 Aug 1984
          FOOTBALL
League Division One, The Hawthorns
WEST BROM              2 1   EVERTON
Hunt 57                      Heath 89(pen)
Thompson 81

Everton Line-Up
1 Neville Southall, 2 Gary Stevens,
3 John Bailey, 4 Kevin Ratcliffe,
5 Derek Mountfield, 6 Peter Reid,
7 Terry Curran, 8 Adrian Heath,
9 Graeme Sharp, 10 Trevor Steven,
11 Kevin Richardson

Manager Howard Kendall Attendance 14,062

P2 W0 D0 L2 F2 A6 Pts0 Pos21st
Match Report Results Tables Fixtures
```

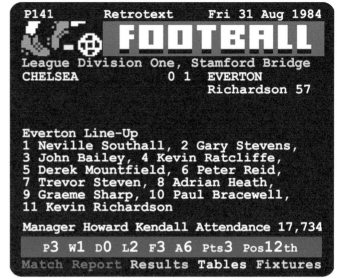

```
P141      Retrotext      Fri 31 Aug 1984
          FOOTBALL
League Division One, Stamford Bridge
CHELSEA                0 1   EVERTON
                             Richardson 57

Everton Line-Up
1 Neville Southall, 2 Gary Stevens,
3 John Bailey, 4 Kevin Ratcliffe,
5 Derek Mountfield, 6 Peter Reid,
7 Trevor Steven, 8 Adrian Heath,
9 Graeme Sharp, 10 Paul Bracewell,
11 Kevin Richardson

Manager Howard Kendall Attendance 17,734

P3 W1 D0 L2 F3 A6 Pts3 Pos12th
Match Report Results Tables Fixtures
```

Despite winning the FA Cup and reaching the League Cup Final, the club's financial accounts had revealed a loss of over £175,000.

This was largely due to investment in players, namely Trevor Steven, Andy Gray, Terry Curran and Paul Bracewell, plus additional payments to Liverpool and Tranmere for Alan Harper and Derek Mountfield respectively.

The annual report also revealed that in 1983-84, average attendances had dropped from 20,276 to 19,290, mainly as a result of the very poor start the club had made to that season.

It also stated that the top earner at the club was on a salary of between £65,000 and £70,000, with six people earning between £35,000 and £40,000 and five between £30,000 and £35,000.

Paul Bracewell missed out on this match after picking up a foot injury on his home debut but thankfully x-rays revealed it wasn't broken. With Kevin Sheedy and Andy Gray also injured, Terry Curran came into the side on the right, with Kevin Richardson moving to the middle and Trevor Steven operating on the left wing.

Two close range headers were the undoing of the Blues and though Inchy was on target again, it was a very underwhelming start to the campaign.

Chelsea had made a very solid start to the new season after being promoted as Division Two champions back in May, drawing 1-1 with Arsenal at Highbury on the opening day and then beating Sunderland 1-0 at Stamford Bridge to sit in fifth spot in the table.

Paul Bracewell had recovered from the injury which had kept him out at the Hawthorns but Andy Gray and Kevin Sheedy were still ruled out.

This Friday night clash was shown live on BBC television but a gusty wind spoilt the match as a spectacle for the viewing public.

The home side had the better of the first-half with Kerry Dixon hitting the bar and missing several other gilt-edged chances.

But after the interval - with harsh words from Howard Kendall ringing in the players' ears and the wind in their favour - the Blues went ahead when Bracewell set up Kevin Richardson to fire into the net.

It was a welcome three points to kick-start the season but the downside was an ankle injury to Peter Reid who faced a battle to be fit for the next game, a midweek match against Ipswich Town at Goodison Park.

It's A Grand Old Team To Play For

Dave Hickson signed for Everton as an eighteen-year-old in 1948 but, due to a stint of National Service in the Army, he didn't make his debut for the club until September 1951, by which time the Blues had been relegated to Division Two. He scored fourteen goals in his first season and another sixteen during the following campaign, including, famously, the winner in a fifth round FA Cup tie in February 1953 against champions Manchester United when he played on despite a bleeding head wound.

Nicknamed 'The Cannonball Kid' for his powerful shot, he scored many crucial goals, including against Birmingham in April 1954 which meant the Blues would be promoted if they beat Oldham in the last game of the season a few days later. Thousands of Evertonians travelled to Boundary Park to witness a 4-0 win with Hickson on target again to take his tally for the season to twenty-eight.

September 1984

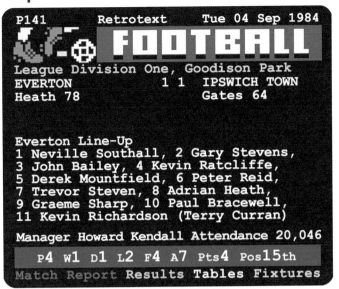

Visitors Ipswich Town had narrowly avoided relegation the previous season and had drawn all their games in the new campaign, 0-0 at West Ham on the opening day plus 1-1 draws at Portman Road against Sunderland and Manchester United respectively.

Everton were looking to bounce back from the shock of the hammering Spurs handed out to them in the first game of the campaign but, despite dominating, it was the Suffolk side which went ahead after a superb strike from Eric Gates.

Terry Curran's introduction from the substitute's bench with twenty minutes left injected some much-needed gusto into the Blues' performance and Adrian Heath's third goal of the season ensured a share of the points.

The day after this game, Kevin Sheedy had a chance to gain some match fitness when he appeared for the Reserves at Sheffield United and came through the outing without any ill-effects, though after holding a 2-0 half-time lead, the Blues' second string collapsed in the second period to lose 6-2.

Worryingly, Andy Gray's knee injury had prevented him from getting some much-needed game time.

In the run up to this game, there was encouraging news on club captain Mark Higgins who had been battling an injury problem for almost twelve months. He would be playing for the A Team on Saturday.

The match saw the return of 1970s legend Bob Latchford to Goodison. Bob had left the club just after Howard Kendall took over to join Swansea City, then managed by ex-Liverpool striker John Toshack. He had a very successful spell at the Vetch Field before he briefly joined Dutch side NAC Breda then moved back to England with Coventry City and he was captain for the day.

After his energetic performance in midweek against Ipswich Town, Terry Curran was pushing for a place in the starting line-up but ultimately he had to settle again for a place on the bench.

Just as in midweek, Everton conceded the first goal with Terry Gibson on target in the first half. Once again, it took the introduction of Curran to liven the game up for the Blues who equalised through Trevor Steven and secured a much-needed three points through Graeme Sharp.

After the game, Howard Kendall took an Everton XI to play a centenary celebration match with FC Sion of Switzerland which the Blues lost 3-2.

It's A Grand Old Team To Support

Dave Hickson was my great hero and I know he was Colin Harvey's too. Dave would bang in some great finishes and was also a tremendous competitor. He always seemed to have blood running down some part of his face and I'm not sure all of it was always his, either!

I met up with Dave not so long ago and we shared a laugh about how big and brave he was. He was always so fit and strong - and he still is - and he sent me a nice card when I got the manager's job.

Hickson was a brave, bustling centre-forward and he was the first number nine I was aware of who really knew what that shirt meant to the Goodison fans.
Manager Joe Royle on Dave Hickson, *The Evertonian*, December 1994

EVERTON
NIL SATIS
NISI OPTIMUM
GOODISON
PARK L4

September 1984

```
P141    Retrotext    Sat 15 Sep 1984
       FOOTBALL
League Division One, St James' Park
NEWCASTLE UTD    2 3    EVERTON
Beardsley 12(pen)       Sheedy 25
Wharton 46              Steven 52
                        Gray 88

Everton Line-Up
1 Neville Southall, 2 Gary Stevens,
3 John Bailey, 4 Kevin Ratcliffe,
5 Derek Mountfield, 6 Peter Reid,
7 Trevor Steven, 8 Adrian Heath,
9 Andy Gray, 10 Paul Bracewell,
11 Kevin Sheedy

Manager Howard Kendall Attendance 29,452
 P6 W3 D1 L2 F9 A10 Pts10 Pos5th
Match Report Results Tables Fixtures
```

```
P141    Retrotext    Wed 19 Sep 1984
       FOOTBALL
European Cup Winners' Cup,
Round 1 (1st leg), Tolka Park, Dublin
UCD              0 0    EVERTON

Everton Line-Up
1 Neville Southall, 2 Gary Stevens,
3 John Bailey, 4 Kevin Ratcliffe,
5 Derek Mountfield, 6 Peter Reid,
7 Trevor Steven (Terry Curran),
8 Adrian Heath, 9 Graeme Sharp,
10 Paul Bracewell, 11 Kevin Sheedy

Manager Howard Kendall Attendance 10,000
      Nil Satis Nisi Optimum
Match Report Results Tables Fixtures
```

This was a bad-tempered affair, with John Bailey booked after only a couple of minutes, and it was the home side who struck first from the penalty spot after Kevin Ratcliffe was ruled to have fouled Chris Waddle, Peter Beardsley converting.

The visitors rode their luck but equalised on twenty-six minutes courtesy of a left foot volley from, who else, Kevin Sheedy.

The second half was only a minute old when Everton found themselves behind again, Derek Mountfield making the mistake which allowed Ken Wharton to nip in and make it 2-1. The Toffees then upped the pressure and were level again on fifty-two minutes as Trevor Steven latched on to a defence-splitting ball from Kevin Ratcliffe.

With time running out, Kevin Sheedy's corner was headed into the net by Andy Gray to send the hoardes of visiting fans into raptures and move the Blues into a share of top spot in the table, with seven teams on ten points.

The Newcastle boss Jack Charlton was fulsome in his praise of the Blues, saying: "Everton had all of the things that I like in the game. They hustle you, play the ball early and are probably the best balanced side in the First Division at the moment."

At the Shareholders Celebration Evening held at Goodison Park earlier in the month, Peter Reid received the Everton Player of the Year trophy having earned no less than ten man-of-the-match awards in the Liverpool Echo the previous season.

Also honoured was first-team coach Colin Harvey, who played 380 games for the Blues between 1963 and 1974, and was now a key element of the backroom team bringing the glory days back to the club.

But the modest Harvey was quick to play down his part in the revival, saying:

"At the end of the day you must lay our success at the feet of the manager. Before Christmas people were calling for Howard's head, but he worked hard to get things right. He sparked us towards the FA Cup success. Mick Heaton played an important role as well and we continue to work as a team."

Apart from the semi-final against Bayern Munich, the games with University College Dublin - a mixture of mature students and seasoned professionals - were probably the most difficult the Blues played in on the road to European glory and the return leg at Goodison was to prove just as tough as this one.

If You Know Your History

At the end of Everton's first season in Division Two, the team finished in seventh place having lost fifteen games, and they performed even worse in the following campaign, languishing in a lowly sixteenth spot just five points above the relegation places.

The 1953-54 season was much more positive with this victory in the last home game keeping alive the Blues' hopes of promotion back to the top flight. Second-placed Blackburn had played all their matches and stood one point ahead of Everton who had one game left, away at Oldham. On the Thursday after this victory, thousands of fans headed to Boundary Park, with the return coach fare costing seven shillings, to see the Blues win 4-0 and book a return to Division One.

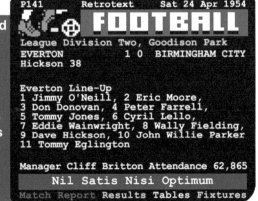

```
P141    Retrotext    Sat 24 Apr 1954
       FOOTBALL
League Division Two, Goodison Park
EVERTON          1 0    BIRMINGHAM CITY
Hickson 38

Everton Line-Up
1 Jimmy O'Neill, 2 Eric Moore,
3 Don Donovan, 4 Peter Farrell,
5 Tommy Jones, 6 Cyril Lello,
7 Eddie Wainwright, 8 Wally Fielding,
9 Dave Hickson, 10 John Willie Parker,
11 Tommy Eglington

Manager Cliff Britton Attendance 62,865
      Nil Satis Nisi Optimum
Match Report Results Tables Fixtures
```

September 1984

Jim Arnold had been one of Howard Kendall's first purchases when he became Everton manager back in 1981 and after months of uncertainty the Blues' boss was delighted when the experienced 'keeper signed a new contract, providing a solid and reliable backup for Neville Southall.

On the negative side, Terry Curran had verbally requested a transfer after becoming frustrated with his lack of first team action despite impressing when coming off the bench, but eventually the manager was able to convince him not to submit a formal request.

Before the Southampton game, it was announced that Everton had agreed a fee of £100,000 with Birmingham City for the transfer of 23-year-old left-back Pat van den Hauwe.

The manager felt this was a position which needed strengthening and Birmingham boss Ron Saunders was happy to do business to fund his own transfer plans.

Everton flew out of the traps against the Saints and established a two goal lead inside ten minutes. Against the run of play, the visitors pulled one back before half-time and a defensive mix-up allowed them to level the game up from the penalty spot.

Pat van den Hauwe's first game for the Blues was in a Reserve team match against Stoke City which they won 5-0. On the same day, x-rays revealed flaking of the bone on the top of Andy Gray's foot, an injury that would require careful management.

This was a thrilling encounter at Bramall Lane with Everton showing great resilience against their lower League opponents to equalise twice after falling behind.

Graeme Sharp scored the first and just when it looked as if the Blues might be making an early exit from the competition after reaching the Final the season before, Derek Mountfield converted a Kevin Sheedy cross to earn a replay two weeks later.

Thoughts then turned to the weekend encounter with Watford, recalling memories of the great day in May when the Blues beat Graham Taylor's side to win the FA Cup, as well as the dramatic 4-4 draw in the League.

Watford had just completed the signing of goalkeeper Tony Coton for £300,000 and he would be replacing Steve Sherwood who had been at fault for Andy Gray's goal at Wembley which had sealed the FA Cup success.

If You Know Your History

Both Everton and Liverpool had installed floodlights and to commemorate the switching on of both systems in 1957, two friendly matches were arranged between the old foes to win the Liverpool County Football Association 75th Anniversary Cup.

On October 9th, Goodison Park's lights were switched on for the first time and Everton won the game 2-0 watched by a huge crowd of 58,771. The return match under Anfield's new lights was played three weeks later, when Liverpool won 3-2 on the night but the Blues lifted the trophy 4-3 on aggregate. Everton's first League match under the floodlights was against Arsenal, with Ian Buchan's side twice coming from behind to earn a draw.

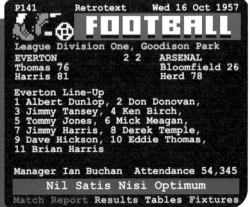

September 1984

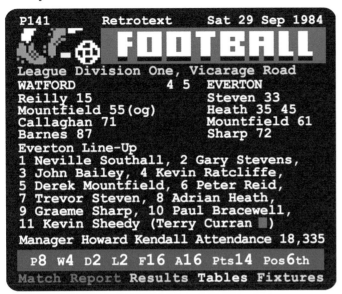

```
P141      Retrotext      Sat 29 Sep 1984
            FOOTBALL
League Division One, Vicarage Road
WATFORD              4 5  EVERTON
Reilly 15                 Steven 33
Mountfield 55(og)         Heath 35 45
Callaghan 71              Mountfield 61
Barnes 87                 Sharp 72
Everton Line-Up
1 Neville Southall, 2 Gary Stevens,
3 John Bailey, 4 Kevin Ratcliffe,
5 Derek Mountfield, 6 Peter Reid,
7 Trevor Steven, 8 Adrian Heath,
9 Graeme Sharp, 10 Paul Bracewell,
11 Kevin Sheedy (Terry Curran  )
Manager Howard Kendall Attendance 18,335

P8 W4 D2 L2 F16 A16 Pts14 Pos6th
Match Report Results Tables Fixtures
```

```
P257 CEEFAX 257  Sun  3 May  23:00/01
            100 YEARS OF THE        3/5
            FA CUP
            75 YEARS AGO
        EVERTON 1-0 NEWCASTLE
Newcastle were deprived of the League
and Cup double in 1905 when Aston Villa
beat them 2-0 in the Cup final.

A year later their luck was no better.
Everton were the underdogs but had the
fortune to catch the Tynesiders on
their bogey ground - Crystal Palace.

Scottish international centre-forward
Young scored the only goal after a fine
run and cross from Taylor in the 75th
minute.
                          More in a moment
```

After the excitement of the eight-goal thriller served up by these sides at Vicarage Road in February, few could have expected this encounter would be even more enthralling.

After falling behind, the Blues showed a great attitude to turn the game on its head and lead 3-1 at the break. Before the hour mark, Derek Mountfield had scored for both teams and though Nigel Callaghan reduced the arrears to a single goal, Graeme Sharp quickly re-established the two-goal advantage.

John Barnes notched a fourth for the home side near the end to ensure a nervy finish but the Blues held on to extend their unbeaten run to eight games, though substitute Terry Curran was sent off in injury time apparently for dissent after an altercation with a linesman.

Curran had come on as substitute for the injured Kevin Sheedy who was expected to be out of action for a fortnight or so.

As Curran's suspension would not start for a couple of weeks, he was free to continue playing and Howard Kendall named him in the line-up for the second leg of the European Cup-Winners' Cup tie against University College Dublin.

This is an original Ceefax page recovered from an old VHS recording.

It was part of a series of pages created to commemorate the 100th FA Cup Final in May 1981 between Manchester City and Tottenham Hotspur and looked back on the very first Final as well as those from 25, 50 and 75 years ago. Everton won the Cup for the first time in 1906.

It's A Grand Old Team To Play For

Alex Young was signed from Hearts by Everton manager Johnny Carey for £40,000 in November 1960 but his debut was delayed for three weeks due to a knee injury. After that one game, a 3-1 home defeat to Bill Nicholson's Tottenham side which would go on to win the double, he was sidelined again until early February.

He finished with six League goals in his first season but contributed fourteen during the next campaign and twenty-two in 1962-63, as the club won the Division One title under new boss Harry Catterick.

Alex was revered by Everton fans, earning the nickname 'The Golden Vision' for his grace and style on the pitch and this was also the name of a famous TV play in the 1960s which featured the Scot and his adoring fans.

October 1984

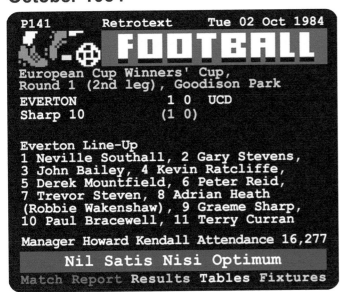

```
P141        Retrotext      Tue 02 Oct 1984
       FOOTBALL
European Cup Winners' Cup,
Round 1 (2nd leg), Goodison Park
EVERTON            1 0    UCD
Sharp 10               (1 0)


Everton Line-Up
1 Neville Southall, 2 Gary Stevens,
3 John Bailey, 4 Kevin Ratcliffe,
5 Derek Mountfield, 6 Peter Reid,
7 Trevor Steven, 8 Adrian Heath
(Robbie Wakenshaw), 9 Graeme Sharp,
10 Paul Bracewell, 11 Terry Curran

Manager Howard Kendall Attendance 16,277

        Nil Satis Nisi Optimum
Match Report  Results Tables Fixtures
```

```
P141        Retrotext      Sat 06 Oct 1984
       FOOTBALL
League Division One, Highbury
ARSENAL            1 0    EVERTON
Nicholas 45(pen)


Everton Line-Up
1 Neville Southall, 2 Gary Stevens,
3 Pat Van Den Hauwe, 4 Kevin Ratcliffe
5 Derek Mountfield, 6 Peter Reid,
7 Trevor Steven, 8 Adrian Heath,
9 Graeme Sharp, 10 Paul Bracewell,
11 Kevin Richardson

Manager Howard Kendall Attendance 37,049

P9 W4 D2 L3 F16 A17 Pts14 Pos8th
Match Report  Results Tables Fixtures
```

With five substitutes allowed for European games, Howard Kendall was able to include club captain Mark Higgins in the squad for this second leg match against UCD, whose manager, Theo Dunne, was a member of the Everton Supporters Club in Dublin.

Dunne had done a terrific job in the first leg to restrict the Blues to a handful of chances but when Graeme Sharp scored after just ten minutes many in the crowd expected the floodgates to open. That it didn't happen is testament to his organisational skills and the commitment of his part-time players.

Neville Southall was untroubled throughout the ninety minutes but if the Irish minnows had been able to find a late equaliser then the Blues would have been out of the competition on the away goals rule.

As it was, Kendall's men made it safely, if not convincingly, into the second round where they were drawn against Inter Bratislava.

John Bailey injured his hamstring in this game, potentially opening the door for new signing Pat van den Hauwe to make his first-team debut in the weekend game at Arsenal. Meanwhile, Andy Gray's troublesome foot had been put in plaster in an attempt to resolve his injury issue.

On the morning of this match, it was announced that the great comedy actor and keen Everton supporter Leonard Rossiter had died, aged 57. He was most famous for his roles as Rigsby in Rising Damp and The Fall and Rise of Reginald Perrin.

As expected, Pat van den Hauwe made his full debut for the Blues as John Bailey had failed to shake off the knock he suffered in midweek. Also out was Terry Curran who had picked up an injury in training and was replaced by Kevin Richardson.

Arsenal had made a great start to the season and coming into the match they were joint top of the table with Tottenham and Nottingham Forest, which each club having accrued sixteen points from their opening eight games.

The only difference between the teams was a controversial penalty on the stroke of half-time.

It involved a coming together between Charlie Nicholas and Kevin Ratcliffe but the referee gave a throw-in before being alerted to the linesman's flag being held aloft.

Nicholas converted the spot kick and the victory gave Arsenal a two-point lead at the top of the table as Tottenham lost 1-0 at Southampton and Forest drew 1-1 at the City Ground with Stoke.

If You Know Your History

The 1962-63 season was severely affected by the Big Freeze when ice and snow engulfed most of the country.

On December 22nd, Everton were top of the table but due to the adverse conditions they didn't play another League game until February 12th, a 3-1 defeat at double-chasing Leicester City.

At the end of March, the Blues lay in third spot but a twelve match unbeaten run between April 1st and this match in May - including winning six of the last seven games, one of them a crunch clash with Tottenham at Goodison Park settled by a solitary Alex Young goal - ensured a sixth League title for the club.

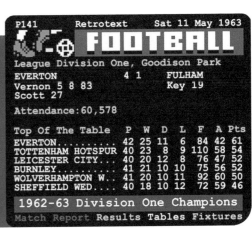

```
P141        Retrotext      Sat 11 May 1963
       FOOTBALL
League Division One, Goodison Park
EVERTON            4 1    FULHAM
Vernon 5 8 83            Key 19
Scott 27

Attendance:60,578
```

Top Of The Table	P	W	D	L	F	A	Pts
EVERTON	42	25	11	6	84	42	61
TOTTENHAM HOTSPUR	40	23	8	9	110	58	54
LEICESTER CITY	40	20	12	8	76	47	52
BURNLEY	41	21	10	10	75	56	52
WOLVERHAMPTON W.	41	20	10	11	92	60	50
SHEFFIELD WED.	40	18	10	12	72	59	46

```
1962-63 Division One Champions
Match Report  Results Tables Fixtures
```

October 1984

P141   Retrotext   Wed 10 Oct 1984

FOOTBALL

League Cup Round 2 (2nd Leg),
Goodison Park
EVERTON   4 0   SHEFFIELD UTD
Mountfield 6   (6 2)
Bracewell 56
Sharp 67 Heath 74
Everton Line-Up
1 Neville Southall, 2 Gary Stevens,
3 Pat Van Den Hauwe, 4 Kevin
Ratcliffe, 5 Derek Mountfield,
6 Peter Reid, 7 Trevor Steven,
8 Adrian Heath, 9 Graeme Sharp,
10 Paul Bracewell, 11 Kevin Richardson
Manager Howard Kendall Attendance 18,740

Nil Satis Nisi Optimum

Match Report Results Tables Fixtures

P141   Retrotext   Sat 13 Oct 1984

FOOTBALL

League Division One, Goodison Park
EVERTON   2 1   ASTON VILLA
Sharp 26   Withe 43
Heath 74

Everton Line-Up
1 Neville Southall, 2 Gary Stevens,
3 Pat Van Den Hauwe, 4 Kevin
Ratcliffe, 5 Derek Mountfield,
6 Peter Reid, 7 Trevor Steven,
8 Adrian Heath, 9 Graeme Sharp,
10 Paul Bracewell, 11 Alan Harper

Manager Howard Kendall Attendance 25,043

P10 W5 D2 L3 F18 A18 Pts17 Pos6th

Match Report Results Tables Fixtures

With John Bailey still out injured, Pat van den Hauwe made his home debut in what turned out to be an emphatic victory for the Blues.

Having drawn 2-2 in the first match, Everton went ahead on aggregate early on when centre-half Derek Mountfield scored his fourth goal in six games.

Surprisingly, given the home side's domination, it was not until the second period that Howard Kendall's side scored again, Paul Bracewell notching his first goal for the club since his move from Sunderland.

Adrian Heath and Graeme Sharp completed the scoring and the one-sided nature of the contest was reflected in the corner count - fifteen for Everton and zero for the visitors.

The third round draw was not kind, though, with the Toffees drawn to play Manchester United at Old Trafford, just three days after facing Ron Atkinson's men in a League match at Goodison Park.

Both games were to be played before the end of October and, with the small matter of a Merseyside derby at Anfield also to come, what a momentous month it promised to be for manager Kendall and his players.

Ahead of the game with Villa and with a hectic schedule of games in October, the Blues were hit by an injury crisis with Kevin Richardson's injured toe forcing him to miss out along with Andy Gray, Kevin Sheedy, Terry Curran, Mark Higgins and John Bailey.

Visitors Villa were coming off a terrific 3-0 over Manchester United the week before and there was lots of media interest in their new French winger, Didier Six.

To add some spice to the occasion, ex-Everton favourite Steve McMahon, who left after a contract dispute, was in the Villa line-up and he soon had the crowd on his back when he clattered into Peter Reid, earning a booking.

Everton went ahead through a thumping Graeme Sharp header but scouser Peter Withe levelled things up on the stroke of half-time.

The Blues had the chance to re-take the lead on the hour mark when Sharp was fouled in the area but Adrian Heath's spot kick hit goalkeeper Mervyn Day's legs.

Inchy was to have the last laugh, though, scoring from a Sharp knock down to give the home side a fully deserved three points.

If You Know Your History

In the early rounds of the 1966 FA Cup, Everton enjoyed 3-0 victories against Sunderland, non-League Bedford and Coventry City to set up a quarter-final clash with Joe Mercer's Manchester City.

Over 63,000 watched that game at Maine Road which finished 0-0 and another 60,000+ crowd crammed into Goodison three days later for the replay, also 0-0. The tie was finally settled at Molineux where the Blues won 2-0, thanks to goals from Derek Temple and Fred Pickering.

In the semi-final at Burnden Park, Bolton, Colin Harvey scored the only goal to put Harry Catterick's side through to Wembley and set up one of the most dramatic Finals in the competition's history.

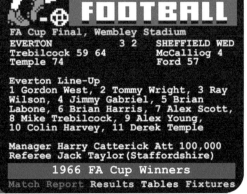

P141   Retrotext   Sat 14 May 1966

FOOTBALL

FA Cup Final, Wembley Stadium
EVERTON   3 2   SHEFFIELD WED
Trebilcock 59 64   McCalliog 4
Temple 74   Ford 57

Everton Line-Up
1 Gordon West, 2 Tommy Wright, 3 Ray
Wilson, 4 Jimmy Gabriel, 5 Brian
Labone, 6 Brian Harris, 7 Alex Scott,
8 Mike Trebilcock, 9 Alex Young,
10 Colin Harvey, 11 Derek Temple

Manager Harry Catterick Att 100,000
Referee Jack Taylor(Staffordshire)

1966 FA Cup Winners

Match Report Results Tables Fixtures

October 1984

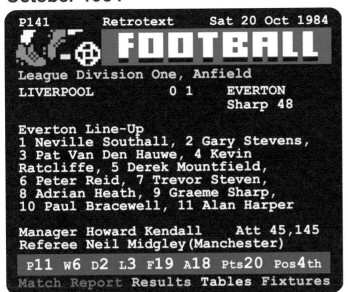

```
P141      Retrotext      Sat 20 Oct 1984
        FOOTBALL
League Division One, Anfield
LIVERPOOL           0 1      EVERTON
                             Sharp 48

Everton Line-Up
1 Neville Southall, 2 Gary Stevens,
3 Pat Van Den Hauwe, 4 Kevin
Ratcliffe, 5 Derek Mountfield,
6 Peter Reid, 7 Trevor Steven,
8 Adrian Heath, 9 Graeme Sharp,
10 Paul Bracewell, 11 Alan Harper

Manager Howard Kendall    Att 45,145
Referee Neil Midgley(Manchester)
P11 W6 D2 L3 F19 A18 Pts20 Pos4th
Match Report Results Tables Fixtures
```

```
P141      Retrotext      Wed 24 Oct 1984
        FOOTBALL
European Cup Winners' Cup,
Round 2 (1st leg), Stadion Pasienky
INTER BRATISLAVA  0 1   EVERTON
                         Bracewell 5

Everton Line-Up
1 Neville Southall, 2 Gary Stevens,
3 John Bailey, 4 Kevin Ratcliffe,
5 Derek Mountfield, 6 Peter Reid,
7 Trevor Steven, 8 Adrian Heath,
9 Graeme Sharp, 10 Paul Bracewell,
11 Alan Harper

Manager Howard Kendall Attendance 15,000
        Nil Satis Nisi Optimum
Match Report Results Tables Fixtures
```

Ahead of the weekend's clash with Liverpool, the Blues were boosted by the return from injury of both Andy Gray and John Bailey. The pair played for the Reserves against Manchester United at Goodison Park in midweek, with Gray on the scoresheet in a 2-1 defeat.

Though not deemed fit enough to start, Gray earned himself a place on the substitute's bench at Anfield as the Blues looked to extend their unbeaten run to twelve games.

The bad news for Everton was that arch nemesis Ian Rush was declared fit enough to make his first start of the season after recovering from a cartilage operation. Liverpool had struggled in his absence and coming into the match were in the bottom half of the table with only two wins from eleven games.

Seeking a first win at Anfield since 1970, the only goal of the game was scored by Rush's opposite number, Graeme Sharp, just after half-time.

The Scottish striker controlled a long ball from Gary Stevens with his left foot and then volleyed an unstoppable shot with his right foot past goalkeeper Bruce Grobbelaar.

Such was the quality, it would later be named Match of the Day's 'Goal of the Season'.

Having struggled to see off the minnows of University College Dublin in the first round, Everton then faced Czech side Inter Bratislava in what would ultimately be a glorious European Cup-Winners' Cup campaign.

Ahead of the game, Howard Kendall reminisced about his own European experience, the season after Everton had been crowned 1969-70 League champions. He said:

"We had a fairly easy win over Keflavik from Iceland, then we got through against Borussia Moenchengladbach on penalties. They were a very strong side at the time so we felt confident against Panathinaikos of Greece. Unfortunately, we drew at Goodison and again in the return and went out on the away goals rule."

The manager was boosted by the availability of Andy Gray, Terry Curran, Kevin Sheedy and John Bailey for the tie, with Bailey returning after a four-match injury absence in the place of the ineligible Pat van den Hauwe.

An early Paul Bracewell header was enough to settle the first leg which the Blues largely controlled without threatening too much to add to the scoreboard.

It's A Grand Old Team To Play For

Derek Temple is most fondly remembered by Evertonians for scoring the winning goal for the Blues in the 1966 FA Cup Final, when Harry Catterick's side came from 2-0 down to win 3-2.

But Derek also played a key role in helping the team to reach Wembley, scoring in the third round against Sunderland, notching a double in the fourth round against non-League Bedford, and another in the fifth round success against Coventry. That set up a sixth round tie with Manchester City which was finally settled in the second replay, with Temple on target together with Fred Pickering.

Having made his debut in March 1957, Derek was transferred to Preston in September 1967 for a fee of £40,000 after 275 appearances and 83 goals.

October 1984

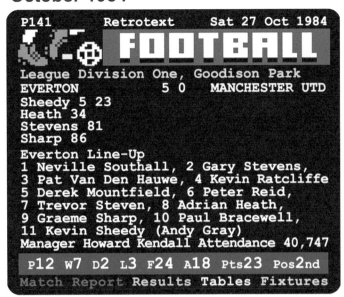

```
P141      Retrotext      Sat 27 Oct 1984
        FOOTBALL
League Division One, Goodison Park
EVERTON           5 0    MANCHESTER UTD
Sheedy 5 23
Heath 34
Stevens 81
Sharp 86
Everton Line-Up
1 Neville Southall, 2 Gary Stevens,
3 Pat Van Den Hauwe, 4 Kevin Ratcliffe
5 Derek Mountfield, 6 Peter Reid,
7 Trevor Steven, 8 Adrian Heath,
9 Graeme Sharp, 10 Paul Bracewell,
11 Kevin Sheedy (Andy Gray)
Manager Howard Kendall Attendance 40,747
P12 W7 D2 L3 F24 A18 Pts23 Pos2nd
Match Report Results Tables Fixtures
```

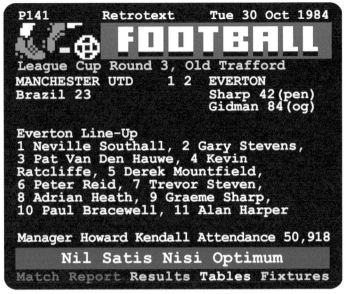

```
P141      Retrotext      Tue 30 Oct 1984
        FOOTBALL
League Cup Round 3, Old Trafford
MANCHESTER UTD    1 2    EVERTON
Brazil 23                Sharp 42(pen)
                         Gidman 84(og)

Everton Line-Up
1 Neville Southall, 2 Gary Stevens,
3 Pat Van Den Hauwe, 4 Kevin
Ratcliffe, 5 Derek Mountfield,
6 Peter Reid, 7 Trevor Steven,
8 Adrian Heath, 9 Graeme Sharp,
10 Paul Bracewell, 11 Alan Harper

Manager Howard Kendall Attendance 50,918
Nil Satis Nisi Optimum
Match Report Results Tables Fixtures
```

Having defeated Liverpool at Anfield, the Toffees were full of confidence for this clash and tore into the visitors from the first whistle.

Kevin Sheedy opened the scoring after just five minutes, deftly placing a header from Derek Mountfield's cross past United keeper Gary Bailey, clashing heads with Kevin Moran as he did so.

In the twenty-third minute, Sheedy was on the mark again, latching onto a pass from Adrian Heath to fire home.

When a concussed Moran was forced to leave the field to be substituted by Frank Stapleton, 'Inchy' got on the scoresheet himself and the Blues went in at the interval three goals to the good.

After totally outclassing their opponents in the first period, the match was slightly more even after half-time but, with ten minutes left, Gary Stevens scored from 25 yards and four minutes from time Graeme Sharp made it 5-0 to complete the rout.

Afterwards former Blues player and ex-Manchester City manager Joe Mercer said, "It was the best performance by any Everton side I can remember" while Howard Kendall commented that "everyone did their job and the amount of work our midfield got through was unbelievable."

Three days later, the two teams met again at Old Trafford in the Milk (League) Cup, with the Toffees again coming out on top.

Without Kevin Sheedy, who had left the pitch early on Saturday due to a groin injury and despite falling behind to an Alan Brazil strike, Everton advanced to the next round thanks to a Graeme Sharp penalty and a John Gidman own goal.

When the draw for the fourth round was made, the Blues were pitted against the winners of the Grimsby Town versus Rotherham replay.

It was Grimsby who were emphatic 6-1 winners of that one to earn the right to play at Goodison Park. Many fans thought it would be an easy stepping stone to the quarter-finals and a number of bookmakers agreed, making Everton favourites to lift the trophy.

It had been a sensational month for the Blues with seven wins from eight games played, the only reverse being the defeat at Arsenal and that was to a controversial penalty.

Indeed, that was Everton's only loss since the first two games of the League season and the irresistible form of Howard's Kendall's side would soon see them on top of the Division One table.

If You Know Your History

Goodison Park hosted three group games during the 1966 World Cup tournament, all featuring Brazil who had won the trophy in 1958 and 1962. The South Americans were strong favourites to advance to the quarter-final stage but, after a winning start against Bulgaria, defeats by Hungary and Portugal saw them eliminated.

Friday 15 July, 1966
BRAZIL 1 (Tostao 14) HUNGARY 3 (Bene 2, Farkas 64, Mészöly 73 pen)
Attendance 51,387
Tuesday 19 July, 1966
BRAZIL 1 (Rildo 73) PORTUGAL 3 (Simões 15, Eusébio 27, 85)
Attendance 58,479

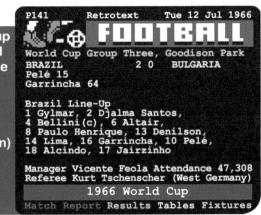

```
P141      Retrotext      Tue 12 Jul 1966
        FOOTBALL
World Cup Group Three, Goodison Park
BRAZIL            2 0    BULGARIA
Pelé 15
Garrincha 64

Brazil Line-Up
1 Gylmar, 2 Djalma Santos,
4 Bellini(c), 6 Altair,
8 Paulo Henrique, 13 Denilson,
14 Lima, 16 Garrincha, 10 Pelé,
18 Alcindo, 17 Jairzinho
Manager Vicente Feola Attendance 47,308
Referee Kurt Tschenscher (West Germany)
1966 World Cup
Match Report Results Tables Fixtures
```

November 1984

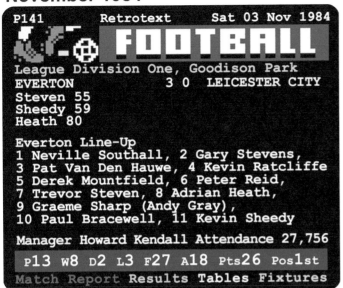

P141   Retrotext   Sat 03 Nov 1984

FOOTBALL

League Division One, Goodison Park
EVERTON   3 0   LEICESTER CITY
Steven 55
Sheedy 59
Heath 80

Everton Line-Up
1 Neville Southall, 2 Gary Stevens,
3 Pat Van Den Hauwe, 4 Kevin Ratcliffe
5 Derek Mountfield, 6 Peter Reid,
7 Trevor Steven, 8 Adrian Heath,
9 Graeme Sharp (Andy Gray),
10 Paul Bracewell, 11 Kevin Sheedy

Manager Howard Kendall Attendance 27,756

P13 W8 D2 L3 F27 A18 Pts26 Pos1st

Match Report Results Tables Fixtures

P141   Retrotext   Wed 07 Nov 1984

FOOTBALL

European Cup Winners' Cup,
Round 2 (2nd leg), Goodison Park
EVERTON   3 0   INTER BRATISLAVA
Sharp 42 (pen)
Sheedy 44
Heath 63
Everton Line-Up
1 Neville Southall, 2 Gary Stevens,
3 John Bailey, 4 Kevin Ratcliffe,
5 Derek Mountfield, 6 Peter Reid
(Alan Harper), 7 Trevor Steven,
8 Adrian Heath, 9 Graeme Sharp,
10 Paul Bracewell, 11 Kevin Sheedy
(John Morrissey)
Manager Howard Kendall Attendance 25,007

Nil Satis Nisi Optimum

Match Report Results Tables Fixtures

Everton were seeking their seventh straight victory in this clash against a Leicester City side featuring future one-season Blues star Gary Lineker, as well as former player, Peter Eastoe.

Howard Kendall had won the Bell's Manager of the Month award after the series of impressive wins.

All this success came just one year on from calls for him to be sacked, with leaflets being handed out at Goodison Park following a narrow 3-2 aggregate Milk Cup success over Chesterfield.

After a goalless first-half and with the wind at their backs, the Blues upped the tempo in the second period and the visitors had no answer.

On fifty-five minutes, Trevor Steven hammered home after good interplay with Kevin Sheedy and Adrian Heath, and just a few minutes later Sheedy made it two. Ten minutes from time 'Inchy' rounded things off with his ninth goal of the season.

The victory took Kendall's side to the top of the Division One table for the first time since February 10th, 1979 when a 4-1 victory over Bristol City saw them leapfrog Liverpool and West Brom.

Andy King hit a hat-trick that day, with centre-half Billy Wright also on target.

Two goals just before half-time from Graeme Sharp and Kevin Sheedy put the Blues firmly in the driving seat and Adrian Heath made it 3-0 on the night just after the hour mark for a convincing 4-0 aggregate victory.

The draw for the next round was made a couple of days later though the matches themselves would not take place until March.

The teams left in at the quarter-final stage in addition to Everton were Celtic, Roma, Bayern Munich, Moscow Dynamo, Fortuna Sittard, Larissa and Dinamo Dresden, with the Toffees drawn to face Dutch side Sittard.

Celtic had beaten the Austrian outfit Rapid Vienna 3-0 on the night to go through 4-3 on aggregate but this result was later annulled due to various controversial incidents and ultimately ordered to be replayed at Old Trafford in December, when Celtic went out 1-0 on the night, 4-1 on aggregate.

As all Evertonians know, their opponents would make full use of their second chance to go on and reach the final of the competition in May.

Before the game, the club had revealed the signing of utility player Ian Atkins from Sunderland for a fee reported to be £70,000.

If You Know Your History

Amongst the legendary players who graced the Goodison Park pitch during the 1966 World Cup was Edson Arantes Do Nascimento, better known as Pelé. As a 17-year-old, he had scored one of the goals in Brazil's 1958 World Cup Final victory over Sweden but missed his country's win in the 1962 Final due to injury.

Pelé scored in Brazil's opening group game against Bulgaria but he was on the receiving end of many heavy tackles and missed the defeat against Hungary. Pelé was back in the team for Brazil's crucial final match in Group Three against Portugal, who had won both their games, but he was again targeted by the opposition and one particularly heavy challenge on the half-hour mark resulted in him having to leave the field for five minutes. When he returned, he was a hobbling passenger and Brazil were eliminated after a 3-1 defeat.

November 1984

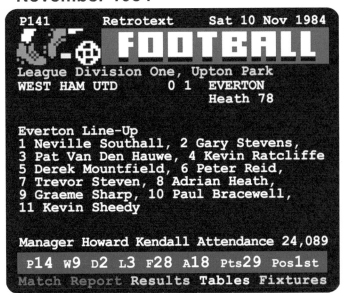

```
P141      Retrotext      Sat 10 Nov 1984
      FOOTBALL
League Division One, Upton Park
WEST HAM UTD      0 1   EVERTON
                         Heath 78

Everton Line-Up
1 Neville Southall, 2 Gary Stevens,
3 Pat Van Den Hauwe, 4 Kevin Ratcliffe
5 Derek Mountfield, 6 Peter Reid,
7 Trevor Steven, 8 Adrian Heath,
9 Graeme Sharp, 10 Paul Bracewell,
11 Kevin Sheedy

Manager Howard Kendall Attendance 24,089
P14 W9 D2 L3 F28 A18 Pts29 Pos1st
Match Report  Results Tables Fixtures
```

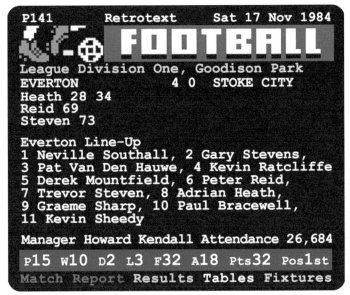

```
P141      Retrotext      Sat 17 Nov 1984
      FOOTBALL
League Division One, Goodison Park
EVERTON          4 0   STOKE CITY
Heath 28 34
Reid 69
Steven 73

Everton Line-Up
1 Neville Southall, 2 Gary Stevens,
3 Pat Van Den Hauwe, 4 Kevin Ratcliffe
5 Derek Mountfield, 6 Peter Reid,
7 Trevor Steven, 8 Adrian Heath,
9 Graeme Sharp, 10 Paul Bracewell,
11 Kevin Sheedy

Manager Howard Kendall Attendance 26,684
P15 W10 D2 L3 F32 A18 Pts32 Pos1st
Match Report  Results Tables Fixtures
```

Although England manager Bobby Robson ignored the claims of both Peter Reid and Adrian Heath, international recognition was given to Gary Stevens and Derek Mountfield, with the pair selected to play for England B in a match against New Zealand, while Trevor Steven and Paul Bracewell were named in the England Under-21 squad.

On the injury front, there was bad news for Kevin Richardson as he was ruled out for up to six weeks after an operation on his troublesome toe.

After being ineligible for the game against Inter Bratislava, Pat van den Hauwe was brought back into the Everton line-up at Upton Park, much to the disappointment of John Bailey who indicated he would be having a chat with the manager.

A solitary strike from Adrian Heath was enough to secure the three points and consolidate Everton's position at the top of the table.

The victory also equalled the club's record of nine straight wins set between March 2nd and April 15th, 1968.

This run included a 6-2 hammering of West Brom at the Hawthorns just weeks before the Blues lost in the FA Cup Final to the same team.

Before the game, popular player Mark Higgins was warmly applauded by the crowd after he had announced his retirement earlier in the week due to injury issues.

After almost a year of problems, Mark seemed to be over the worst when he was named on the substitutes' bench for the second leg of the European Cup-Winners' Cup tie against University College Dublin at the beginning of October.

But, alas, a specialist confirmed that we would have no option but to hang up his boots.

Everton set a post-war club record with this thumping of Stoke City, notching a tenth straight victory and consolidating the side's position at the top of the Division One table.

Adrian Heath was on target twice in the first half, his twelfth and thirteenth goals of the season, to put the Blues firmly in control at the interval against the division's bottom side.

More Everton pressure continued in the second period but the third goal didn't arrive until near the seventy minute mark, Peter Reid scoring his first of the campaign, and Trevor Steven made it 4-0.

If You Know Your History

In the long history of Goodison Park, this was one of the most astonishing matches ever played there. Portugal were expected to brush aside their opponents after winning all three of their group games, though North Korea had shocked the football world by beating Italy 1-0 to reach this knockout phase of the tournament.

The spectators inside the stadium could not believe their eyes when the underdogs raced into a three-goal lead inside the first twenty-five minutes but then the player of the tournament to this point, Eusébio, began the comeback and before half-time he reduced the arrears further. The Benfica star scored two more in the second period and Jose Augusto added a fifth to set up a semi-final clash with England.

```
P141      Retrotext      Sat 23 Jul 1966
      FOOTBALL
World Cup Quarter-Final,Goodison Park
PORTUGAL          5 3   NORTH KOREA
Eusébio 27 43(pen)        Seung Zin 1
57 61(pen)                Dong Woon 20
Augusto 80                Seung Kook 22
Portugal Line-Up
3 José Pereira, 17 Morais,
20 Alexandre Baptista, 4 Vicente,
9 Hilário, 16 Jaime Graça,
10 Mário Coluna(c), 12 José Augusto,
13 Eusébio, 18 José Torres,
11 António Simões

Manager Otto Glória Attendance 40,248
      1966 World Cup
Match Report  Results Tables Fixtures
```

November 1984

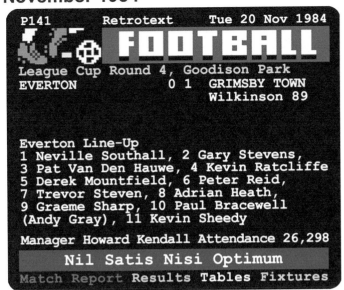

```
P141        Retrotext        Tue 20 Nov 1984
      FOOTBALL
League Cup Round 4, Goodison Park
EVERTON               0 1   GRIMSBY TOWN
                            Wilkinson 89


Everton Line-Up
1 Neville Southall, 2 Gary Stevens,
3 Pat Van Den Hauwe, 4 Kevin Ratcliffe
5 Derek Mountfield, 6 Peter Reid,
7 Trevor Steven, 8 Adrian Heath,
9 Graeme Sharp, 10 Paul Bracewell
(Andy Gray), 11 Kevin Sheedy

Manager Howard Kendall Attendance 26,298
        Nil Satis Nisi Optimum
Match Report Results Tables Fixtures
```

```
P141        Retrotext        Sat 24 Nov 1984
      FOOTBALL
League Division One, Carrow Road
NORWICH CITY          4 2   EVERTON
Deehan 15 64                Sharp 27
Gordon 17                   Sheedy 50
Donowa 25

Everton Line-Up
1 Neville Southall, 2 Gary Stevens,
3 Pat Van Den Hauwe (Andy Gray),
4 Kevin Ratcliffe, 5 Derek Mountfield,
6 Peter Reid, 7 Trevor Steven,
8 Adrian Heath, 9 Graeme Sharp,
10 Paul Bracewell, 11 Kevin Sheedy

Manager Howard Kendall Attendance 16,477
 P16 W10 D2 L4 F34 A22 Pts32 Pos1st
Match Report Results Tables Fixtures
```

There was no squad rotation for Cup games in the 1980s and the Blues were at full strength for what on paper seemed like it would be a routine win over lower League opponents.

There was no sense of complacency either as Howard Kendall himself had been to watch the 6-1 replay victory which booked Grimsby's place in this round.

As well as a clutch of promising young players in their ranks, including England Under-21 international Paul Wilkinson, Grimsby also had veteran Chris Nicholl at the heart of their defence.

Blues' fans had painful memories of Nicholl, as the centre-half scored one of Aston Villa's goals in the 3-2 League Cup Final victory over Everton in 1977.

From start to finish, the home side mounted attack after attack but failed to put any of the numerous chances into the net.

The corner count of nineteen to zero in favour of the Blues told it's own story, but there is only one statistic that really matters and that is the goal tally.

With just seconds left and a replay at Blundell Park looking likely, it was Grimsby striker Wilkinson who put the ball in the back of the net to leave most of the 26,000 present stunned into silence.

Though disappointed by the result against Grimsby, Howard Kendall had no complaints about the performance of his side and vowed to name the same starting eleven for the weekend clash with Norwich City, injuries permitting.

Grimsby's reward for their giantkilling was the opportunity to do it again, with a plum home draw in the quarter-final against the Blues' next opponents. But the Mariners' dreams of Wembley glory were dashed by the East Anglian side who would go on to lift the League Cup against Sunderland in March.

The Carrow Road faithful were in dreamland when their team raced into a 3-0 lead against the table-toppers within twenty-five minutes of the start.

Though Graeme Sharp pulled one back almost immediately and Kevin Sheedy narrowed the arrears in the second half, John Deehan's second of the match ensured the Blues would head back to Goodison Park empty-handed.

But the defeat was not too costly, as nearest pursuers Manchester United lost 3-2 at Sunderland, Tottenham drew 1-1 with Chelsea and Arsenal were beaten 2-1 by Sheffield Wednesday so the Blues still had a three-point cushion at the top of the table.

If You Know Your History

Eusébio da Silva Ferreira, to give him his full name, was one of the greatest players of his generation who scored no less than six goals at Goodison Park during the 1966 World Cup.

In the group stages, Portugal's first two games were played at Old Trafford, where they beat Hungary 3-1 and Bulgaria 3-0, Eusébio scoring one. Portugal's final game in Group Three was at Goodison against Brazil and he scored twice to confirm his country's place in the quarter-final. He almost single-handedly dragged Portugal into the semi-final against England, scoring four times as they beat North Korea 5-3. Eusébio's penalty in a 2-1 loss to Sir Alf Ramsey's men at Wembley and another in a 2-1 win for Portugal against the Soviet Union to clinch third place saw him finish the tournament as top scorer with nine goals.

December 1984

```
P141        Retrotext      Sat 01 Dec 1984
        FOOTBALL
League Division One, Goodison Park
EVERTON           1 1   SHEFFIELD WED.
Sharp 28(pen)           Blair 7


Everton Line-Up
1 Neville Southall, 2 Gary Stevens,
3 Pat Van Den Hauwe, 4 Kevin Ratcliffe
5 Derek Mountfield, 6 Peter Reid,
7 Trevor Steven, 8 Adrian Heath
(Andy Gray), 9 Graeme Sharp,
10 Paul Bracewell, 11 Kevin Sheedy

Manager Howard Kendall Attendance 35,409
P17 W10 D3 L4 F35 A23 Pts33 Pos1st
Match Report Results Tables Fixtures
```

```
P141        Retrotext      Sat 08 Dec 1984
        FOOTBALL
League Division One, Loftus Road
QPR               0 0   EVERTON
Stainrod ■             Van Den Hauwe ■


Everton Line-Up
1 Neville Southall, 2 Gary Stevens,
3 Pat Van Den Hauwe, 4 Kevin Ratcliffe
5 Derek Mountfield, 6 Peter Reid,
7 Trevor Steven, 8 Andy Gray,
9 Graeme Sharp, 10 Paul Bracewell,
11 Kevin Sheedy

Manager Howard Kendall Attendance 14,338
P18 W10 D4 L4 F35 A23 Pts34 Pos1st
Match Report Results Tables Fixtures
```

Sheffield Wednesday had been one of the leading Division One sides in the 1960s but dropped into Division Three during the 1970s.

Under manager Howard Wilkinson, the club was enjoying a resurgence and in season 1983-84 earned promotion back to the top flight, enabling three ex-players to grace the Goodison Park pitch again - striker Imre Varadi, goalkeeper Martin Hodge and, in particular, defender Mike Lyons.

In the 1970s, Mike Lyons was the equivalent of Seamus Coleman - he was a player who had blue blood coarsing through his veins and would fight for the shirt whether playing in defence or attack, as he was often called upon to do.

The Blues went behind early on but worse was to follow on seventeen minutes when Adrian Heath was left in a heap after a heavy challenge by Brian Marwood, having to leave the field as a result.

Marwood was booked and was later on the receiving end of a full-blooded Peter Reid tackle for which the midfielder was also booked. Marwood did not re-appear for the second half.

Though Graeme Sharp equalised from the spot, the day was soured by the injury to Inchy as everyone waited for news on the extent of the damage.

On the Sunday after the Sheffield Wednesday match, Inchy had an operation on his damaged knee ligaments and it looked probable that he would miss the rest of the season, a huge blow to the player and the team as he was joint leading scorer with thirteen goals.

Howard Kendall did not think Brian Marwood's tackle was malicious and he contacted Wednesday to ask them to inform the player that he should not feel responsible for Adrian's likely long layoff.

The manager now turned his attention to the next game against QPR on the unique plastic surface at Loftus Road which he described as similar to playing on an icy pitch.

QPR had just sacked their manager Alan Mullery so caretaker boss Frank Sibley was in the dugout when the two teams kicked off.

Andy Gray replaced the unfortunate Heath and he was involved in the game's major talking point ten minutes before half-time.

The Scottish striker made a robust challenge on Gary Waddock which the QPR players reacted to and, after the resulting melee, Pat van den Hauwe and Simon Stainrod were dismissed, with Gray booked.

If You Know Your History

There was uproar in the city of Liverpool before this match as FIFA had indicated ahead of the World Cup starting that should England reach the semi-final, the game would be played at Goodison Park, partly to counter criticism that the home country had an unfair advantage by playing all its fixtures at Wembley Stadium.

However, the FIFA organising committee said the England versus Portugal match should be switched to the venue where it could be watched by the most people. It was still a huge honour for Everton to have had its stadium selected to host five games at the World Cup, reflecting the prestigious position the club and the ground held in English football at this time.

```
P141        Retrotext      Mon 25 Jul 1966
        FOOTBALL
World Cup Semi-Final, Goodison Park
WEST GERMANY      2 1   U.S.S.R.
Haller 43               Porkuyan 88
Beckenbauer 68


West Germany Line-Up
1 Hans Tilkowski, 3 Karl-Heinz
Schnellinger, 5 Willi Schulz,
6 Wolfgang Weber, 14 Friedel Lutz,
4 Franz Beckenbauer, 8 Helmut Haller,
12 Wolfgang Overath, 9 Uwe Seeler(c),
10 Siegfried Held, 11 Lothar Emmerich
Manager Helmut Schön Attendance 38,273
        1966 World Cup
Match Report Results Tables Fixtures
```

December 1984

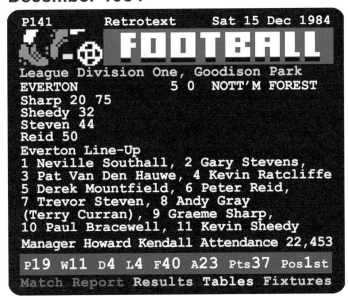

```
P141        Retrotext      Sat 15 Dec 1984
        FOOTBALL
League Division One, Goodison Park
EVERTON          5 0   NOTT'M FOREST
Sharp 20 75
Sheedy 32
Steven 44
Reid 50
Everton Line-Up
1 Neville Southall, 2 Gary Stevens,
3 Pat Van Den Hauwe, 4 Kevin Ratcliffe
5 Derek Mountfield, 6 Peter Reid,
7 Trevor Steven, 8 Andy Gray
(Terry Curran), 9 Graeme Sharp,
10 Paul Bracewell, 11 Kevin Sheedy
Manager Howard Kendall Attendance 22,453
P19 W11 D4 L4 F40 A23 Pts37 Pos1st
Match Report  Results Tables Fixtures
```

```
P141        Retrotext      Sat 22 Dec 1984
        FOOTBALL
League Division One, Goodison Park
EVERTON          3 4   CHELSEA
Bracewell 35            Davies 9 40 72
Sharp 69 88(pens)       Pates 61

Everton Line-Up
1 Neville Southall, 2 Gary Stevens,
3 John Bailey, 4 Kevin Ratcliffe,
5 Derek Mountfield, 6 Peter Reid,
7 Trevor Steven, 8 Andy Gray,
9 Graeme Sharp, 10 Paul Bracewell,
11 Kevin Sheedy
Manager Howard Kendall Attendance 29,867
P20 W11 D4 L5 F43 A27 Pts37 Pos3rd
Match Report  Results Tables Fixtures
```

As the second round FA Cup matches had been played on the Saturday, as usual the draw for the third round was made on Monday afternoon. Holders Everton were drawn away to Leeds United, then managed by Eddie Gray, with the game subsequently chosen for live TV coverage.

Howard Kendall confirmed that Pat van den Hauwe would be suspended for games against Chelsea and Sunderland over the Christmas period due to his dismissal at the weekend.

In midweek, 40,000 Celtic fans travelled to Old Trafford for a European Cup-Winners' Cup clash with Rapid Vienna. UEFA had ordered the match to be replayed at a neutral venue after crowd trouble when the Scottish side beat their Austrian counterparts 3-0 in November to seemingly advance to the next round 4-3 on aggregate.

But there were more terrible scenes in Manchester as Rapid players Herbert Feurer and Peter Pacult were attacked by Celtic supporters. Rapid won the game 1-0 to book their place in the quarter-final at the Scottish side's expense.

Come Saturday, Everton maintained top spot in Division One with this thumping of Brian Clough's Nottingham Forest, for a first win in five matches.

The day before the game with Forest, the draw had been made for the quarter-finals of the European Cup Winners' Cup with Everton paired against Dutch side Fortuna Sittard, the game to be played over two legs in March. The rest of the draw was:

Larissa (Greece) v Dynamo Moscow (Soviet Union); Bayern Munich (West Germany) v AS Roma (Italy); Rapid Vienna (Austria) v Dynamo Dresden (East Germany)

The day after the 5-0 win, a healthy crowd of over 16,000 saw a Merseyside XI beat a Manchester XI 6-5 in Mark Higgins' Testimonial Match, with current players from Everton, Liverpool, City and United taking part which would be unthinkable today.

With Pat van den Hauwe serving the first of his two-match ban, John Bailey made a welcome return to the starting line-up for this match with Chelsea.

The man of the match for the visitors was their recent £90,000 signing from Fulham, Gordon Davies, whose hat-trick gave them the three points in a seven-goal thriller.

The defeat saw the Blues drop to third in the table, after Manchester United beat Ipswich 3-0 and Spurs won 2-1 at Norwich City.

If You Know Your History

Franz Beckenbauer was just twenty-years-old when he played for West Germany during the 1966 World Cup but he was instrumental in his country's progress to the Final against England. Though a midfielder, he scored two goals in the group stages, another in the 4-0 quarter-final victory over Uruguay and a crucial second goal in the 2-1 semi-final win over the Soviet Union played at Goodison Park.

As well as finishing runners-up in 1966, West Germany finished third in 1970 when a Beckenbauer-inspired comeback saw his country beat England 3-2 at the quarter-final stage. After being appointed captain in 1971, 'Der Kaiser' led West Germany to World Cup glory in 1974 and in 1990, as boss of the national team, he won the World Cup again, one of only three men to have lifted the Jules Rimet trophy as both a player and a manager.

December 1984

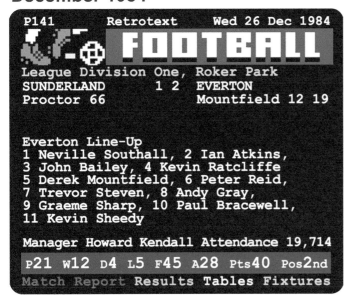

In his programme notes for the Chelsea match, Howard Kendall gave an insight into how his players would be spending the festive period.

He said that they would be at home for Christmas morning and then report for a light workout after lunch. The travelling party would then set off by coach later in the afternoon for an overnight stop ahead of the Boxing Day clash at Roker Park.

Gary Stevens would not be involved in the game as he had suffered a dead leg in the game with Chelsea. This meant a debut for new signing Ian Atkins, ironically against his former club, and it was also a return to the North East for Paul Bracewell, who left Sunderland in the summer.

Centre-half Derek Mountfield had not found the back of the net since the League Cup tie with Sheffield United back in October, but inside the first twenty minutes he had put that right with his first-ever double.

Though the home side pulled one back, the Blues held on for the three points which took them level on points with Tottenham at the top of the table, after Spurs surrendered a two-goal lead at home to West Ham to draw 2-2.

Ahead of the long-trip to East Anglia for the club's last game of the year, Howard Kendall had mixed news on the injury front.

Andy Gray was ruled out by an ankle injury he picked up on Boxing Day but Gary Stevens had recovered from his dead leg, though he subsequently failed a late fitness test. Pat van den Hauwe was back in the squad after his suspension and Terry Curran would start in place of Gray.

Young striker Rob Wakenshaw, a member of the FA Youth Cup winning team of the previous season who had just celebrated his nineteenth birthday, was also in the travelling party. He had scored all six goals in a Reserve team match against Bradford earlier in the month.

The Everton fans who made the journey to Suffolk had an anxious wait to see if the match would even go ahead due to overnight frost and persistent fog but the referee gave it the go-ahead a couple of hours before kick-off time.

After Derek Mountfield hit a double at Roker Park, it was Graeme Sharp's turn to grab a brace at Portman Road to keep the Blues neck-and-neck with Tottenham at the top of the final League table of 1984.

It's A Grand Old Team To Play For

Everton signed Alan Ball from Blackpool in August 1966, just a couple of weeks after he had starred for England in the World Cup Final, for a record fee of £110,000.

'Bally' immediately endeared himself to the Goodison faithful as he scored twice in a 3-1 win over Liverpool in only his third game for the club. He also grabbed the only goal later in the season as the Blues beat the Reds in an FA Cup fifth round tie watched by over 64,000 at Goodison and over 40,000 at Anfield via CCTV.

In season 1969/70, together with Howard Kendall and Colin Harvey, he was part of the famous midfield trio which helped Everton secure their seventh League title. There was disbelief among Evertonians when Alan was sold to Arsenal in December 1972 for another record fee of £220,000.

January 1985

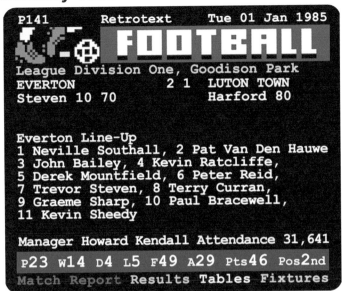

On New Year's Eve, Howard Kendall commented on reports that the Blues were keen to sign Ipswich striker Eric Gates to bolster the attacking options now that Adrian Heath was out of action.

The manager confirmed the club's interest in the 29-year-old but stated that as the team had been finding the net regularly in recent games, no transfer activity was imminent.

On New Year's Day, there was an early kick-off for Tottenham who had a tough assignment against Arsenal at Highbury.

Tony Woodcock gave the home side the lead in the first half but in the second period Spurs hit back strongly and goals from Garth Crooks and Mark Falco gave them victory and took them three points clear of Everton.

The Blues knew that a handsome victory over Luton Town would see them leapfrog their rivals on goal difference and the team certainly created enough chances to have done so.

In the end, though, only Trevor Steven's two goals were recorded and Evertonians had a few anxious moments near the end after Mick Harford pulled one back for the visitors.

As well as Arsenal, who were in fourth spot in the table, the challenge of third-placed Manchester United also looked to be faltering after the New Year's Day matches as Ron Atkinson's side were beaten 2-1 at Old Trafford by Sheffield Wednesday, with Imre Varadi grabbing both goals for the visitors.

Those results meant there was now a five-point gap between Tottenham and Everton at the top and the chasing pack as the title chase really hotted up.

But the teams now had a break from League action with the third round of the FA Cup and the Blues were involved in the first match of the weekend, a Friday night fixture against Leeds live on BBC1.

Howard Kendall was boosted by the return of Gary Stevens and Andy Gray from minor injury setbacks, as well as by the Leeds team news as top scorer Andy Ritchie and veteran goalkeeper David Harvey were both missing.

The visitors went ahead after a handball in the area gave Graeme Sharp the chance to register his twentieth goal of the campaign from the penalty spot.

Kevin Sheedy added a second late on, as the Blues began the defence of their trophy strongly.

It's A Grand Old Team To Support

Alan Ball says scoring the match-winner on his debut at Fulham and then twice in a 3-1 win over Liverpool at Goodison, all in his first week, triggered an instant relationship with the Everton fans.

"I couldn't have had a better start to a career than I had at Everton. They were the best days of my life, football-wise. The affection and the passion from the people... just going and playing at Goodison, against whoever, was special.

I always remember my father saying, the day I signed, that Everton fans wanted me to play football the way they supported it. That meant playing with everything I could possibly give. Those words stuck with me."

From The Evertonian, February 1995

EVERTON
NIL SATIS
NISI OPTIMUM
GOODISON
PARK L4

January 1985

```
P141        Retrotext      Sat 12 Jan 1985
    FOOTBALL
League Division One, Goodison Park
EVERTON           4 0   NEWCASTLE UTD
Sharp 17
Mountfield 32
Sheedy 62 86

Everton Line-Up
1 Neville Southall, 2 Gary Stevens,
3 Pat Van Den Hauwe, 4 Kevin Ratcliffe
5 Derek Mountfield, 6 Peter Reid,
7 Trevor Steven, 8 Andy Gray,
9 Graeme Sharp, 10 Paul Bracewell,
11 Kevin Sheedy

Manager Howard Kendall Attendance 32,156
P24 W15 D4 L5 F53 A29 Pts49 Pos1st
Match Report  Results Tables Fixtures
```

```
P141        Retrotext      Sat 26 Jan 1985
    FOOTBALL
FA Cup 4th Round, Goodison Park
EVERTON           2 0   DONCASTER R.
Steven 19
Stevens 33


Everton Line-Up
1 Neville Southall, 2 Gary Stevens,
3 Pat Van Den Hauwe, 4 Kevin Ratcliffe
5 Derek Mountfield, 6 Peter Reid,
7 Trevor Steven, 8 Andy Gray,
9 Graeme Sharp, 10 Paul Bracewell,
11 Kevin Sheedy

Manager Howard Kendall Attendance 37,537
Nil Satis Nisi Optimum
Match Report  Results Tables Fixtures
```

After the FA Cup win over Leeds, Everton were drawn at home to third division Doncaster Rovers in the fourth round, a team managed by Leeds legend Billy Bremner.

It would be a good opportunity for the Blues to progress further in the competition, but Howard Kendall reminded everyone of the struggle his side had at this stage last year against Gillingham.

Another Leeds legend, Jack Charlton, brought his Newcastle side to Goodison Park on the back of a poor run which had yielded just seven points from a possible twenty-seven and without one of his best players, Peter Beardsley, who had a stomach strain.

The Blues were in no mood to show any favours to the visitors, going ahead on seventeen minutes when Graeme Sharp headed home a Pat van den Hauwe cross for his tenth goal in ten games.

Just after the half-hour mark, Derek Mountfield forced home a second from close range for his seventh strike of the campaign.

Kevin Sheedy struck twice more in the second period to record his ninth and tenth goals as Everton ran out emphatic winners.

With Tottenham only drawing 2-2 at QPR, it meant that the victory over Newcastle returned the Blues to the top of the table for the first time since the 4-3 home defeat by Chelsea.

With no new injury concerns, Howard Kendall would have a free week to prepare for the massive clash with Tottenham at the weekend which would have a huge bearing on the destination of the Division One title. Spurs, though, would have a midweek FA Cup replay to play against Charlton.

However, later in the week, the south of the country was hit with an icy blast which meant the postponement of Tottenham's Cup replay at Charlton and put the top-of-the-table clash with Spurs in doubt as the White Hart Lane pitch was frozen and there was no undersoil heating.

When four inches of snow fell on top as well, officials bowed to the inevitable and the match was postponed.

The winter weather had eased sufficiently by the following weekend to allow most of the FA Cup fourth round matches to go ahead. Roared on by 8,000 visiting fans, Doncaster Rovers put up a good show at Goodison but ultimately the quality of the Blues shone through and they earned their place in the next round.

If You Know Your History

This was the fourth derby clash of the season between the previous season's champions and FA Cup holders. Liverpool had won the Charity Shield 1-0 back in August, but Everton beat the Reds 3-1 in a League match two weeks later and the third game, on New Year's Eve, was drawn 0-0.

Eight huge screens were erected at Anfield so anyone without a ticket for Goodison could watch the action via closed-circuit television, as well as a half-hour preview show featuring interviews and match clips. Though Everton advanced to the quarter-finals, they were beaten 3-2 by Nottingham Forest at the City Ground with Ian Storey-Moore scoring the winner a minute from time.

```
P141        Retrotext      Sat 11 Mar 1967
    FOOTBALL
FA Cup Fifth Round, Goodison Park
EVERTON           1 0   LIVERPOOL
Ball 45

Everton Line-Up
1 Gordon West, 2 Tommy Wright, 3 Ray
Wilson, 4 John Hurst, 5 Brian Labone,
6 Colin Harvey, 7 Alex Young, 8 Alan
Ball, 9 Derek Temple, 10 Jimmy
Husband, 11 Johnny Morrissey

Manager Harry Catterick
Attendance 64,851. 40,149 also
watched the game on CCTV at Anfield.
Nil Satis Nisi Optimum
Match Report  Results Tables Fixtures
```

February 1985

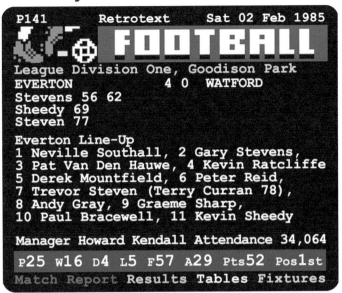

```
P141      Retrotext      Sat 02 Feb 1985
         FOOTBALL
League Division One, Goodison Park
EVERTON              4 0   WATFORD
Stevens 56 62
Sheedy 69
Steven 77

Everton Line-Up
1 Neville Southall, 2 Gary Stevens,
3 Pat Van Den Hauwe, 4 Kevin Ratcliffe
5 Derek Mountfield, 6 Peter Reid,
7 Trevor Steven (Terry Curran 78),
8 Andy Gray, 9 Graeme Sharp,
10 Paul Bracewell, 11 Kevin Sheedy

Manager Howard Kendall Attendance 34,064
P25 W16 D4 L5 F57 A29 Pts52 Pos1st
Match Report  Results Tables Fixtures
```

```
P141      Retrotext      Sat 16 Feb 1985
         FOOTBALL
FA Cup 5th Round, Goodison Park
EVERTON              3 0   TELFORD UNITED
Reid 67
Sheedy 72 (pen)
Steven 89

Everton Line-Up
1 Neville Southall, 2 Gary Stevens,
3 Pat Van Den Hauwe, 4 Kevin Ratcliffe
5 Derek Mountfield, 6 Peter Reid,
7 Trevor Steven, 8 Andy Gray,
9 Graeme Sharp (Alan Harper),
10 Paul Bracewell, 11 Kevin Sheedy

Manager Howard Kendall Attendance 47,402
Nil Satis Nisi Optimum
Match Report  Results Tables Fixtures
```

On the transfer front, two more names had been added to that of Eric Gates as possible striker re-inforcements for the Blues - Peter Davenport of Nottingham Forest and Gary Lineker of Leicester.

But the manager told the Liverpool Echo,"We are the leading scorers in the country, so who would I leave out if I brought someone in?"

The previous two League meetings with Graham Taylor's Watford had finished 4-4 and 4-5 so goals were expected in this latest encounter. They duly arrived but all four went to Everton.

England boss Bobby Robson had recently indicated that two of Everton's stars, Gary Stevens and Trevor Steven, were increasingly in his thoughts for a call-up to the full national squad and neither did themselves any harm here.

Both were on the scoresheet, full-back Stevens twice, with Kevin Sheedy completing the rout. With nearest pursuers Tottenham dropping points at Luton Town in a 2-2 draw, the Blues extended their lead at the top of the table to four points.

Earlier in the week, Howard Kendall had received his award for being named Liverpool Echo's Merseyside Sports Personality of 1984, having been the first winner of it back in 1972.

When the fifth round draw paired the Blues with the winners of the Darlington versus Telford tie which had been postponed on the Saturday, Howard Kendall, Colin Harvey and Mick Heaton all attended the re-arranged match to gauge the strength of their opponents.

The game finished 1-1 at Feethams and, in the replay, non-League Telford earned the trip to Goodison Park, winning 3-0.

The management team then set about preparing for the weekend game with Coventry City and there was concern about the participation of midfield dynamo Peter Reid whose lengthy run of successive matches for the Blues was under threat because of a hamstring strain.

However, the wintry weather made a comeback across much of the country and the game in the Midlands was called off along with many others.

The famous Pools Panel, which had been created by pools companies Littlewoods, Vernons and Zetters during the great freeze of 1962-63 to maintain their revenue, deemed that the match would have been a Score Draw.

Better weather a week later allowed this FA Cup tie to take place - with Reid in the line-up - and the Blues booked their place in the quarter-finals.

If You Know Your History

Everton could not have asked for a tougher start to the 1969-70 season with away games at Arsenal and Manchester United, but they won 1-0 at Highbury and 2-0 at Old Trafford.

With the campaign having begun early due to the 1970 World Cup, by the end of August the Blues had played seven League matches, winning six and drawing one, and sat proudly on top of the table.

Harry Catterick's side remained in the top two throughout the season and another blistering unbeaten run from March saw the team win eight of their last nine matches to finish nine points clear of the rest and secure a seventh Division One League title for the club.

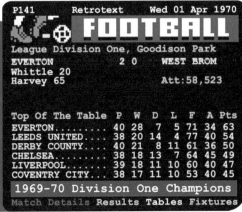

```
P141      Retrotext      Wed 01 Apr 1970
         FOOTBALL
League Division One, Goodison Park
EVERTON              2 0   WEST BROM
Whittle 20
Harvey 65                 Att:58,523


Top Of The Table   P  W  D  L  F  A Pts
EVERTON.........   40 28  7  5 71 34 63
LEEDS UNITED....   38 20 14  4 77 40 54
DERBY COUNTY....   40 21  8 11 61 36 50
CHELSEA.........   38 18 13  7 64 45 49
LIVERPOOL.......   39 18 11 10 60 40 47
COVENTRY CITY...   38 17 11 10 53 40 45
1969-70 Division One Champions
Match Details  Results Tables Fixtures
```

February 1985

From The Teletext Archive

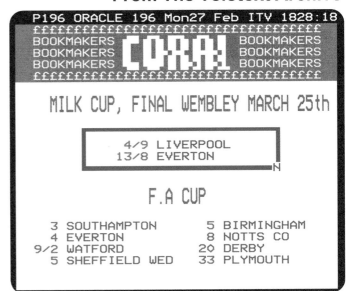

Though the match with Telford had been tough, the Blues were in the hat for the quarter-final and they were drawn at home again against the winners of the Ipswich Town versus Sheffield Wednesday replay, after their match was postponed.

There was also good news on the international front with England boss Bobby Robson finally recognising the claims of Gary Stevens with a call-up to the full-squad but there was still no room for Peter Reid or Paul Bracewell, though an injury to Bryan Robson later enabled Trevor Steven to step up from the Under-21 squad.

In transfer news, the Liverpool Echo reported that Nottingham Forest had turned down a £400,000 bid for the Birkenhead-born striker Peter Davenport, while Terry Curran had asked for a move due to his lack of first-team opportunities.

Before this match, Andy Gray had only scored one goal in a stop-start, injury-hit season. But Howard Kendall had no worries about his lack of goals, making it clear how much he valued Gray's intelligence on the field which created space for others in the team.

Gray broke his five-month drought with a double at Filbert Street to maintain the Blues' four-point lead at the top of the table.

This is an original Oracle page recovered from an old VHS recording. The corruption is caused by the retrieval process.

Ceefax was a non-commercial service but bookmakers were major advertisers on Oracle, mostly promoting football and horse racing odds. This page is from 1984 before the Milk and FA Cup Finals in March and May respectively.

After the FA Cup third round win over Stoke City in January 1984 and the draw for the fourth round which paired the Blues with Gillingham, you could still have had 14/1 on Everton lifting the trophy.

It's A Grand Old Team To Play For

Referred to by his manager, Harry Catterick, as the last of the great Corinthians, centre-half Brian Labone was renowned for his sportsmanship and good humour while remaining a fierce competitor.

Having joined the club in 1957, Brian was a member of the Everton side which won the Division One title in season 1962-63 and was captain of the team which landed the FA Cup in 1966 and another League title in 1969-70.

In his remarkable fifteen year career, Brian made 534 appearances for the Blues, scoring two goals - both in the same 1965-66 campaign and not surprisingly both headers; one at Goodison against Blackburn in October 1965 and the other away at Burnley in February 1966.

March 1985

```
P141      Retrotext      Sat 02 Mar 1985
        FOOTBALL
League Division One, Old Trafford
MANCHESTER UTD      1  1    EVERTON
Olsen 36                    Mountfield 41


Everton Line-Up
1 Neville Southall, 2 Gary Stevens,
3 Pat Van Den Hauwe, 4 Kevin Ratcliffe
5 Derek Mountfield, 6 Peter Reid,
7 Trevor Steven, 8 Terry Curran,
9 Andy Gray, 10 Paul Bracewell,
11 Kevin Sheedy

Manager Howard Kendall Attendance 51,150
P27 W17 D5 L5 F60 A31 Pts56 Pos1st
Match Report  Results Tables Fixtures
```

```
P141      Retrotext      Wed 06 Mar 1985
        FOOTBALL
European Cup Winners' Cup,
Quarter-Final(1st Leg), Goodison Park
EVERTON          3  0    FORTUNA SITTARD
Gray 48 74 76


Everton Line-Up
1 Neville Southall, 2 Gary Stevens,
3 Pat Van Den Hauwe, 4 Kevin Ratcliffe
5 Derek Mountfield, 6 Peter Reid
(Kevin Richardson), 7 Trevor Steven,
8 Terry Curran, 9 Andy Gray,
10 Paul Bracewell, 11 Kevin Sheedy

Manager Howard Kendall Attendance 25,782
      Nil Satis Nisi Optimum
Match Report  Results Tables Fixtures
```

On the international scene, Trevor Steven was named in the England team to play a World Cup qualifier against Northern Ireland in Belfast, his first cap, triggering an extra £25,000 payment to his former club, Burnley.

He also became the first Everton player to gain such recognition since Bob Latchford in 1979.

Having been thrashed 5-0 at Goodison earlier in the season and then knocked out of the League Cup by the Blues a few days later, Manchester United were keen to get their revenge at Old Trafford.

Ron Atkinson's side were seven points behind Howard Kendall's table-toppers in third spot but were coming off an excellent 1-0 at Highbury against Arsenal the week before.

An incident-packed match finished 1-1 but both sides missed penalties - Gordon Strachan having his saved by Neville Southall after just four minutes and Gary Bailey stopping Kevin Sheedy's spot-kick eight minutes from time to deny the Blues all three points.

At the Victoria Ground, a Garth Crooks goal gave Tottenham victory over Stoke City which reduced the points arrears with Everton to just two, both teams having played twenty-seven games.

The Blues' task of winning this trophy had been made easier by the shock elimination of favourites Barcelona in the first round.

Then managed by future England boss Terry Venables, the Spanish giants had beaten French club Metz 4-2 away in the first leg and went 5-2 up on aggregate in the second leg at home, before Metz scored four times without reply to go through.

Ahead of this game, Howard Kendall again stressed the importance of not conceding an away goal as this had been so costly in Everton's 1970-71 European Cup campaign when he was a player.

The Blues went out of the competition at the quarter-final stage that season without losing a game, having drawn 1-1 at Goodison and 0-0 in Athens against Panathinaikos.

As it was, his side gained an emphatic victory over the Dutch side, who had ex-Ipswich Town star Frans Thijssen in their ranks.

It was a memorable night for Andy Gray, who recorded his first goals of the season at Goodison, all scored at the Gwladys Street end of the ground, and registered the first hat-trick of his Everton career on his European debut for the club.

It's A Grand Old Team To Support

For 12 years, Brian Labone was the rock on which the Everton defence was built. It seemed he would be around for ever, but he was forced out of the game in October 1971 with an Achilles injury, aged just 32.

For many, it is Labone they think of when they think of Everton. He grew up on Merseyside and was an Everton fanatic. Liverpool and Manchester United were after him but he said: "There was only one club for me. When I knew Everton were interested I didn't think twice, I signed."

That was back in 1957 and he made his debut the next year. By 1959 he was a regular and he stayed an automatic choice until forced to quit.
From the match programme versus Wolves, 6th September 1980

EVERTON
NIL SATIS
NISI OPTIMUM
GOODISON
PARK L4

March 1985

```
P141      Retrotext      Sat 09 Mar 1985
         FOOTBALL
FA Cup 6th Round, Goodison Park
EVERTON           2 2   IPSWICH TOWN
Sheedy 5                Wilson 15
Mountfield 85           Zondervan 31


Everton Line-Up
1 Neville Southall, 2 Gary Stevens,
3 Pat Van Den Hauwe, 4 Kevin Ratcliffe
5 Derek Mountfield, 6 Peter Reid,
7 Trevor Steven, 8 Terry Curran,
9 Andy Gray, 10 Paul Bracewell,
11 Kevin Sheedy

Manager Howard Kendall Attendance 36,468
       Nil Satis Nisi Optimum
Match Report Results Tables Fixtures
```

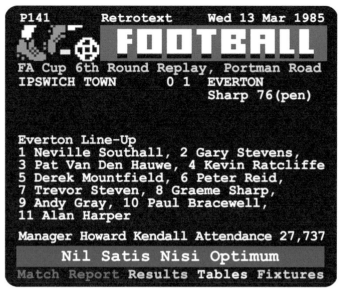

```
P141      Retrotext      Wed 13 Mar 1985
         FOOTBALL
FA Cup 6th Round Replay, Portman Road
IPSWICH TOWN      0 1   EVERTON
                        Sharp 76(pen)


Everton Line-Up
1 Neville Southall, 2 Gary Stevens,
3 Pat Van Den Hauwe, 4 Kevin Ratcliffe
5 Derek Mountfield, 6 Peter Reid,
7 Trevor Steven, 8 Graeme Sharp,
9 Andy Gray, 10 Paul Bracewell,
11 Alan Harper

Manager Howard Kendall Attendance 27,737
       Nil Satis Nisi Optimum
Match Report Results Tables Fixtures
```

Everton didn't know who their opponents would be in this quarter-final clash until the Monday before the game as the fifth round tie between Ipswich Town and Sheffield Wednesday had been postponed due to bad weather.

It was the East Anglian side who came out on top at Portman Road, winning 3-2 courtesy of a late Alan Sunderland goal. Two days later, the Tractor Boys were beaten 2-0 by fierce rivals Norwich City in the second leg of their League Cup semi-final, missing out on a Wembley place 2-1 on aggregate.

So, it had been a busy week for the visitors and they fell behind after just five minutes to Kevin Sheedy's famous free-kick from the edge of the area. He curled his first effort to goalkeeper Paul Cooper's right only for the referee to say it had to be re-taken, so Kevin stepped up and planted the ball into the net again, this time to Cooper's left.

A rare error by Neville Southall, who allowed a shot to squirm under his body, levelled things up and before half-time Ipswich went ahead through Romeo Zondervan.

The home side dominated the second period and after Steve McCall was sent off for a foul on Trevor Steven, Derek Mountfield's ninth goal of the season earned them a replay.

Just minutes after the thrilling FA Cup tie with Ipswich on Saturday, former Everton boss Harry Catterick collapsed in the directors' box after a heart attack and died. He was aged just sixty-five.

Under the chairmanship of Sir John Moores, Catterick had led Everton to title success in 1962-63 and again in 1969-70, as well as winning the FA Cup in 1966 and he will be forever remembered as one of the great football managers of his era.

In the 1980s, Cup replays took place just a few days after the first game so the Everton players and fans faced a long midweek trek to Suffolk to see which team would go through to the semi-final.

Ahead of the match, the draw for the last four was made and it set up the prospect of the first all-Merseyside FA Cup Final, with the Blues facing the winners of Luton Town versus Millwall and Liverpool drawn against Manchester United. Both ties would be played on Saturday 13th April.

Graeme Sharp returned to the starting eleven after a four-game injury absence but Kevin Sheedy missed out due to thigh strain, with Terry Curran dropping to the bench. A tight match was decided from the penalty spot, with Sharp claiming his twenty-second goal of the campaign.

If You Know Your History

Ex-Everton player Harry Catterick was appointed manager of the club in April 1961 by chairman John Moores on a four-year contract with a salary of £3,500. He replaced Johnny Carey who was infamously sacked by Moores during a taxi journey and who subsequently sued the club for breach of contract.

Just two years later, Catterick led the Blues to the Division One League title and won the FA Cup in 1966 after an epic win against his former club, Sheffield Wednesday.

In season 1969-70, Everton won the Division One title again and in such style that Catterick was rewarded with a six-year contract. But the expected success didn't materialise and, coupled with ill-health, this led to him being replaced as manager by Billy Bingham in April 1973.

March 1985

```
P141        Retrotext       Sat 16 Mar 1985
         FOOTBALL
League Division One, Villa Park
ASTON VILLA        1 1    EVERTON
Evans 83(pen)            Richardson 42


Everton Line-Up
1 Neville Southall, 2 Gary Stevens,
3 Pat Van Den Hauwe, 4 Kevin Ratcliffe
5 Derek Mountfield, 6 Kevin Richardson
7 Trevor Steven, 8 Graeme Sharp,
9 Andy Gray, 10 Paul Bracewell,
11 Alan Harper

Manager Howard Kendall Attendance 22,265
P28 W17 D6 L5 F61 A32 Pts57 Pos1st
Match Report  Results Tables Fixtures
```

```
P141        Retrotext       Wed 20 Mar 1985
         FOOTBALL
European Cup Winners' Cup,
Quarter-Final(2nd Leg), De Baandert
FORTUNA SITTARD    0 2    EVERTON
                  (0 5)   Sharp 15
                          Reid 76
Everton Line-Up
1 Neville Southall, 2 Gary Stevens,
3 Pat Van Den Hauwe, 4 Kevin Ratcliffe
(Ian Atkins), 5 Derek Mountfield,
6 Peter Reid, 7 Trevor Steven,
8 Terry Curran, 9 Graeme Sharp
(Robbie Wakenshaw), 10 Alan Harper,
11 Kevin Richardson

Manager Howard Kendall Attendance 20,000
       Nil Satis Nisi Optimum
Match Report  Results Tables Fixtures
```

Before the replay with Ipswich Town, the Blues' title hopes had been boosted by the 2-1 home defeat of Tottenham by Manchester United. The loss kept Spurs two points behind Everton but having played a game more, with Ron Atkinson's United in third spot four points behind Kendall's boys having played two games more.

Peter Reid was suspended for the match at Villa Park, bringing to an end his long run of consecutive games for the Toffees. His manager also revealed to the Liverpool Echo that the midfield dynamo had been playing through the pain barrier since the game against Watford at the beginning of February when he suffered two broken ribs.

Reliable utility player Kevin Richardson stepped in for Reid and Alan Harper did the same for the injured Kevin Sheedy. Neville Southall would later say that without the contribution of these two players, the team would have won nothing.

It was Richardson who gave the visitors a deserved lead shortly before half-time when he intercepted a poor backpass from ex-Blue Steve McMahon but a late penalty meant the game ended all-square. With Spurs winning at Anfield for the first time in seventy-three years, the boys from White Hart Lane drew level on points but having played a game more.

On the night Everton booked their FA Cup semi-final spot, the club discovered who their opponents would be. It was Luton Town who won the delayed quarter-final tie with Millwall 1-0, but the game featured some of the worst football violence ever seen as some Millwall fans rioted both in the ground and later in the town.

Hooliganism had been the scourge of English football at home and abroad for many years but in 1985 it was reaching its peak. Further incidents later in the season would have tragic consequences and have a severe impact on the game in general and Everton in particular.

For this match in Holland, the Everton hierarchy asked the fans not to travel with all the tickets sold to home supporters. However, it was estimated around a thousand Evertonians made it into the Baandert Stadium and there was no trouble.

The team were without the injured Kevin Sheedy, Paul Bracewell and Andy Gray but Peter Reid was back from suspension and Terry Curran came back into the side.

Goals from Graeme Sharp and Reid ensured a comfortable 5-0 aggregate success and thoughts now turned to who the Blues would play in the semi-final of this competition.

It's A Grand Old Team To Play For

When Johnny Morrissey made the switch from Anfield to Goodison Park in August 1962 for a fee of £10,000 it almost led to the resignation of legendary Liverpool boss Bill Shankly, who had not sanctioned the move which was dealt with by directors.

Shankly's anger was justified as Morrissey hit the ground running for the Blues and scored in a 2-2 draw with his former team just a few weeks later before notching a hat-trick against West Brom. In total, he scored seven goals in the 1962-63 season as Harry Catterick's side were crowned League champions.

Though he missed out on a place in the 1966 FA Cup Final to Derek Temple, Morrissey was a key member of the Everton team which won the Division One title again in 1969-70.

March 1985

```
P141        Retrotext        Sat 23 Mar 1985
       FOOTBALL
League Division One, Goodison Park
EVERTON              2  0  ARSENAL
Gray 27
Sharp 89


Everton Line-Up
1 Neville Southall, 2 Gary Stevens,
3 Pat Van Den Hauwe, 4 Kevin Ratcliffe
5 Derek Mountfield, 6 Peter Reid,
7 Trevor Steven, 8 Graeme Sharp,
9 Andy Gray, 10 Alan Harper,
11 Kevin Richardson

Manager Howard Kendall Attendance 36,364

P29 W18 D6 L5 F63 A32 Pts60 Pos1st
Match Report Results Tables Fixtures
```

```
P141        Retrotext        Sat 30 Mar 1985
       FOOTBALL
League Division One, The Dell
SOUTHAMPTON          1  2  EVERTON
Jordan 90                 Richardson 48 51


Everton Line-Up
1 Neville Southall, 2 Gary Stevens,
3 Pat Van Den Hauwe, 4 Kevin Ratcliffe
5 Derek Mountfield, 6 Peter Reid,
7 Trevor Steven, 8 Graeme Sharp
(Paul Wilkinson), 9 Andy Gray,
10 Paul Bracewell, 11 Kevin Richardson

Manager Howard Kendall Attendance 18,754

P30 W19 D6 L5 F65 A33 Pts63 Pos1st
Match Report Results Tables Fixtures
```

In the other European Cup-Winners' Cup quarter-finals, Bayern Munich beat Roma 4-1 on aggregate, Rapid Vienna overturned a 3-0 first-leg loss to go through 5-3 on aggregate against Dynamo Dresden and Dynamo Moscow eliminated Larissa 1-0 on aggregate.

In the semi-final draw, the Blues were paired with the bookmakers' favourites Bayern Munich but their manager Udo Lattek had great respect for his opponents, saying: "Bayern against Everton, that's really the final. Whoever wins this semi-final will also win the Cup."

But Everton were chasing honours in three competitions and the focus turned back to the title race and this home game with Arsenal.

It was an opportunity for Kendall's side to avenge the controversial defeat back in October and Andy Gray set them on the way with his seventh goal of the campaign, Graeme Sharp securing the points near the end.

Tottenham boosted their goal difference with a 5-1 win over Southampton to stay neck-and-neck with the Blues at the top of the table, while third-placed Manchester United hammered Aston Villa 4-0 to stay four points behind the two leaders.

On the Sunday after the Arsenal game, Peter Reid was named Player Of The Year by the Professional Footballers' Association, with three other team-mates included in the PFA All-Star team - Kevin Ratcliffe, Gary Stevens and Kevin Sheedy.

Trevor Steven was on international duty with England for the second time and he crowned an impressive performance with a goal in the 2-1 win over the Republic of Ireland.

Having scored the goal for Grimsby Town which knocked Everton out of the League Cup earlier in the season, Paul Wilkinson was a name supporters were familiar with. He obviously made an impression on Howard Kendall as the Blues' boss announced he had bought the England Under-21 player for a fee of £250,000.

If Everton were to maintain their title charge, they would have to improve on an appalling record at the Dell where Southampton had won the last seven meetings. Paul Bracewell was fit again and there was a place on the bench for new boy Wilkinson.

With goals shared throughout the team all season, it was Kevin Richardson who stepped up to the plate with two quickfire strikes just after half-time which were enough to give the visitors the points.

If You Know Your History

Everton sailed through the first round of the European Cup with a 9-2 aggregate victory over Icelandic side Keflavik and then faced the German champions Borussia Moenchengladbach with the first leg ending in a 1-1 draw thanks to a Howard Kendall goal.

At Goodison, Johnny Morrissey put the Blues ahead but Herbert Laumen pulled the visitors level and, after extra-time, the teams faced the first-ever penalty shootout in this competition.

Goalkeeper Andy Rankin was the Everton hero, saving the fifth spot kick, to set up a quarter-final clash with Greece's Panathinaikos which the Blues lost on the away goals rule.

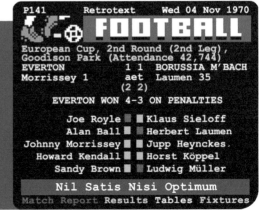

```
P141        Retrotext        Wed 04 Nov 1970
       FOOTBALL
European Cup, 2nd Round (2nd Leg),
Goodison Park (Attendance 42,744)
EVERTON              1  1  BORUSSIA M'BACH
Morrissey 1      aet    Laumen 35
                    (2 2)
EVERTON WON 4-3 ON PENALTIES

   Joe Royle  ■ ■ Klaus Sieloff
   Alan Ball  ■ ■ Herbert Laumen
Johnny Morrissey ■ ■ Jupp Heynckes
Howard Kendall ■ ■ Horst Köppel
  Sandy Brown  ■ ■ Ludwig Müller
      Nil Satis Nisi Optimum
Match Report Results Tables Fixtures
```

April 1985

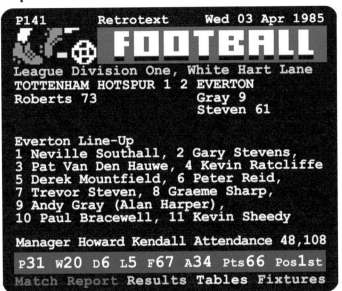

```
P141        Retrotext      Wed 03 Apr 1985
      FOOTBALL
League Division One, White Hart Lane
TOTTENHAM HOTSPUR 1 2 EVERTON
Roberts 73              Gray 9
                        Steven 61


Everton Line-Up
1 Neville Southall, 2 Gary Stevens,
3 Pat Van Den Hauwe, 4 Kevin Ratcliffe
5 Derek Mountfield, 6 Peter Reid,
7 Trevor Steven, 8 Graeme Sharp,
9 Andy Gray (Alan Harper),
10 Paul Bracewell, 11 Kevin Sheedy

Manager Howard Kendall Attendance 48,108
P31 W20 D6 L5 F67 A34 Pts66 Pos1st
Match Report  Results Tables Fixtures
```

```
P141        Retrotext      Sat 06 Apr 1985
      FOOTBALL
League Division One, Goodison Park
EVERTON            4 1      SUNDERLAND
Gray 34 37                  Wallace 2
Steven 50
Sharp 68
Everton Line-Up
1 Neville Southall, 2 Gary Stevens,
3 John Bailey, 4 Kevin Ratcliffe,
5 Derek Mountfield, 6 Peter Reid,
7 Trevor Steven, 8 Graeme Sharp,
9 Andy Gray, 10 Paul Bracewell,
11 Kevin Sheedy (Alan Harper)
Manager Howard Kendall Attendance 35,898
Referee Vic Callow (Solihull)
P32 W21 D6 L5 F71 A35 Pts69 Pos1st
Match Report  Results Tables Fixtures
```

The price of success for football teams when fighting on multiple fronts is often fixture congestion and Everton secretary Jim Greenwood had the headache of fitting in postponed games against West Ham, Coventry, West Brom and Liverpool between now and the end of the season.

If they won both upcoming semi-finals, Everton would face seventeen matches before the end of the campaign.

Tottenham had surprisingly slipped up at home to Aston Villa at the weekend, handing the Blues a three-point advantage ahead of this crunch midweek clash at White Hart Lane.

The Blues welcomed back Kevin Sheedy after a five match absence with Kevin Richardson the unlucky player to miss out. Andy Gray gave the visitors the lead when he latched on to a misdirected defensive header to rifle home from the edge of the area, Trevor Steven made it 2-0 in the second half when he dispossessed Mark Bowen, rounded the keeper and slotted the ball home.

A Graham Roberts piledriver brought Spurs back into it and they almost equalised near the end when Mark Falco's powerful point-blank header was somehow kept out by Neville Southall, undoubtedly one of the saves of this, or any other, season.

The win over Spurs pushed Everton six points clear of them at the top of the table with a game in hand. After a 2-1 win at home to Leicester the same evening, Manchester United were now the Blues' nearest pursuers though still four points behind having played two games more.

Transfer-listed John Bailey was back in the line-up against Sunderland, replacing the suspended Pat van den Hauwe.

The Blues shrugged off the shock of going behind early on to put on a sensational performance featuring goals of the highest quality. Having only scored one goal up to the game at Leicester at the end of February, Andy Gray grabbed his ninth and tenth of the campaign, both stunning diving headers to finish off flowing Everton moves.

Those two goals were good but the third from Trevor Steven was simply magnificent. Paul Bracewell hit a breathtaking pass on the volley to the opposite side of the pitch where the new England international anticipated the ball dropping over the defender's head, took it in his stride, advanced on goal and smashed it into the net.

Graeme Sharp completed the scoring in more mundane fashion and the Blues moved another step closer to the title.

If You Know Your History

Having won the League title in 1969-70, Everton struggled during the following campaign finishing in a lowly fourteenth place and being knocked out of a European Cup quarter-final and an FA Cup semi-final within the space of three days. They even lost a play-off for third and fourth spot in the FA Cup 3-2 to Stoke City after leading 2-0.

This match was the highlight of another poor campaign in 1971-72 in which the Blues finished fifteenth in the table. The lowest crowd of the season at Goodison braved a snow storm to see the home side lead 5-0 at the interval and go on to score eight goals for the first time since 1962 when they beat Cardiff 8-3. Earlier in the season, Southampton had knocked Everton out of the League Cup.

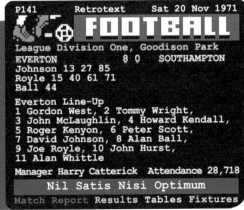

```
P141        Retrotext      Sat 20 Nov 1971
      FOOTBALL
League Division One, Goodison Park
EVERTON            8 0      SOUTHAMPTON
Johnson 13 27 85
Royle 15 40 61 71
Ball 44

Everton Line-Up
1 Gordon West, 2 Tommy Wright,
3 John McLaughlin, 4 Howard Kendall,
5 Roger Kenyon, 6 Peter Scott,
7 David Johnson, 8 Alan Ball,
9 Joe Royle, 10 John Hurst,
11 Alan Whittle
Manager Harry Catterick Attendance 28,718
      Nil Satis Nisi Optimum
Match Report  Results Tables Fixtures
```

April 1985

P141   Retrotext   Wed 10 Apr 1985

FOOTBALL

European Cup Winners' Cup,
Semi-Final(1st Leg), Olympic Stadium
BAYERN MUNICH   0 0   EVERTON

Everton Line-Up
1 Neville Southall, 2 Gary Stevens,
3 Pat Van Den Hauwe, 4 Kevin Ratcliffe
5 Derek Mountfield, 6 Peter Reid
7 Trevor Steven, 8 Alan Harper,
9 Graeme Sharp, 10 Paul Bracewell,
11 Kevin Richardson

Manager Howard Kendall Attendance 67,000

Nil Satis Nisi Optimum

Match Report   Results   Tables   Fixtures

P141   Retrotext   Sat 13 Apr 1985

FOOTBALL

FA Cup Semi-Final, Villa Park
EVERTON   2 1   LUTON TOWN
Sheedy 85   aet   Hill 36
Mountfield 114

Everton Line-Up
1 Neville Southall, 2 Gary Stevens,
3 Pat Van Den Hauwe, 4 Kevin
Ratcliffe, 5 Derek Mountfield,
6 Peter Reid, 7 Trevor Steven,
8 Graeme Sharp, 9 Andy Gray,
10 Paul Bracewell, 11 Kevin Sheedy

Manager Howard Kendall Attendance 45,289

Nil Satis Nisi Optimum

Match Report   Results   Tables   Fixtures

While Everton were beating Sunderland, Manchester United had thrashed Stoke City 5-0 to maintain their challenge but in midweek, as the Blues prepared to face Bayern Munich, United lost 1-0 away at Sheffield Wednesday and now trailed the champions-elect by four points having played three games more.

Before this first-leg match, Mick Heaton had been sent out to watch Bayern's German Cup semi-final with Borussia Moenchendgladbach.

It was the first time in the European campaign that Mick had been on a 'spying' mission. Previously, Colin Harvey had been to Ireland to watch University College Dublin, while the club relied on videos on Inter Bratislava and Howard Kendall watched Fortuna Sittard himself.

Like Everton, Bayern were chasing success on three fronts, standing on top of the Bundesliga and in the German Cup Final as well as seeking European glory.

The Blues were without the injured Andy Gray and Kevin Sheedy, but the ever-reliable duo of Kevin Richardson and Alan Harper stepped up and both played their part in a resolute Everton performance which gave the team an excellent chance in the second-leg to reach the club's first European Final.

Though they had beaten bottom club Stoke City 4-0 away before this semi-final, Luton were in relegation danger and Everton were hot favourites to reach Wembley again after a twenty-game unbeaten run featuring no less than sixteen victories.

But the underdogs were the dominant team in the first half and but, for the brilliance of Neville Southall, David Pleat's side could have scored more than the one goal.

Howard Kendall's men improved after the break but it was not until five minutes from the end of normal time that Kevin Sheedy brought them level.

The Blues were much more like their normal selves in the extra-time period and Sheedy was again involved in the winner, crossing for Derek Mountfield to nod home is tenth goal of the season.

In the other semi-final, played at Goodison Park, Paul Walsh scored an equaliser for Liverpool in the last minute of extra-time to earn a replay against Manchester United.

So, the Blues would have to wait a little longer to find out who their opponents in the Final would be.

If You Know Your History

In his first three full seasons at Everton, Bob Latchford scored a respectable seventeen, twelve and seventeen goals. But after manager Gordon Lee signed the mercurial winger Dave Thomas in the summer of 1977 for £200,000, 'Big Bob' really found his scoring boots and ended the 1977-78 campaign with thirty League goals.

Thomas's pinpoint crosses created numerous opportunities for Everton's number nine, with the partnership seen to maximum effect in the 5-1 thrashing of QPR at Loftus Road, where Latchford scored four, and a 6-0 demolition of Coventry at Goodison, where he hit a hat-trick. The Blues finished third in the Division One table and were top scorers with seventy-six goals.

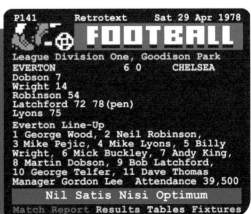

P141   Retrotext   Sat 29 Apr 1978

FOOTBALL

League Division One, Goodison Park
EVERTON   6 0   CHELSEA
Dobson 7
Wright 14
Robinson 54
Latchford 72 78(pen)
Lyons 75

Everton Line-Up
1 George Wood, 2 Neil Robinson,
3 Mike Pejic, 4 Mike Lyons, 5 Billy
Wright, 6 Mick Buckley, 7 Andy King,
8 Martin Dobson, 9 Bob Latchford,
10 George Telfer, 11 Dave Thomas
Manager Gordon Lee   Attendance 39,500

Nil Satis Nisi Optimum

Match Report   Results   Tables   Fixtures

April 1985

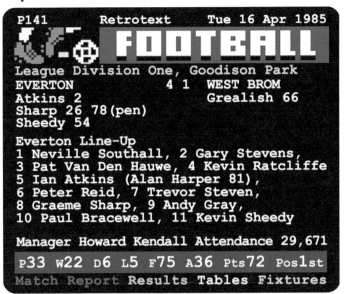

```
P141        Retrotext      Tue 16 Apr 1985
    FOOTBALL
League Division One, Goodison Park
EVERTON              4  1   WEST BROM
Atkins 2                    Grealish 66
Sharp 26 78(pen)
Sheedy 54

Everton Line-Up
1 Neville Southall, 2 Gary Stevens,
3 Pat Van Den Hauwe, 4 Kevin Ratcliffe
5 Ian Atkins (Alan Harper 81),
6 Peter Reid, 7 Trevor Steven,
8 Graeme Sharp, 9 Andy Gray,
10 Paul Bracewell, 11 Kevin Sheedy

Manager Howard Kendall Attendance 29,671
P33 W22 D6 L5 F75 A36 Pts72 Pos1st
Match Report  Results Tables Fixtures
```

```
P141        Retrotext      Sat 20 Apr 1985
    FOOTBALL
League Division One, Victoria Ground
STOKE CITY           0  2   EVERTON
                            Sharp 23
                            Sheedy 46

Everton Line-Up
1 Neville Southall, 2 Gary Stevens,
3 Pat Van Den Hauwe, 4 Kevin Ratcliffe
5 Ian Atkins, 6 Peter Reid,
7 Trevor Steven, 8 Graeme Sharp,
9 Andy Gray, 10 Paul Bracewell,
11 Kevin Sheedy

Manager Howard Kendall Attendance 18,344
P34 W23 D6 L5 F77 A36 Pts75 Pos1st
Match Report  Results Tables Fixtures
```

Having played in all the previous games in this magnificent season, FA Cup semi-final hero Derek Mountfield was forced to miss this match with a knee injury.

His replacement in the number five shirt. Ian Atkins, got the home team off to a flyer but it was the visitors who were on top after the goal, forcing Neville Southall to make a number of super saves.

Somewhat against the run of play, Graeme Sharp established a two-goal lead mid-way through the half before Kevin Sheedy and Sharp again from the penalty spot secured three more points.

With two games in hand, Everton now stood seven points clear of nearest pursuers Manchester United and eight clear of one-time challengers Tottenham, who lost their third successive home match, 2-0 to North London rivals Arsenal.

The next day, United met Liverpool at Maine Road to see who would join The Blues in the FA Cup Final.

Joe Fagan's side went ahead through a Paul McGrath own goal but Bryan Robson and Mark Hughes struck in the second period to put the Red Devils through to Wembley.

Before the next game, Howard Kendall announced that Terry Curran had been released from his contract and was free to find another club, while John Bailey had agreed a new one-year deal.

The playing squad, meanwhile, travelled down to Abbey Road Studios in London to record the traditional FA Cup Final record. Named 'Here We Go', the single would be in all good record shops from April 29th.

Stoke City were well adrift at the foot of the League table and relegation was inevitable so Everton did not have to be at their best to claim victory. Two of the scorers from the midweek win over West Brom were again on target, with Graeme Sharp registering his twenty-eighth goal of the campaign and Kevin Sheedy his sixteenth.

The Blues had now established a ten point lead at the top of the table and there was more good news the following day when second-placed Manchester United lost 2-1 at Luton Town.

It was also announced by Wales boss Mike England that Pat van den Hauwe would be in his next squad. Pat had relinquished his Belgian nationality and, having an English mother and being born outside the UK, was eligible to play for any of the home nations.

It's A Grand Old Team To Play For

Everton manager Billy Bingham signed Bob Latchford in February 1974 in a record transfer valued at £350,000. The deal involved Blues' legend Howard Kendall and left-back Archie Styles moving to Birmingham City, with those players valued at £180,000 and £90,000 respectively, plus £80,000 cash.

Bob famously scored thirty League goals during the 1977-78 season which won him a £10,000 prize offered by the Daily Express, his final two goals coming in a 6-0 demolition of Chelsea.

After that game, Bob met Dixie Dean who congratulated him on his achievement but joked that - in the 50th anniversary season of Dixie's amazing sixty goal tally - he was still only half the player he had been!

April 1985

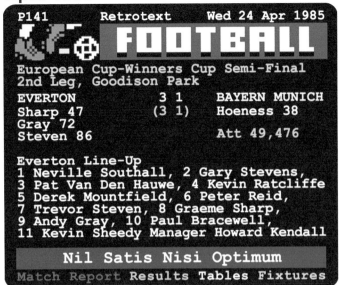

In his Captain's Column ahead of the second leg, Kevin Ratcliffe commented on the first game, saying: "We knew Bayern were a good team and that not many teams had held them in the Olympic Stadium in the past.

As we expected, they put us under a lot of pressure in the first-half but we defended well and gradually came more into the game. I think it will be our turn to put them under pressure tonight, but we will have to keep a sharp eye on them when they break."

They were prophetic words from the skipper as the two men Mick Heaton had identified as dangers combined for the opening goal of the second leg. Kogl was put in the clear only for Neville Southall to block his shot but the ball rebounded to Hoeness who coolly picked his spot with defenders on the line to slot home.

The home side roared back in the second period with Graeme Sharp nodding home to level the tie then Bayern keeper Pfaff living up to his name, allowing Andy Gray to sweep the Blues in front.

Trevor Steven sealed the momentous victory after a slide rule pass from Kevin Sheedy was deftly knocked into his path by Andy Gray and 'Tricky Trev' buried his shot into the Gwladys Street net.

After the euphoria of one of the greatest nights in the club's illustrious history, the players returned to the nitty gritty of League action with the title tantalisingly close.

The Blues were without the injured pair of Peter Reid and Kevin Sheedy but Kevin Richardson and Alan Harper stepped into their shoes seamlessly as they had done so often during this remarkable season.

Everton's defeat at Carrow Road back in November, when they lost 4-2 after being 3-0 down inside the first twenty-five minutes, was probably the worst performance of the whole campaign. But there was never a danger of a repeat once Derek Mountfield's eleventh goal of the season gave the home side a lead just before half-time.

With Trevor Steven and Paul Bracewell also on target, the Blues' lead at the top over second-placed Manchester United was nine points and Ron Atkinson's side had played three games more.

Howard Kendall's team had played eight games in April, including two Cup semi-finals, winning seven and drawing one, yet, unbelievably, they still had nine more matches to play in just twenty-four days before the end of the season.

It's A Grand Old Team To Support

I was lucky enough to be at Goodison on the memorable night when the mighty Bayern Munich were overwhelmed by an Everton team powered by the intensity and energy of a crowd that would not settle for anything less than victory.

One goal up on aggregate after a goal-less first leg (and with their away goal counting double in the event of a draw), there was a swagger about the Bayern players as they left the field at half-time and I remember saying to friends, "They think they've won." But the roar as the players came out for the second half was deafening and I'll never forget how the Blues tore into the German side in a brilliant forty-five minutes of football, scoring three great goals in front of almost 50,000 ecstatic Evertonians! Happy days!

Steven Doran

EVERTON
NIL SATIS
NISI OPTIMUM
GOODISON
PARK L4

May 1985

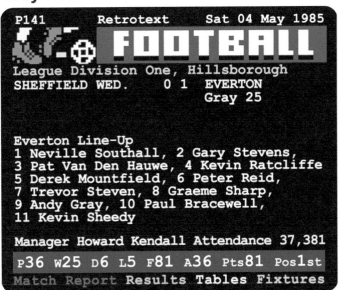

P141   Retrotext   Sat 04 May 1985

FOOTBALL

League Division One, Hillsborough
SHEFFIELD WED.   0 1   EVERTON
                                Gray 25

Everton Line-Up
1 Neville Southall, 2 Gary Stevens,
3 Pat Van Den Hauwe, 4 Kevin Ratcliffe
5 Derek Mountfield, 6 Peter Reid,
7 Trevor Steven, 8 Graeme Sharp,
9 Andy Gray, 10 Paul Bracewell,
11 Kevin Sheedy

Manager Howard Kendall Attendance 37,381

P36 W25 D6 L5 F81 A36 Pts81 Pos1st
Match Report Results Tables Fixtures

P141   Retrotext   Mon 06 May 1985

FOOTBALL

League Division One, Goodison Park
EVERTON   2 0   QPR
Mountfield 25
Sharp 82   Att: 50,317

Top Of The Table	P	W	D	L	F	A	Pts
EVERTON.........	37	26	6	5	83	36	84
MANCHESTER UNITED	40	21	10	9	73	41	73
TOTTENHAM HOTSPUR	39	21	8	10	74	46	71
LIVERPOOL........	37	19	10	8	58	29	67
ARSENAL.........	41	19	8	14	59	47	65
SOUTHAMPTON......	40	18	10	12	53	45	64

1984-85 Division One Champions
Match Report Results Tables Fixtures

Lifelong Evertonian and club legend Mike Lyons had been a spectator at Goodison Park a few weeks earlier to witness the unforgettable triumph over Bayern Munich, but on this day, as Sheffield Wednesday captain, he would be doing his best to deny his beloved Blues victory.

With a 'spine' of ex-Everton players in their ranks - Martin Hodge in goal, Lyons at centre-half and Imre Varadi at centre-forward - Wednesday had enjoyed a terrific season back in the top flight under their young manager Howard Wilkinson, who would go on to win the Division One title with Leeds.

Lyons had also become a legend at Wednesday and before kick-off he was presented with an inscribed watch on behalf of both clubs by Blues' chairman Philip Carter in recognition of recently playing his 500th League game.

Mathematically, only Liverpool - champions for the three previous seasons - could now prevent their local rivals from taking the League title away from them.

After winning 1-0 thanks to Andy Gray's twelfth goal of the campaign, Everton could have become champions at Hillsborough but Liverpool's 4-3 win over Chelsea meant Evertonians would have to wait another couple of days at least.

Over 50,000 fans crammed into Goodison Park to see Everton become Division One champions for the first time since 1970. Derek Mountfield's twelfth goal of the season and Graeme Sharp's thirtieth gave the Blues an unassailable lead at the top of the table with five games left to play.

Before the game, Howard Kendall picked up his Manager of the Month award for April and it became known that Neville Southall had been voted Player of the Season by the Football Writers' Association for his outstanding contribution to a record-breaking season.

This was the team's twenty-seventh game without defeat, a run stretching back to 22nd December, of which twenty-three games had been victories with only four draws. The line-up on the day was:

1 Neville Southall, 2 Gary Stevens, 3 Pat Van Den Hauwe, 4 Kevin Ratcliffe, 5 Derek Mountfield, 6 Peter Reid, 7 Trevor Steven, 8 Graeme Sharp, 9 Andy Gray, 10 Paul Bracewell, 11 Kevin Sheedy. Substitute Kevin Richardson

The terraces rang out with "We're going to win the lot" as the small squad did a lap of honour around the pitch, with the Canon League trophy itself to be presented to the new champions before the home match against West Ham on Wednesday.

It's A Grand Old Team To Play For

Mark Higgins made his debut for Everton as an 18-year-old in December 1976, the Blues drawing 2-2 with a Manchester City team whose line-up included Joe Royle.

He served the Blues with distinction at centre-half and midway through the 1982-83 season Howard Kendall made him club captain. In November of the following campaign, he developed a persistent groin injury which would eventually lead to his premature retirement at the age of just 26. He played his last game in a 2-0 League Cup replay win against West Ham at Goodison Park in December 1984 and twelve months later his testimonial match draw a crowd of 16,000, generating £35,000 in gate receipts.

Mark did return to professional football in 1986 for a brief spell with Manchester United before joining Bury and then Stoke City.

May 1985

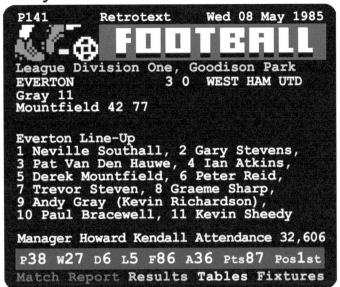

Kevin Ratcliffe was presented with the Canon League trophy before the kick-off but that was as far as his involvement on the evening went as the skipper was forced to miss his first match of the season due to injury, Ian Atkins stepping in to replace him.

West Ham were one of a number of clubs at the bottom of the table still battling against relegation and with Everton having secured the League title John Lyall's side may have hoped the new champions would not be on their best form.

As it was, there was no complacency in the Blues' ranks and Andy Gray set them on the way to another three points with his thirteenth goal of the season.

Derek Mountfield doubled the advantage just before half-time and the free-scoring centre-half grabbed another in the second period to take his total for the campaign to an astonishing fourteen.

The hectic fixture schedule was inevitably taking its toll on the players with Andy Gray, Graeme Sharp, Peter Reid and Paul Bracewell all rated as doubtful for the match with Nottingham Forest on Saturday when the Blues would be seeking to extend their unbeaten run to twenty-nine games.

With two Cup finals to play in the next week, not surprisingly Howard Kendall did not take risks with his quartet of walking wounded.

Garry Birtles put the home side ahead on ten minutes and that proved to be the decisive moment of the game.

Despite having plenty of the ball and with good performances from the replacement strikeforce of Paul Wilkinson and Ian Atkins, the Blues couldn't find an equaliser and the amazing unbeaten run came to end.

From the shock 4-3 home reverse to Chelsea on the Saturday before Christmas, Everton had gone twenty-eight games without losing and only four of those matches were draws, the rest were victories.

But this was also the day of the Bradford fire which claimed the lives of fifty-six people. The blaze broke out just before half-time during the match between Bradford City and Lincoln City and engulfed the main stand in a matter of minutes.

Sadly, it was not the only tragedy on this day. At Birmingham City's game against Leeds United rioting broke out which resulted in a wall collapsing, killing a fifteen-year-old fan.

If You Know Your History

Coming into this derby, Everton were unbeaten after eleven League games and stood in second spot in the table, four points behind leaders Liverpool, with Bob Paisley's side also yet to lose a match.

Mike Lyons had suffered a badly gashed knee at QPR the week before and was ruled out, so veteran Roger Kenyon came into the defence. Kenyon had been in the last Everton side to beat the Reds back in November 1971, thanks to a goal by David Johnson.

Andy King hit the memorable winner from the edge of the area to crown a brilliant derby display by the Blues and earn a fully deserved victory which narrowed the gap at the top to just two points.

May 1985

```
P141        Retrotext       Wed 15 May 1985
    FOOTBALL
European Cup-Winners Cup Final,
Feyenoord Stadium, Rotterdam
EVERTON          3 1      RAPID VIENNA
Gray 58                   Krankl 85
Steven 73
Sheedy 86

Everton Line-Up
1 Neville Southall, 2 Gary Stevens,
3 Pat Van Den Hauwe, 4 Kevin Ratcliffe,
5 Derek Mountfield, 6 Peter Reid,
7 Trevor Steven, 8 Graeme Sharp,
9 Andy Gray, 10 Paul Bracewell,
11 Kevin Sheedy
Manager Howard Kendall Attendance 38,500
        Nil Satis Nisi Optimum
Match Report Results Tables Fixtures
```

```
P141        Retrotext       Sat 18 May 1985
    FOOTBALL
FA Cup Final, Wembley Stadium
EVERTON          0 1      MANCHESTER UTD
                  aet  Whiteside 110


Everton Line-Up
1 Neville Southall, 2 Gary Stevens,
3 Pat Van Den Hauwe, 4 Kevin Ratcliffe
5 Derek Mountfield, 6 Peter Reid,
7 Trevor Steven, 8 Graeme Sharp,
9 Andy Gray, 10 Paul Bracewell,
11 Kevin Sheedy

Manager Howard Kendall Attendance 100,000
Referee Peter Willis (County Durham)
        Nil Satis Nisi Optimum
Match Report Results Tables Fixtures
```

Ahead of Everton's involvement in two Cup Finals, the achievements of the players were recognised on the international front, with Graeme Sharp and Andy Gray called into the Scotland squad, and Peter Reid and Paul Bracewell joining Gary Stevens and Trevor Steven in the England squad.

In his programme notes for the home game with West Ham, Howard Kendall had given an insight into the team's preparations for the European Cup-Winners' Cup Final against Rapid Vienna.

"We will have a training session on Tuesday before leaving for Rotterdam, where we will be staying in the hotel which Aston Villa used before their European Cup Final appearance three years ago. On the Wednesday morning, we'll do nothing more energetic than go for a walk, which is what we would normally do on a matchday, and in the afternoon, the players will rest before having tea and toast prior to our departure to the stadium."

The Final itself was completely dominated by the Blues who enjoyed a fully deserved 2-0 lead when Hans Krankl briefly pulled one back to threaten an unlikely comeback for the Austrian outfit. But Kevin Sheedy swiftly restored Everton's two-goal advantage and the Blues secured their first European trophy in emphatic fashion.

After the Final in Rotterdam, there was high praise not only for Everton's almost perfect performance but also for the up to 25,000 Evertonians who had behaved impeccably before, during and after the match, even at one stage having an impromptu kickabout with Dutch police.

Everton had played Manchester United three times already this season without defeat and had torn Ron Atkinson's side apart in the 5-0 drubbing at Goodison back in October, but in a one-off game such as a Final, anything can happen.

Before the match kicked off there was a minute's silence for the victims of the terrible fire at Bradford a week before.

Peter Reid went closest for the Blues, hitting the woodwork with a volley after ten minutes, and the midfield maestro was involved in the game's major incident on seventy-eight minutes.

He was fouled by Kevin Moran who was then sent off for denying a goalscoring opportunity, the first player ever dismissed in an FA Cup Final.

In extra-time, United's ten men grew in strength as the Blues tired, not surprisingly playing in their sixth match in just fourteen days, and Norman Whiteside curled one home to take the FA Cup to Old Trafford.

It's A Grand Old Team To Play For

Andy King signed for Everton from Luton Town in March 1976 for a fee of £35,000 but due to injury only made his debut in April with three games of the 1975-76 season left. The 19-year-old was an instant hit with the Goodison faithful and scored two goals in his second match as the Blues finished the campaign with three straight wins.

He is most fondly remembered for scoring the goal in October 1978 which gave Everton a first victory over Liverpool in seven years and also for being pushed off the pitch by a policeman whilst being interviewed after the match.

Gordon Lee was boss when King moved to QPR in 1980, then onto West Brom, from where in 1982 Howard Kendall brought him back to the club in a swop deal with Peter Eastoe.

May 1985

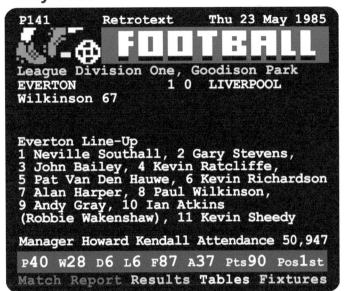

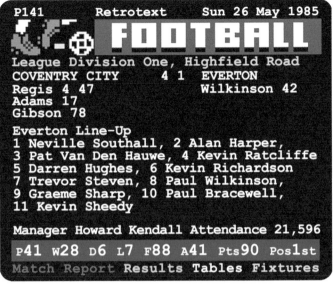

On the Sunday after the FA Cup Final, 250,000 fans put the disappointment of missing out on the treble by welcoming the players home, many with signs saying "Two Will Do." The open-topped bus went on a twelve-mile tour of the city with the European Cup-Winners' Cup and the Canon League trophy prominently displayed.

Incredibly, Everton still had three League fixtures to fulfill and one of them, away to Coventry City, would determine whether the Sky Blues or Norwich City would be relegated so there was pressure from the Carrow Road team for the Blues to play a full strength side.

The first match, though, Everton's last home game of a momentous season, would be a derby against Liverpool for which the injured Derek Mountfield was already ruled out while four players had been away with the England team in Finland.

An entertaining clash was settled by a Paul Wilkinson goal on his full debut for the club. The victory took Everton's points tally to ninety, surpassing the previous best set by Liverpool.

Off the field, Howard Kendall was named Bell's Manager of the Year and it was announced that the club had secured a lucrative three-year sponsorship deal with Japanese electronics firm NEC.

The Football League had ruled that Everton must field their strongest team available at Highfield Road, which Howard Kendall did, but with this being the eighth game in three weeks for many players there were inevitably tired minds and bodies in the Blues' line-up.

Darren Hughes was making his first appearance of the season with his only previous game in the first team being a 3-0 defeat at Wolves in December 1983, just before Kendall began to turn around his own and Everton's fortunes.

Coventry had looked dead and buried, needing to win their last three games to stay up, but having beaten Stoke and Luton, three points in this Sunday morning match with an 11.30 kick-off, would secure their Division One status.

Paul Wilkinson scored his second goal in two games but it was just a consolation as the home team were emphatic winners, sending League Cup winners Norwich City down to Division Two, along with Sunderland and Stoke City.

Though there was still one fixture to fulfill, Howard Kendall was already planning for next season and revealed that the club had signed goalkeeper Bobby Mimms from Rotherham for £150,000.

It's A Grand Old Team To Play For

After his debut in March 1971, lifelong Evertonian Mike Lyons made 473 appearances for the Blues, scoring 59 goals. He was club captain from 1976 to 1982 and would give everything he had in every single game, whether at centre-half or centre-forward.

In 1981-82, he was an ever-present during Howard Kendall's first season in charge at Everton until a groin injury in February forced him to step down, allowing Billy Wright to come in and form an impressive central defensive partnership with Mark Higgins.

Sheffield Wednesday manager Jack Charlton signed Lyons for £80,000 in the summer of 1982 and he went on to earn legendary status at Hillsborough, too. In his first season, the club reached the FA Cup semi-final and, in his second, he played in all 42 League games as promotion to Division One was secured.

May 1985

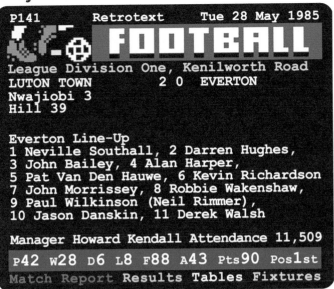

```
P141        Retrotext        Tue 28 May 1985
      FOOTBALL
League Division One, Kenilworth Road
LUTON TOWN          2  0  EVERTON
Nwajiobi 3
Hill 39

Everton Line-Up
1 Neville Southall, 2 Darren Hughes,
3 John Bailey, 4 Alan Harper,
5 Pat Van Den Hauwe, 6 Kevin Richardson
7 John Morrissey, 8 Robbie Wakenshaw,
9 Paul Wilkinson (Neil Rimmer),
10 Jason Danskin, 11 Derek Walsh

Manager Howard Kendall Attendance 11,509
P42 W28 D6 L8 F88 A43 Pts90 Pos1st
Match Report  Results Tables Fixtures
```

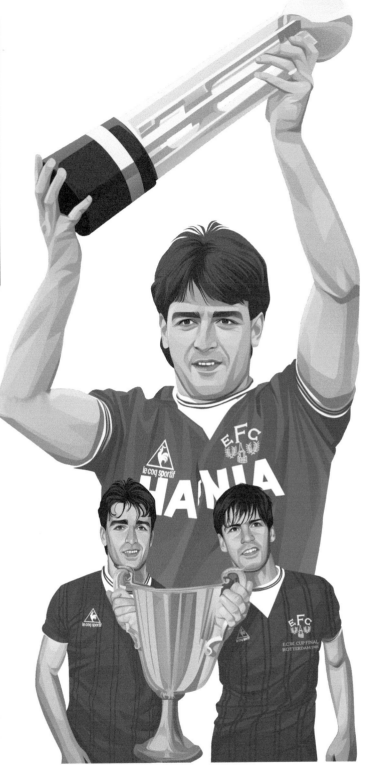

This was the the sixty-third and last game of Everton's marathon season which had begun in August with a Charity Shield victory over Liverpool and goalkeeper Neville Southall had played in every one. The FWA Player of the Season was made captain in the absence of so many first-teamers and was man-of-the-match,

Youngsters John Morrissey (son of 1960's legend Johnny), Jason Danskin, Derek Walsh and Neil Rimmer made their debuts, while right back Darren Hughes was making only his third appearance.

Despite losing three of their last four League games, Everton had set a new points record in securing the Division One title for the first time since 1969-70 and added two more trophies to go with the FA Cup won in 1984.

Not only that but Howard Kendall could now plan for a European Cup campaign to potentially erase his frustration at being eliminated from that competition as a player in 1970-71 at the quarter-final stage without losing a game.

Everton would be one of the favourites to lift the trophy, having been described by legendary Bayern Munich coach Udo Lattek earlier in the season as the best team in Europe.

It's A Grand Old Team To Support

Writing in the match programme a few days before his testimonial match in September, 1980, Mike Lyons said:

"Everton, of course, have always been my life. Since I was a kid who stood on the terraces, it was my dream to play for them and I jumped quickly when I got the chance to join them straight from school. It's been a happy time for me at Goodison, not only playing for the club but also captaining it."

The testimonial game was between a team of current players and a team of former ones, including Howard Kendall, Colin Harvey, Joe Royle and Martin Dobson. It finished 5-5, before a crowd of 12,851 which generated receipts of £25,000.

**EVERTON
NIL SATIS
NISI OPTIMUM
GOODISON
PARK L4**

May 1985

Twenty-four hours after Everton's final game of the 1984-85 season, dreams of a European Cup campaign in 1985-86 had vanished due to events at the Heysel Stadium in Brussels, which was hosting the European Cup Final.

Poor segregation allowed a section of Liverpool fans to charge Juventus supporters who fled in panic, leading to thirty-nine people being killed and many more injured.

After pressure from Downing Street, the Football Association withdrew all English clubs from the following season's European competitions. However, in early June, UEFA announced an indefinite ban on them.

Back in 1985, after years of seeing violence at grounds on TV screens at home and abroad, many supporters couldn't have cared less about missing out on the European Cup. People had died going to watch a football match and everything else seemed insignificant.

The new reality for Howard Kendall and his team was that there was to be no opportunity for them to prove Udo Lattek's assertion against the likes of Bayern Munich (again), Barcelona and Juventus in UEFA's premier club competition. Instead, there would be a new Super Cup to try and fill the void.

These are original Ceefax pages recovered from an old VHS recording. The corruption is caused by the retrieval process.

They provided the latest information as it was known at the time, just a few hours after the Heysel Stadium disaster had occurred.

It's A Grand Old Team To Support

Everton and their royal blue army were the pride of Europe today after last night's magnificent and historic European Cup Winners' Cup win in Rotterdam. The 20,000 Evertonians who descended on the city won a huge tribute from the Dutch authorities.

A senior police spokesman said: "It was a pleasure having the Everton supporters here in Rotterdam. They were a credit to their country."

Everton chairman Mr Philip Carter said: "Our supporters have been absolutely marvellous. Our fans have upheld the reputation of Everton F.C. and given a tremendous boost to the British image abroad. I am proud of our team and I am proud of our supporters."

From the *Liverpool Echo*, Thursday 16th May 1985

EVERTON NIL SATIS NISI OPTIMUM GOODISON PARK L4

Three: 1985-1986
EVERTON FC*

HOWARD KENDALL - MANAGER

COLIN HARVEY - COACH

MICK HEATON - COACH

JOHN CLINKARD - PHYSIO

ADRIAN HEATH

ALAN HARPER

BOBBY MIMMS

DEREK MOUNTFIELD

GARY LINEKER

GARY STEVENS

GRAEME SHARP

IAN ATKINS

IAN MARSHALL

JOHN BAILEY

KEVIN RATCLIFFE

KEVIN RICHARDSON

KEVIN SHEEDY

NEVILLE SOUTHALL

PAT VAN DEN HAUWE

PAUL BRACEWELL

PAUL WILKINSON

PETER REID

TREVOR STEVEN

*as at the start of the season

August 1985

The big transfer news of the summer was Everton's £800,000 acquisition of Leicester City's prolific striker, Gary Lineker, who had scored seventy-seven goals for his hometown club in the previous three seasons.

The signing meant the Blues had an embarrassment of riches up front and there was much speculation as to who would make way for the England star. That question was answered in mid-July when Andy Gray returned to his first English club, Aston Villa.

Gray told the Liverpool Echo: "I had this vision of playing out my career with Everton, but I've been long enough in the game to accept that things can change very quickly in football."

After returning from a short pre-season tour of Canada, the Blues warmed up for the Charity Shield clash with Manchester United with a reserve game at Crewe, allowing Peter Reid and Adrian Heath to prove their fitness. Both came through okay with Inchy on the scoresheet in a 2-1 win.

The traditional season-opener offered Everton the opportunity of a modicum of revenge for the FA Cup Final defeat of three months earlier at the hands of United and they took it with a fully deserved win over Ron Atkinson's side.

Ahead of the first League game of the new season, Everton played Liverpool in Phil Neal's Testimonial match, with the Blues coming from 2-0 down to win 3-2 thanks to goals from Derek Mountfield and Inchy (two).

The big decision manager Howard Kendall had to make before the season-opener at Filbert Street was who would partner Gary Lineker up front, with Adrian Heath in such good goal-scoring form after his long injury lay-off. In the end, Kendall opted to start with Graeme Sharp with Inchy on the bench.

Just as they did twelve months earlier, Everton began the campaign with a defeat, despite taking the lead through the prolific Derek Mountfield. The home side equalised on the stroke of half-time and claimed the points in the second period with a brace of goals from Mark Bright.

Before the next game, at home to West Brom, Kendall announced that defender Ian Atkins and young striker Rob Wakenshaw would be allowed to leave the club when an acceptable offer was received.

The manager explained that the emergence of Ian Marshall would limit Atkins' playing opportunities, while Wakenshaw would find it difficult to displace the top quality strikers at the club.

It's A Grand Old Team To Play For

When Howard Kendall took over at Everton in 1981, he signed seven new players, including two goalkeepers - Jim Arnold, who he knew well from his days as manager of Blackburn Rovers, and Neville Southall, a £150,000 purchase from Bury.

Neville and Jim both had periods when one or the other was first choice 'keeper and at one point the Welsh stopper was loaned out to Port Vale for a brief spell.

Arnold claimed the number one shirt at the start of the 1983-84 season but after seven games Southall regained that position and from then on went on to establish himself as the best goalkeeper in the world during the most successful era in Everton's history. He was voted Football Writers' Player Of The Season in 1984-85 and won another FA Cup winners medal with the Blues in 1995.

August 1985

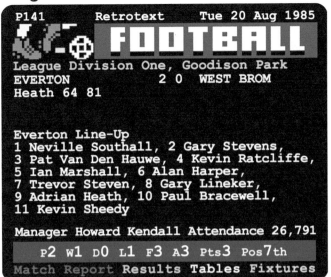

P141   Retrotext   Tue 20 Aug 1985
FOOTBALL
League Division One, Goodison Park
EVERTON   2 0   WEST BROM
Heath 64 81

Everton Line-Up
1 Neville Southall, 2 Gary Stevens,
3 Pat Van Den Hauwe, 4 Kevin Ratcliffe,
5 Ian Marshall, 6 Alan Harper,
7 Trevor Steven, 8 Gary Lineker,
9 Adrian Heath, 10 Paul Bracewell,
11 Kevin Sheedy

Manager Howard Kendall Attendance 26,791

P2 W1 D0 L1 F3 A3 Pts3 Pos7th

Match Report **Results Tables Fixtures**

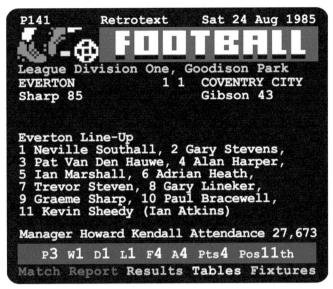

P141   Retrotext   Sat 24 Aug 1985
FOOTBALL
League Division One, Goodison Park
EVERTON   1 1   COVENTRY CITY
Sharp 85   Gibson 43

Everton Line-Up
1 Neville Southall, 2 Gary Stevens,
3 Pat Van Den Hauwe, 4 Alan Harper,
5 Ian Marshall, 6 Adrian Heath,
7 Trevor Steven, 8 Gary Lineker,
9 Graeme Sharp, 10 Paul Bracewell,
11 Kevin Sheedy (Ian Atkins)

Manager Howard Kendall Attendance 27,673

P3 W1 D1 L1 F4 A4 Pts4 Pos11th

Match Report **Results Tables Fixtures**

After Everton had lost their opener against Tottenham the previous season, the team were beaten by West Brom in their second game. Coincidentally, the Blues' second game this season was also against the Baggies but, with home advantage this time around, Howard Kendall's side notched their first win of the campaign despite being without three influential players.

Peter Reid's achilles injury had flared up again while Derek Mountfield had damaged his knee and Graeme Sharp was suffering from a hamstring strain.

Mountfield's absence meant a debut for young Ian Marshall, who was captain of the successful FA Youth Cup side in 1984, and the 19-year-old coped well with the speed of ex-Everton striker Imre Varadi, now in the West Brom ranks.

Adrian Heath was making up for lost time having been out of the team since the incident with Brian Marwood which had ended his season in December 1984.

He had scored after coming on as substitute in the Charity Shield and in this, his first full game in almost nine months, he nabbed two more to get the Blues off the mark for the campaign.

Following his impressive display against West Brom, Ian Marshall was in the starting line-up again for the Blues with Kevin Ratcliffe joining Derek Mountfield on the physio's table allowing Alan Harper to come into the back four.

Peter Reid again missed out but Graeme Sharp was fit enough to return. Transfer-listed Ian Atkins was named on the substitute's bench.

With Paul Bracewell as captain for the day, the home side dominated the first half but fell behind to a sucker punch just before the break when the diminuitive Terry Gibson prodded home.

The second period was more of the same but with time running out and a second defeat of the season looking a distinct possibility, in-form Adrian Heath turned provider when his corner was nodded home by Graeme Sharp.

Four points from three games was a very modest return for the defending champions.

The Blues now faced a tricky trip to White Hart Lane on Bank Holiday Monday to play a Tottenham side which had pushed them all the way in the title race in the previous campaign, though they too had made a poor start to the new season.

It's A Grand Old Team To Support

I tend to look back on the bad games. The five-nil against Liverpool and things like that. Maybe that's because I try and use the bad ones to make sure I have good ones.

When it comes to good memories, I suppose the Bayern Munich semi-final was the one. After that, the final was almost an anti-climax. Not being able to carry on in Europe was a blow but nothing like what happened to people who died at Heysel and Hillsborough.

At the end of the road, I will look back and honestly say that I had a good time here. I couldn't have gone to a better club and I couldn't have played for better supporters.

Neville Southall in the match programme versus Wimbledon, May 1994

EVERTON
NIL SATIS
NISI OPTIMUM
GOODISON
PARK L4

August 1985

```
P141      Retrotext      Mon 26 Aug 1985
[LOGO] FOOTBALL
League Division One, White Hart Lane
TOTTENHAM HOTSPUR 0 1 EVERTON
                      Lineker 75


Everton Line-Up
1 Neville Southall, 2 Gary Stevens,
3 Pat Van Den Hauwe, 4 Kevin Ratcliffe
5 Ian Marshall, 6 Alan Harper,
7 Trevor Steven, 8 Gary Lineker,
9 Adrian Heath (Graeme Sharp),
10 Paul Bracewell, 11 Kevin Sheedy

Manager Howard Kendall Attendance 29,720

P4 W2 D1 L1 F5 A4 Pts7 Pos6th
Match Report  Results Tables Fixtures
```

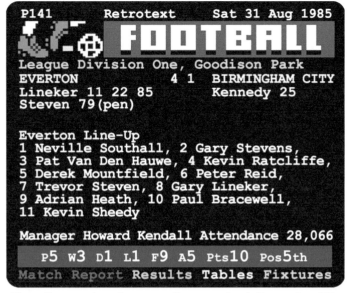

```
P141      Retrotext      Sat 31 Aug 1985
[LOGO] FOOTBALL
League Division One, Goodison Park
EVERTON           4 1  BIRMINGHAM CITY
Lineker 11 22 85       Kennedy 25
Steven 79(pen)


Everton Line-Up
1 Neville Southall, 2 Gary Stevens,
3 Pat Van Den Hauwe, 4 Kevin Ratcliffe,
5 Derek Mountfield, 6 Peter Reid,
7 Trevor Steven, 8 Gary Lineker,
9 Adrian Heath, 10 Paul Bracewell,
11 Kevin Sheedy

Manager Howard Kendall Attendance 28,066

P5 W3 D1 L1 F9 A5 Pts10 Pos5th
Match Report  Results Tables Fixtures
```

This was Everton's third successive victory at White Hart Lane, following a 2-1 win in September 1983 (Reid and Sheedy the scorers) and the famous 2-1 win in April this year which did so much to secure the Division One title for the Blues.

Gary Lineker's first goal for the club since his £800,000 move from Leicester City was enough to secure the three points and move the Blues up the table. It was something of a transfer coup for the champions as Manchester United and Liverpool had also been vying for his signature.

Lineker's arrival in June had seemingly increased the competition for places amongst the strikers, with the 24-year-old England international joining Andy Gray, Graeme Sharp, Paul Wilkinson and Adrian Heath in the battle for a starting berth.

The following month, though, came the shock news that Andy Gray was leaving and re-joining Aston Villa, the club he had moved to from Dundee in 1975. The Scottish striker had a massive impact on the Blues on and off the field during the eighteen months he had been an Everton player.

Manager Howard Kendall told the Liverpool Echo: "From my point of view, I couldn't let the chance of signing Gary Lineker pass us by and that meant we were overloaded in the front positions."

Despite scoring the equaliser against Coventry City which earned a point, Graeme Sharp found himself on the bench for the trip to White Hart Lane as the Gary Lineker/Adrian Heath partnership flourished.

Ahead of the weekend game with Birmingham, Sharp played for the reserves in a 0-0 draw at Hull City, together with Derek Mountfield. The Scottish striker was clearly not happy with the situation and with his contract up at the end of the season he was keeping all his options open.

Another player feeling frustrated though for different reasons was Peter Reid, but his groin and achilles injuries had responded to treatment and he was hopeful of being in the starting eleven come Saturday. On matchday, Reid and Mountfield both came back in but Sharp would have to make do with a place on the bench.

Gary Lineker scored twice to put the Blues in the ascendency but after Andy Kennedy pulled one back the visitors made a game of it. The key moment came midway through the second half when Birmingham defender Ken Armstrong was sent off and the Blues made their numerical advantage count with Trevor Steven converting a penalty and Lineker notching his first hat-trick for Howard Kendall's team.

It's A Grand Old Team To Play For

Gary Stevens came through Everton's youth ranks, making his debut in a League Cup tie with Coventry in the 1981-82 season and going on to make 19 appearances in total during that campaign. He lost his place to Brian Borrows at the start of the 1982-83 season but regained it after the infamous 5-0 defeat at Goodison Park by Liverpool.

He provided an assist in the 1984 FA Cup Final, setting up Graeme Sharp who scored the first goal in that 2-0 win over Watford, and was an integral part of the team which won two Division One League titles and the European Cup-Winners' Cup.

With English teams banned from Europe after the Heysel Stadium disaster at the end of the 1985 season, Gary was sold by manager Colin Harvey to big-spending Glasgow Rangers in the summer of 1988 for £1.25 million.

September 1985

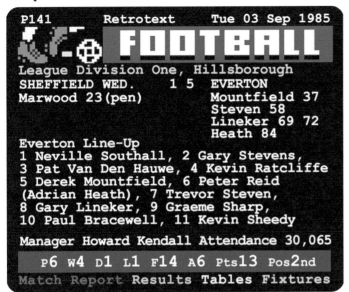

P141　　　Retrotext　　　Tue 03 Sep 1985

FOOTBALL

League Division One, Hillsborough
SHEFFIELD WED.　　1 5　　EVERTON
Marwood 23(pen)　　　　Mountfield 37
　　　　　　　　　　　　Steven 58
　　　　　　　　　　　　Lineker 69 72
　　　　　　　　　　　　Heath 84
Everton Line-Up
1 Neville Southall, 2 Gary Stevens,
3 Pat Van Den Hauwe, 4 Kevin Ratcliffe
5 Derek Mountfield, 6 Peter Reid
(Adrian Heath), 7 Trevor Steven,
8 Gary Lineker, 9 Graeme Sharp,
10 Paul Bracewell, 11 Kevin Sheedy
Manager Howard Kendall Attendance 30,065
P6 W4 D1 L1 F14 A6 Pts13 Pos2nd
Match Report **Results Tables Fixtures**

P141　　　Retrotext　　　Sat 07 Sep 1985

FOOTBALL

League Division One, Loftus Road
QPR　　　　　　　3 0　　EVERTON
Bannister 29 55
Byrne 42

Everton Line-Up
1 Neville Southall, 2 Gary Stevens,
3 Pat Van Den Hauwe, 4 Kevin Ratcliffe
5 Derek Mountfield, 6 Peter Reid,
7 Trevor Steven, 8 Gary Lineker,
9 Graeme Sharp, 10 Paul Bracewell,
11 Adrian Heath
Manager Howard Kendall Attendance 14,006
P7 W4 D1 L2 F14 A9 Pts13 Pos4th
Match Report **Results Tables Fixtures**

Bobby Robson announced his England squad for a World Cup qualifier, with Mexico 86 now only a few months away, and there were no less than five Everton players in it - Peter Reid, Paul Bracewell, Trevor Steven, Gary Stevens and Gary Lineker.

Graeme Sharp and ex-crowd favourite Andy Gray, now at Aston Villa, were in the Scotland squad and Kevin Sheedy in the Republic of Ireland's. On top of that, two younger members of Howard Kendall's side were in the Under-21 squad - goalkeeper Bobby Mimms and striker Paul Wilkinson.

The manager made a surprise announcement ahead of the midweek game at Hillsborough with Graeme Sharp coming into the side at the expense of Adrian Heath, possibly anticipating an aerial bombardment from a strong and physical Sheffield Wednesday side.

The home side had started the season well, coming into this match unbeaten in five matches, recording four wins and a draw, and they took the lead from the penalty spot.

Derek Mountfield equalised before half-time and the visitors turned on the style in the second period with Trevor Steven, Gary Lineker (twice) and substitute Adrian Heath all on target.

Before the weekend League game on QPR's plastic pitch, the draw for the second round of the Milk (League) Cup was made, with Everton tied against Bournemouth in a two-legged clash.

Graeme Sharp was expected to retain his place in the starting line-up after his performance at Hillsborough with Inchy again on the bench, but Kevin Sheedy was a late withdrawal so both players were involved from the kick-off, with Ian Marshall on the sub's bench.

The Blues had a poor record on Loftus Road's artificial surface and the team's five-match unbeaten run came to end as the home side's advantage of playing on a pitch they knew better shone through.

The defeat dropped Kendall's men from second to fourth in the Division One table, losing further ground on Manchester United who had won all seven games and were already eight points clear of the Blues.

Speaking of United, there was shock news that Mark Higgins, who had been forced to retire because of injury at the age of twenty-six, had taken up an offer from Old Trafford boss Ron Atkinson to train with them for three months to see if his pelvic problem could withstand the rigours of top flight football.

It's A Grand Old Team To Play For

Pat van den Hauwe joined Everton from Birmingham City for a fee of £100,000 and made his debut in a 1-0 defeat at Arsenal in October 1984, almost immediately establishing himself as first-choice left-back at the expense of John Bailey.

His no-nonsense approach soon endeared him to the Goodison Park faithful and earned him the affectionate nickname 'Psycho'. His reputation as a hardman was enhanced in December when he was sent off at QPR for fighting, leading to a two-match suspension.

As well as a dependable left-back, Pat was also a reliable stand-in at centre-back when called upon. He became a key member of the side which carried all before it in 1984-85 and he is also fondly remembered for scoring the goal at Norwich City in May 1987 which gave the Blues a second League title in three seasons.

September 1985

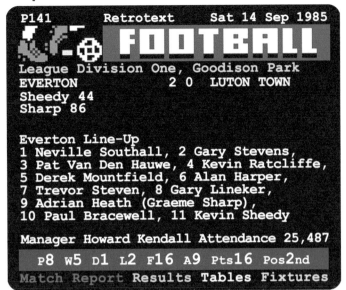

```
P141      Retrotext      Sat 14 Sep 1985
      FOOTBALL
League Division One, Goodison Park
EVERTON        2  0   LUTON TOWN
Sheedy 44
Sharp 86

Everton Line-Up
1 Neville Southall, 2 Gary Stevens,
3 Pat Van Den Hauwe, 4 Kevin Ratcliffe,
5 Derek Mountfield, 6 Alan Harper,
7 Trevor Steven, 8 Gary Lineker,
9 Adrian Heath (Graeme Sharp),
10 Paul Bracewell, 11 Kevin Sheedy

Manager Howard Kendall Attendance 25,487
P8 W5 D1 L2 F16 A9 Pts16 Pos2nd
Match Report Results Tables Fixtures
```

```
P141      Retrotext      Wed 18 Sep 1985
      FOOTBALL
Screen Sport Super Cup First Round,
Old Trafford
MANCHESTER UTD    2  4   EVERTON
Robson 45(pen)           Sheedy 23 53
Stapleton 61            Lineker 43
                        Sharp 80

Everton Line-Up
1 Neville Southall, 2 Gary Stevens,
3 Pat Van Den Hauwe, 4 Kevin Ratcliffe
5 Ian Marshall, 6 Alan Harper,
7 Trevor Steven, 8 Gary Lineker
(Adrian Heath), 9 Graeme Sharp,
10 Paul Bracewell, 11 Kevin Sheedy

Manager Howard Kendall Attendance 33,859
Nil Satis Nisi Optimum
Match Report Results Tables Fixtures
```

Many Everton players were on international duty at the start of the week with Peter Reid making his Wembley debut for England in a World Cup qualifier against Romania, together with Gary Stevens and Trevor Steven. Bobby Robson's side drew 1-1, keeping them on course for Mexico '86.

The biggest clash of the week was in Cardiff, where Wales needed to beat Scotland to keep their World Cup hopes alive, while Jock Stein's men needed just a point to virtually guarantee their participation.

Neville Southall, Pat van den Hauwe and Kevin Ratcliffe were in the Wales team, while Graeme Sharp led the Scotland attack.

Wales took an early lead through Mark Hughes but the Scots equalised from a contentious penalty ten minutes from time and the game finished all-square.

However, the match was overshadowed by the death of the legendary Stein - the man who led Celtic to European Cup glory in 1967 - from a heart attack after the final whistle.

Peter Reid returned to Bellefield with a recurrence of his achilles injury and missed the game with Luton, which was decided by a Kevin Sheedy goal seconds before half-time and a header late on by substitute Graeme Sharp.

Though he scored when coming on as a substitute against Luton, Graeme Sharp was not happy at being dropped, sparking speculation that Aston Villa would seek to reunite the Scottish striker with Andy Gray.

Another headache for manager Howard Kendall was the news that Peter Reid's achilles injury required him to rest so he would be out for a few weeks and Derek Mountfield had a cartilage operation which meant up to six weeks out.

With English clubs banned indefinitely from European competitions, midweek saw Everton in their first match of the Football League Super Cup designed to generate revenue for the teams which had qualified for the European Cup (Everton), European Cup Winners' Cup (Manchester United) and UEFA Cup (Liverpool, Norwich City, Southampton and Tottenham).

As well as Ron Atkinson's United, League Cup winners Norwich were in Everton's group.

Though United were flying in the League, having won all eight of their opening matches, they were no match for the defending champions. There was a healthy attendance for this game but generally the new competition failed to excite fans.

It's A Grand Old Team To Play For

A product of the club's youth system, Kevin Ratcliffe made his debut for Everton against Manchester United at Old Trafford in April 1980 and a few days later was in the team which dramatically lost in an FA Cup semi-final replay against West Ham.

He was a regular in the side when Howard Kendall became boss and during the trophy-laden period of 1984 to 1987 was almost an ever-present in the team. Though he made over 350 appearances for the Blues, he scored only two goals - the winner at Carrow Road in January 1983 in a 1-0 win and, famously, against Liverpool in February 1986.

Kevin was appointed club captain in December 1983 and as skipper won the FA Cup in 1984, the Division One title in 1984-85 and 1986-87 plus the European Cup-Winners' Cup in 1985, as well as narrowly missing out on the 'double' in 1985-86.

September 1985

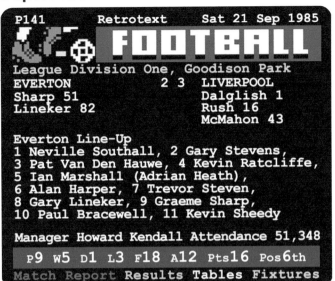

```
P141      Retrotext      Sat 21 Sep 1985
⚽ FOOTBALL
League Division One, Goodison Park
EVERTON           2  3  LIVERPOOL
Sharp 51                 Dalglish 1
Lineker 82               Rush 16
                         McMahon 43

Everton Line-Up
1 Neville Southall, 2 Gary Stevens,
3 Pat Van Den Hauwe, 4 Kevin Ratcliffe,
5 Ian Marshall (Adrian Heath),
6 Alan Harper, 7 Trevor Steven,
8 Gary Lineker, 9 Graeme Sharp,
10 Paul Bracewell, 11 Kevin Sheedy

Manager Howard Kendall Attendance 51,348
P9 W5 D1 L3 F18 A12 Pts16 Pos6th
Match Report  Results Tables Fixtures
```

```
P141      Retrotext      Wed 25 Sep 1985
⚽ FOOTBALL
League Cup 2nd Round (1st Leg),
Goodison Park
EVERTON           3  2  BOURNEMOUTH
Lineker 22               Clarke 1
Marshall 35              Russell 11
Heffernan 54(og)

Everton Line-Up
1 Neville Southall, 2 Gary Stevens,
3 Pat Van Den Hauwe, 4 Kevin Ratcliffe
5 Ian Marshall, 6 Alan Harper,
7 Trevor Steven, 8 Gary Lineker,
9 Graeme Sharp, 10 Paul Bracewell,
11 Kevin Sheedy
Manager Howard Kendall Attendance 13,930
Nil Satis Nisi Optimum
Match Report  Results Tables Fixtures
```

Ahead of the first Merseyside derby of the season, Howard Kendall was presented with the Bell's Manager of the Year Award in recognition of his part in the memorable 1984-85 campaign.

On the pitch, teenager Ian Marshall came in for the injured Derek Mountfield with Alan Harper deputising for Peter Reid. In Liverpool's starting eleven was former Everton player Steve McMahon who had joined the Reds earlier in the month from Aston Villa for a fee of £350,000.

Kenny Dalglish put the visitors ahead inside the first minute and with the home team pushing for the equaliser, Ian Rush made it 2-0. To add insult to injury, old boy McMahon was also on target leaving Kendall's side with a mountain to climb.

Kendall took off the youngster Marshall at half-time, putting Pat van den Hauwe in his position, with Adrian Heath entering the fray. Graeme Sharp pulled one back and another goal from Gary Lineker, making his first appearance in a derby, made for an exciting finish but there was to be no equaliser.

With Manchester United winning 5-1 at West Brom to put them on a maximum twenty-seven points, the Blues dropped to sixth in the table, eleven points behind the runaway leaders.

After conceding two quick goals against Liverpool at the weekend, no doubt Howard Kendall's message to his team before they took to the Goodison Park pitch against Harry Redknapp's Bournemouth was 'keep it tight'.

If it was, the players didn't do so and soon found themselves 2-0 down to the visitors with Colin Clarke's opener hitting the back of the net after just eleven seconds. The team from two divisions below the Blues looked on course for another giantkilling act, as they had knocked Manchester United out of the FA Cup in January 1984.

In-form Gary Lineker got one back for the Blues with a diving header and Ian Marshall levelled things up before the break. With the home side increasing the pressure as the game went on, Tom Heffernan headed into his own net to give Kendall's side a slender victory but with a difficult looking assignment in the second leg still to come.

Meanwhile, Ian Atkins, who joined the club the season before as an experienced squad player, left after making just nine appearances and scoring one goal. He had been courted by both Sunderland boss Lawrie McMenemy and Ipswich manager Bobby Ferguson and he opted to join the Tractor Boys for a fee of £60,000.

It's A Grand Old Team To Support

Kevin Ratcliffe will be walking tall in the name of an illustrious predecessor on Sunday when he picks up his first trophy of the season, the Liverpool Echo's Dixie Dean Memorial Award.

Ratcliffe never met the great man but he was brought up on stories about Goodison heroes of the past. Kevin's family are staunch Blues and his father Bryan used to take him to all the home games, his earliest memory being of the side that won the League title in 1970.

"My dad and my uncles were all Main Stand season ticket holders. It's funny the little things that stick in your mind like Alan Ball's famous white boots. He was my idol, along with Joe Royle and Brian Labone."

From the *Liverpool Echo*, Friday 25th September 1987

EVERTON
NIL SATIS
NISI OPTIMUM
GOODISON
PARK L4

September 1985

From The Teletext Archive

```
P141        Retrotext      Sat 28 Sep 1985
        FOOTBALL
League Division One, Villa Park
ASTON VILLA        0  0        EVERTON


Everton Line-Up
1 Neville Southall, 2 Gary Stevens,
3 Pat Van Den Hauwe, 4 Kevin Ratcliffe,
5 Ian Marshall, 6 Alan Harper,
7 Trevor Steven, 8 Gary Lineker,
9 Graeme Sharp, 10 Paul Bracewell,
11 Kevin Sheedy
Manager Howard Kendall Attendance 22,048
P10 W5 D2 L3 F18 A12 Pts17 Pos5th
Match Report Results Tables Fixtures
```

```
P142 ORACLE 142 Thu14 Dec ITV 0021:38
                                    2/2
FOOTBALL           KENDALL LINES UP
 Transfer news      DOUBLE REUNION
Manchester City's new manager Howard
Kendall has signed Peter Reid from QPR
on a three-year contract to be player-
coach at Maine Road.

Reid, now 33, makes his City debut on
Sunday against his former club Everton
at Goodison Park.

Kendall has also agreed a fee for
another of his Everton old boys, Alan
Harper, 29, of Sheffield Wednesday.

City are prepared to splash out
£150,000 on the Liverpool-born utility
player who Kendall describes as: "A
tremendous asset because he can play in
any number of positions."       >>>>>
    Sport headlines 130  Football 140
Next Report  In Brief  Football TV Guide
```

The game against Aston Villa on Saturday raised the prospect of Andy Gray playing against his old club for this time since his shock transfer in the summer. The talismanic striker had not scored for Villa in his second spell at the club but Graham Turner's team were in good form and unbeaten in seven matches.

New signing Simon Stainrod had scored all four goals for Villa in a League Cup tie with Exeter in midweek and this was the first time the two of them had played together.

Gray caused his former team-mates plenty of problems all afternoon with Neville Southall having to be at his imperious best to keep the home side out, but in the end the spoils were shared.

Southall had injured his ribs in the Bournemouth match and had to have a jab before this clash. He was a doubt for the midweek Super Cup game against Norwich City, with Bobby Mimms put on alert for a possible first team debut.

The result meant that the gap between defending champions Everton and this season's trailblazers Manchester United grew to thirteen points, with Ron Atkinson's side having beaten Southampton 1-0 to make it ten wins from ten games.

This is an original Oracle page recovered from an old VHS recording.

Having left Athletic Bilbao in November, Howard Kendall was appointed manager of Manchester City in December 1989 with the club bottom of the Division One table. But with the help of a number of Everton old boys, by the end of the season he had guided the club to the safety of fourteenth place.

When he left City to rejoin Everton in November 1990, the club were riding high in fifth spot, while the Blues were languishing in seventeenth.

It's A Grand Old Team To Play For

Local lad Derek Mountfield was signed by Howard Kendall for £30,000 from Tranmere Rovers ahead of the 1982-83 season but he didn't make his full debut for the club until the following April when he replaced club captain Mark Higgins in a 1-0 defeat at Birmingham City.

With Higgins continuing to suffer from a persistent groin injury, Derek had more chances at the start of the 1983-84 season to show what he could do and from December he made the centre-half position his own alongside Kevin Ratcliffe.

Derek scored three goals during that campaign but in the unforgettable 1984-85 season, he contributed no less than fourteen goals as the Blues surged to domestic and European honours.

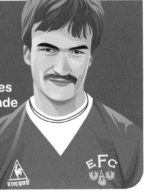

October 1985

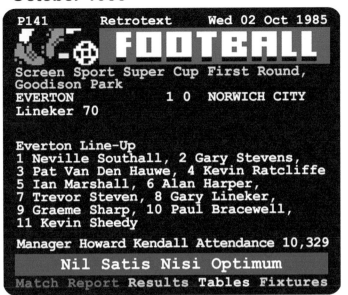

```
P141        Retrotext        Wed 02 Oct 1985
     FOOTBALL
Screen Sport Super Cup First Round,
Goodison Park
EVERTON              1  0   NORWICH CITY
Lineker 70


Everton Line-Up
1 Neville Southall, 2 Gary Stevens,
3 Pat Van Den Hauwe, 4 Kevin Ratcliffe,
5 Ian Marshall, 6 Alan Harper,
7 Trevor Steven, 8 Gary Lineker,
9 Graeme Sharp, 10 Paul Bracewell,
11 Kevin Sheedy

Manager Howard Kendall Attendance 10,329
       Nil Satis Nisi Optimum
Match Report  Results  Tables  Fixtures
```

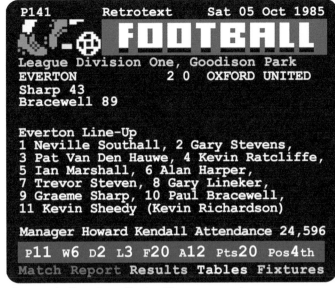

```
P141        Retrotext        Sat 05 Oct 1985
     FOOTBALL
League Division One, Goodison Park
EVERTON              2  0   OXFORD UNITED
Sharp 43
Bracewell 89


Everton Line-Up
1 Neville Southall, 2 Gary Stevens,
3 Pat Van Den Hauwe, 4 Kevin Ratcliffe,
5 Ian Marshall, 6 Alan Harper,
7 Trevor Steven, 8 Gary Lineker,
9 Graeme Sharp, 10 Paul Bracewell,
11 Kevin Sheedy (Kevin Richardson)

Manager Howard Kendall Attendance 24,596
P11 w6 D2 L3 F20 A12 Pts20 Pos4th
Match Report  Results  Tables  Fixtures
```

With Neville Southall's injury improving, Bobby Mimms took his place in a strong looking reserve side for the mini derby with Liverpool, with Kevin Richardson, John Bailey, Paul Wilkinson and Adrian Heath all on show.

Reserve team coach Terry Darracott, who hadn't played a game for the Blues for six years, was a surprise inclusion in Everton's line-up

But the Reds had a strong team too, including Sammy Lee and John Wark and they ran out 2-0 winners, thanks to a brace from Paul Walsh.

Though Everton won the Super Cup clash with Norwich City, virtually guaranteeing a place in the semi-final, it was clear that the competition had not captured the supporters' imagination with only 10,000 fans turning up to watch.

The small turnout obviously affected the atmosphere and a low key match was settled in the same fashion, with a shot that was going wide from Gary Stevens deflecting off Gary Lineker into the net.

On the same evening, the first round matches in the European Cup were concluding with Bayern Munich, Juventus, Ajax and Alex Ferguson's Aberdeen amongst the sides making it through.

Over at Prenton Park, Tranmere player manager Frank Worthington had signed former Everton youngster John Morrissey from the Blues and he made his debut on the Friday night before this match at Southend. The game ended 2-2 with both Worthington and Morrissey on the scoresheet.

The son of 1960's Everton star Johnny Morrissey would go on to have a terrific career with Tranmere, making 470 appearances. He was a member of the team which reached the League Cup semi-final in 1994, only beaten 5-4 on penalties by eventual winners Aston Villa after the game finished 4-4 on aggregate.

Against Oxford United, Everton took the lead just before half-time through Graeme Sharp's fourth goal of the season but the game was in the balance right up to the end.

With time ticking away, Ian Marshall appeared to handle the ball in the area but the referee declined to give a penalty and the home side swept forward with Paul Bracewell sealing the victory to the fury of the Oxford players.

Manchester United's one hundred percent record ended after they drew 1-1 at Luton so the win moved Howard Kendall's side to within eleven points of the runaway leaders.

It's A Grand Old Team To Support

Derek Mountfield used to stand on the Gwladys Street terraces and cheer on the Blues. As a schoolboy, he would dream of playing at Goodison Park and emulating his soccer heroes.

"I was a spectator the last time we scored a League win over Liverpool in 1978 when Andy King grabbed that memorable goal. I saw the FA Cup win against them a few years back and now I'm part of the set-up and I'll fight and battle all the way to help Everton win the Milk Cup."

One of Derek's biggest fans - and critics - is his grandad Roland who used to be in the Liverpool Mounted Police. He was on duty at Goodison the day Dixie Dean scored his memorable 60th League goal in 1928.

From *Mersey Masters*, Liverpool Echo Milk Cup Final Special, March 1984

EVERTON NIL SATIS NISI OPTIMUM GOODISON PARK L4

October 1985

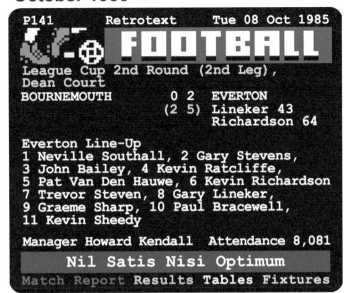

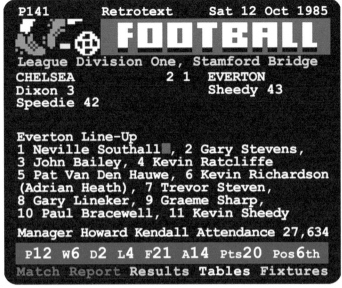

Ahead of a tricky-looking second leg of the League Cup tie with Bournemouth, Howard Kendall was dealing with unrest from Adrian Heath, who was unhappy at being left out of the team at the weekend. But the manager laid down the law in no uncertain terms, telling the Liverpool Echo:

"He is wasting his time moaning. I had fitness tests on three players on Saturday in defensive areas and midfield. Kevin Richardson was my choice as substitute with the possibility of players breaking down. I shouldn't have to justify my decisions to any player."

There was no place for Heath at Dean Court where John Bailey came in at left-back to allow Pat van den Hauwe to play alongside Kevin Ratcliffe, with Kevin Richardson making his first start of the season after injury.

As expected, the Blues came under pressure from Harry Redknapp's side who had shocked Manchester United on this ground two years earlier but they found Neville Southall in his usual sparkling form.

Gary Lineker's eleventh goal of an increasingly fruitful season for him gave the visitors breathing space and Richardson celebrated his return to the side with a second to kill the tie off.

The Blues could now seek to improve their League position and close the yawning gap on Manchester United. But this game against Chelsea would be tough as under manager John Hollins the London side were flying, sitting in third spot in the table a point ahead of Everton.

Chelsea flew out of the traps and were soon ahead through Kerry Dixon. It could have got worse after twenty minutes when David Speedie broke through and was hauled down by Neville Southall. The referee awarded a penalty and booked the Welshman but Nigel Spackman missed the spot kick.

There was to be no respite though and Speedie made it 2-0 just before the break, but the visitors gave themselves hope for the second half when Kevin Sheedy reduced the arrears shortly afterwards.

Graeme Sharp had the chance to level things up when Everton were awarded a penalty but he dragged his shot wide. Worse was to come for Howard Kendall's side when Southall received a second booking for handling outside the area and was sent off, with Kevin Ratcliffe going in goal.

Manchester United beat QPR 2-0 so the defending champions now trailled them by fourteen points.

It's A Grand Old Team To Play For

Blues boss Gordon Lee had tried to sign Peter Reid from Bolton Wanderers for £600,000 in 1980 but it was Howard Kendall who brought Huyton's finest to the club a week before Christmas 1982 for a cut-price £60,000.

Andy Gray credits the introduction of Peter as a second-half substitute in a League Cup tie at Goodison in November 1983 as one of the catalysts for the club's upturn in fortunes, the Blues coming from behind to win 2-1 and eventually reach the Final.

At the end of Everton's momentous 1984-85 season, Peter was voted the PFA Footballer Of The Year and he was a key member of the England squad during the 1986 World Cup.

October 1985

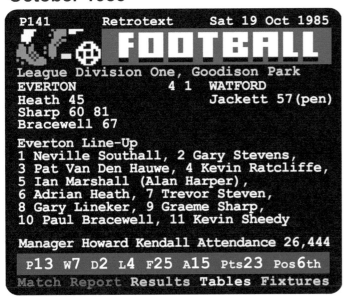

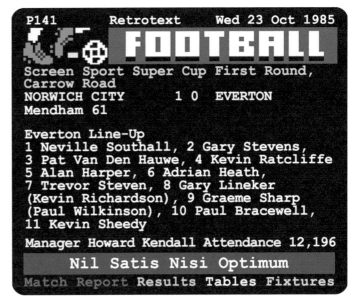

On the run-up to the Watford game, several Everton players were on international duty. Gary Lineker and Gary Stevens were in the England team which booked its place at the Mexico World Cup with a 5-0 drubbing of Turkey, Lineker scoring a hat-trick.

Recent matches against Watford had been goalfests, with the Blues winning 4-0 at Goodison the previous season as well as 5-4 at Vicarage Road. Howard Kendall brought Adrian Heath back into the starting eleven and it was Inchy who broke the deadlock on the stroke of half-time.

Watford's Kenny Jackett levelled things up from the penalty spot early in the second period but the visitors' joy was short-lived as Graeme Sharp's header restored the Blues' advantage. Paul Bracewell added a third before Sharp again rounded off the victory.

With leaders Manchester United held to a 1-1 draw with Liverpool at Old Trafford, Everton cut the deficit at the top to twelve points but remained sixth.

Paul Wilkinson, whose first team opportunities had been limited due to the form of Gary Lineker, Graeme Sharp and Adrian Heath, was the subject of a transfer inquiry by Southampton manager, Chris Nicholl, but Howard Kendall dismissed the approach for the England Under-21 player.

Though Howard Kendall talked up the new Super Cup whenever he could, it was clear some of the players didn't have the same enthusiasm for it.

Peter Reid, who was still suffering from an achilles injury, was particularly scathing of the event, saying in his book Everton Winter, Mexican Summer:

"The lads lost 1-0 at Norwich last night. They evidently didn't play well. I don't think they put too much thought into the game because I don't really think they were in the mood for it. Getting excited about playing Manchester United in a meaningless competition is one thing; being motivated to play at Norwich is another matter."

There was a popular television quiz show in the 1980s called Bullseye. If, at the end of the show, the contestants had missed out on the main prize, host Jim Bowen would say "here's what you could have won."

It must have felt like that for the players as instead of travelling to Carrow Road for this low key match, they could have been turning out at the Olympic Stadium, Munich or Camp Nou, Barcelona.

On this same evening, in the European Cup first leg round of 16 matches, Bayern beat Austria Vienna 4-2 and Terry Venables' Barcelona side defeated Porto 2-0.

It's A Grand Old Team To Support

A boyhood Liverpool fan, Peter Reid now proudly proclaims himself as an Evertonian. When receiving his Everton Giant accolade in 2006, he said: "To have been able to play for this club is fantastic. To be described as a legend is beyond my wildest dreams."

"I lost my dad earlier this year. He, like me, was born a red but converted to an Evertonian. My mum was the one with the brains in the family because she has always been a Blue. This award will take pride of place at my mum's house and every time I look at it I will think of my old fella."
From EvertonFC.com

EVERTON NIL SATIS NISI OPTIMUM GOODISON PARK L4

October 1985

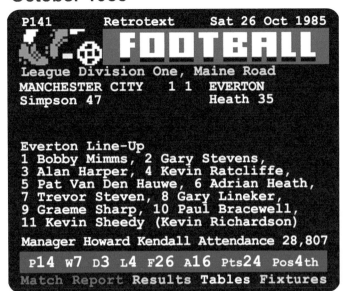

```
P141        Retrotext      Sat 26 Oct 1985
FOOTBALL
League Division One, Maine Road
MANCHESTER CITY    1 1    EVERTON
Simpson 47                Heath 35


Everton Line-Up
1 Bobby Mimms, 2 Gary Stevens,
3 Alan Harper, 4 Kevin Ratcliffe,
5 Pat Van Den Hauwe, 6 Adrian Heath,
7 Trevor Steven, 8 Gary Lineker,
9 Graeme Sharp, 10 Paul Bracewell,
11 Kevin Sheedy (Kevin Richardson)
Manager Howard Kendall Attendance 28,807
P14 W7 D3 L4 F26 A16 Pts24 Pos4th
Match Report  Results Tables Fixtures
```

```
P141        Retrotext      Tue 29 Oct 1985
FOOTBALL
League Cup 3rd Round, Gay Meadow
SHREWSBURY TOWN    1 4    EVERTON
Robinson 51              Sharp 22
                        Hughes 47(og)
                        Sheedy 55
                        Heath 89
Everton Line-Up
1 Neville Southall, 2 Gary Stevens,
3 Alan Harper, 4 Kevin Ratcliffe
5 Pat Van Den Hauwe, 6 Adrian Heath,
7 Trevor Steven, 8 Gary Lineker,
9 Graeme Sharp, 10 Paul Bracewell,
11 Kevin Sheedy
Manager Howard Kendall Attendance 10,346
Nil Satis Nisi Optimum
Match Report  Results Tables Fixtures
```

On the run-up to Saturday's game it was announced that popular left-back John Bailey was moving to Newcastle United for a fee of £100,000.

Together with Andy Gray, John had been one of the great characters in the Everton dressing room and he left the club with everyone's good wishes.

After resting his achilles injury for six weeks in a bid to sort it out, Peter Reid was not too pleased to be told he would, after all, need an operation on it which would be carried out immediately with the midfielder under the care of the same surgeon who dealt with Adrian Heath's injury.

With Neville Southall suspended following his sending off at Chelsea, Howard Kendall gave a debut to Bobby Mimms against Manchester City at Maine Road. The youngster didn't let him down, making a string of fine saves to deny Billy McNeill's side.

Adrian Heath put the visitors ahead but Paul Simpson equalised just after half-time.

The result meant the Blues moved up to fourth spot but fell further behind runaway leaders Manchester United who got back to winning ways after two successive draws to beat Chelsea 2-1 at Stamford Bridge despite playing the second half with only ten men.

The best thing about Cup competitions in the 1980s was that managers always played their best available team. Conscious of the fact that twelve months earlier the Blues had been knocked out of this competition by second division Grimsby, Howard Kendall brought Neville Southall straight back into the line-up against a team with a recent history of giant-killing acts in the FA Cup.

But there was never any chance of a Cup shock in this tie as the Blues put in a thoroughly professional performance which their opponents simply had no answer to. Graeme Sharp put the visitors 1-0 up at the interval and then there was a flurry of goals just after half-time.

Defender Darren Hughes had left Everton during the summer and, under pressure from Graeme Sharp, he put the ball past his own keeper two minutes into the second period. The hosts pulled one back a few minutes later but a superb strike from Kevin Sheedy then effectively ended the contest and Adrian Heath rounded off the scoring near the end.

In the next round, the Blues were drawn against the winners of the Chelsea versus Fulham replay. The teams had drawn 1-1 at Stamford Bridge and it would be Chelsea hosting Everton as a sole Kerry Dixon goal gave them victory at Craven Cottage.

It's A Grand Old Team To Play For

Trevor Steven played 99 games for Burnley, scoring 16 goals, before his transfer to Everton for £300,000 in the summer of 1983. John Bond had just been appointed Burnley boss and sanctioned the sale of Trevor to raise funds for his own acquisitions.

He was a player Howard Kendall had monitored for some time and with Steve McMahon having just left the club to join Aston Villa, the manager opted to invest that money in 'Tricky Trev'. In the first-half of the 1983-84 season, opportunities for him were limited, with Alan Irvine often preferred, but towards the end of the campaign Trevor proved his worth and he played in the 1984 FA Cup Final.

He was a key member of the team in the 1984-85 season, famously scoring the third goal in the greatest-ever Goodison match against Bayern Munich.

November 1985

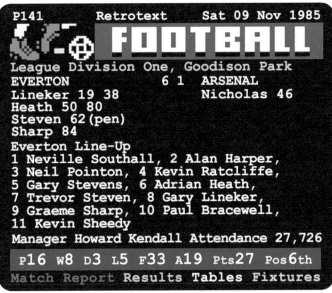

It was back to League action at the weekend and a tricky trip to in-form West Ham, whose two strikers - Frank McAvennie and Tony Cottee - were Division One's top scorers with thirteen and ten respectively.

McAvennie had been in sensational scoring form since his summer move from St Mirren for £340,000 and his double against the Blues, after Trevor Steven had put the visitors ahead, was the fifth time in fifteen games that he had scored two in a match.

Another summer recruit at Upton Park was Mark Ward, a former Everton apprentice, who was signed from Oldham Athletic for £250,000.

Mark had a number of relatives down from Merseyside to watch this game and he would go on to re-join the Blues in 1991.

The victory for John Lyall's side took the Hammers above their opponents in the table and with Manchester United registering their thirteenth win of a so far unbeaten season, Ron Atkinson's men were a colossal seventeen points ahead of the defending champions.

In transfer news, the club announced the signing of 20-year-old left-back Neil Pointon from Scunthorpe United for a fee said to be in the region of £50,000.

New boy Neil Pointon made his debut sooner than he probably anticipated due to an injury crisis at Goodison.

With Derek Mountfield and Ian Marshall out of action, Welsh international Pat van den Hauwe had been operating alongside Kevin Ratcliffe.

But when 'Psycho' was sent home suffering from measles, the young left back was drafted in with the ever reliable utility player Alan Harper switching to right back and Gary Stevens partnering Ratcliffe in the heart of the defence.

Arsenal were above Everton in the League so a tough match was anticipated but it turned out completely differently as Don Howe's side were swamped by the depleted Blues.

Gary Lineker put the home team 2-0 up at half-time and though Charlie Nicholas pulled one back for the Gunners just after the interval, that just spurred the champions on. Adrian Heath with two, Trevor Steven from the spot and Graeme Sharp were all on target in the second period to complete the rout.

There was also good news from Hillsborough, where Sheffield Wednesday brought to an end Manchester United's unbeaten start to the campaign, courtesy of a Lee Chapman strike.

It's A Grand Old Team To Play For

Graeme Sharp joined Everton from Dumbarton for £120,000 in April 1980 and made his debut for the club against Brighton the following month. Then manager Gordon Lee later said Sharp was the best signing he made for the Blues but the Scottish striker had limited first-time opportunities until Howard Kendall's arrival in May 1981.

In Kendall's first season, Sharp scored sixteen goals for the the club and followed that with nineteen goals during the 1982-83 campaign. Injuries restricted his appearances in the FA Cup-winning season but he did score in the Final against Watford.

He found the net twenty-five times in the memorable 1984-85 season and when he left the club in 1991 to join Joe Royle's newly promoted Oldham Athletic, he had scored a total of 159 goals in 446 appearances.

November 1985

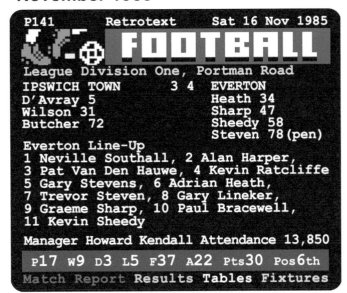

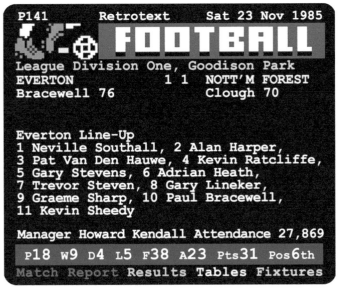

There was an international break on the run-up to the away game at Ipswich Town at the weekend and Paul Bracewell was named in the England team to play Northern Ireland at Wembley, together with Gary Stevens and Gary Lineker, with Trevor Steven on the bench.

Ex-Everton boss Billy Bingham was manager of England's opponents and his side were looking for the point which would secure their place in the World Cup Finals in Mexico. A huge contingent of Northern Ireland fans celebrated a 0-0 draw at the final whistle, with Tottenham's forty-year-old goalkeeper Pat Jennings the hero after making a string of fine saves.

On the domestic front and away from Goodison, Everton legend Mike Lyons had left Sheffield Wednesday to take on the player-manager role at Grimsby Town and he had appointed the Blues' reserve team coach, Terry Darracott, as his assistant.

The game at Portman Road was a cracker, with the visitors 2-0 down at one stage before rallying to lead 3-2 then being pegged back at 3-3.

The thrilling encounter was finally settled from the penalty spot, Trevor Steven converting after Gary Lineker had been fouled.

Howard Kendall was full of praise for his team's performance at Portman Road and told the Liverpool Echo:

"They showed tremendous character and I was very proud of them. After the match I went on to the pitch and shook every one of them by the hand. It's not something I do very often, but they had earned it. You cannot go wrong If you have players like that who are ready to give you everything."

With no midweek game to consider, Kendall, together with club chairman Philip Carter, flew to Paris to receive the European Team of the Year award in recognition of the fantastic achievements of the glorious 1984-85 season, the greatest campaign in Everton's history.

The big game of the week was the first leg of a World Cup playoff match between Scotland and Australia to decide who would be playing in Mexico the following summer. The Scots won the first leg 2-0 with Graeme Sharp coming on as a second half substitute. Sharp would also be involved in the second leg in Melbourne and would miss a couple of Everton games as a result.

Against Forest, Everton had been hoping to record a third consecutive League win but instead needed a late Paul Bracewell goal to salvage a point.

It's A Grand Old Team To Play For

Andy Gray had been the most expensive player in English football in 1979 when he joined Wolves from Aston Villa for £1.5 million but he had endured injury problems and Howard Kendall was ultimately able to secure his services for £250,000 in November 1983.

Kendall would later say that the acquisition of the Scottish striker was one of the key reasons for the change in the team's fortunes from January 1984, citing the impact he had both on and off the field. As well as in the 1984 FA Cup Final win over Watford, Gray scored a host of important goals for the club during the glorious 1984-85 season.

Everton fans - and Andy himself - were shocked when he was sold to Aston Villa in July 1985 following the arrival of Gary Lineker at Goodison Park.

November 1985

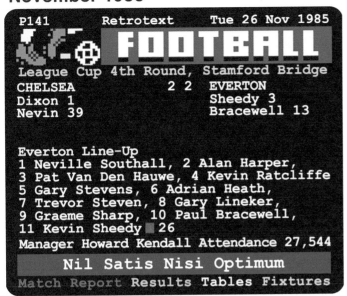

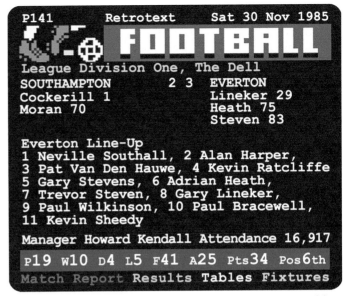

Having already lost at Stamford Bridge this season, Everton knew they were in for a tough match against Chelsea. Back in October, the Blues had been beaten 2-1 by John Hollins's side and had Neville Southall sent off for two bookable offences.

Kerry Dixon had made his England debut earlier in the month and he kicked off a whirlwind start to the tie by scoring in the first minute.

Kevin Sheedy levelled things up with a free-kick and ten minutes later the visitors went ahead with a well-worked goal finished off by Paul Bracewell.

Sheedy was sent off on the half-hour mark for nothing more than swearing at the referee and before a breathless first-half was over, Pat Nevin had made it 2-2.

The ten-men Blues settled for a draw in the second period and earned a replay at Goodison two weeks later.

Sheedy's harsh dismissal earned him a two-game ban, meaning would miss the replay with Chelsea as well as the home game against Leicester.

In other news, the Football League announced that Milk Marketing Board's sponsorship of the League Cup would be ending, with the new sponsor being Liverpool-based firm, Littlewoods.

With Graeme Sharp away on World Cup duty with Scotland in Australia, 21-year-old Paul Wilkinson came into the side to partner Gary Lineker .

The Blues had developed a habit this season for conceding early goals and after Kerry Dixon had scored after fifty-three seconds in midweek, Glenn Cockerill put the home side ahead inside the first minute here.

The visitors recovered and Gary Lineker's fourteenth goal of the season had levelled things up by half-time.

Howard Kendall's side fell behind again with twenty minutes left but, just as at Portman Road a couple of weeks earlier, the players showed great character to fight back, with Adrian Heath making it 2-2 and then a Trevor Steven piledriver earning all three points.

Manchester United, meanwhile, having been fifteen games unbeaten at the beginning of November, in four games since then had lost two and drawn two.

As the month came to a close, Ron Atkinson's side had seen a ten point advantage over second-placed Liverpool reduced to just two, with Everton also edging closer, trailling the leaders by nine points back in sixth spot.

It's A Grand Old Team To Support

It is nice to think I played a part in what Everton achieved but Colin Harvey's promotion, the emergence of Peter Reid and, of course, Adrian Heath's famous goal at Oxford all contributed to turning things around.

I rate my time at Everton as the two greatest years of my career. Although I scored more goals during my early days at Aston Villa, I would be happy to be remembered for what I did at Everton.

To be in at the beginning of such a dramatic turnaround - when things went from being as bad as they could be in 1983 to take off so quickly - was a joy.

Andy Gray, *The Evertonian*, December 1994

EVERTON
NIL SATIS
NISI OPTIMUM
GOODISON
PARK L4

December 1985

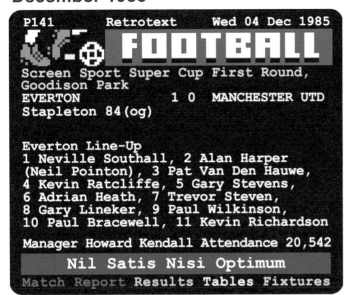

Manchester United boss Ron Atkinson was facing such an injury crisis that he requested that the Football League allow him to play ex-Blues' skipper Mark Higgins, who was trying to resurrect his career after being forced to retire in 1985, as a non-contract player but his request was denied.

With Graeme Sharp 'Down Under', Paul Wilkinson kept his place in the side but manager Howard Kendall left out Kevin Sheedy so Kevin Richardson could have a run-out.

In a healthy crowd of over 20,000, there were only five hundred United fans and they witnessed a largely one-sided match with the Blues missing a host of chances before Frank Stapleton's own goal settled the tie. The win confirmed Everton's spot in the semi-final of this new competition.

Over in Melbourne, Scotland drew 0-0 with Australia to secure the final place at the 1986 World Cup in Mexico, Alex Ferguson's team going through 2-0 on aggregate.

Meanwhile, the draw had been made for the quarter-finals of the European Cup which would be played in March: Bayern Munich v Anderlecht, Steaua Bucharest v Kuusysi, Aberdeen v Gothenburg, Barcelona v Juventus.

Before the next League game, Howard Kendall announced that Footballer of the Year Neville Southall had signed a new six-year contract, one of the longest deals ever given to an Everton player and testament to the part he had played in the club's recent revival.

West Brom were bottom of the Division One table and England World Cup winner Nobby Stiles had just replaced Johnny Giles as manager.

The visitors were two up inside fifteen minutes through Kevin Sheedy and Pat van den Hauwe, his first for the club. Goal-machine Gary Lineker rattled home his fifteenth of the campaign in the second half and the only black spot on the afternoon was a booking for Kevin Ratcliffe which would mean a two-match ban for the skipper.

But the win didn't affect Everton's League position and they still lagged behind Manchester United (who beat Ipswich 1-0) and Liverpool (who beat Aston Villa 3-0) by nine and seven points respectively.

Already without the injured Derek Mountfield, the prospect of losing Kevin Ratcliffe for a couple of games as well prompted Howard Kendall to sign defender Kevin Steggles on a month's loan from Ipswich Town.

It's A Grand Old Team To Play For

Paul Bracewell had just been named Sunderland's Player Of The Year by supporters when Howard Kendall signed him in May 1984 as he prepared to strengthen the team which had just won the FA Cup and he made his debut in August's Charity Shield match.

On New Year's Day 1986, he injured his ankle against Newcastle United and bravely played through the pain barrier for the remainder of the campaign. Rest over the summer failed to resolve the problem and he missed the entire title-winning 1986-87 season and made only four appearances in 1987-88. After six operations, Bracewell played a full part in helping Everton reach the FA Cup Final in 1989 but that proved to be his last game for the Blues. He moved to Sunderland in August, joined Newcastle in 1992 and returned to Roker Park in the summer of 1995 where Peter Reid was now manager, helping the club to gain promotion to the Premier League.

December 1985

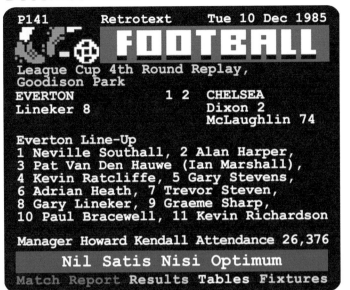

Having been knocked out of the competition at this stage the season before, the Blues were determined to book a place in the semi-final, particularly after surviving at Stamford Bridge for more than half the match with only ten men after Kevin Sheedy's dismissal.

But the curse of the early goal struck yet again and the home side found themselves a goal behind with only a couple of minutes on the clock, Kerry Dixon continuing his prolific season in front of goal.

Gary Lineker buried a pinpoint cross from Trevor Steven to level things up but Everton were unable to get their noses in front. Midway through the second half, Chelsea were reduced to ten men after Darren Wood scythed down Pat van den Hauwe.

That should have been the signal for Howard Kendall's team to turn the screw but it was the visitors' Joe McLaughlin who settled the tie in the London team's favour.

On the plus side, Howard Kendall was delighted to find out that Kevin Ratcliffe's booking at Southampton did not trigger a suspension so the captain would be available for the games over the Christmas period at Coventry and home to Manchester United.

Ahead of Saturday's game, FIFA announced that the worldwide ban on English clubs playing abroad would be lifted next season. This meant teams like Everton could arrange tours and friendlies with foreign clubs again to try and boost revenues severely impacted by the indefinite UEFA ban.

Leicester City had shocked the Blues on the opening day of the season when Gordon Milne's side had come from behind to win 3-1, with Mark Bright scoring two. The home side were without Pat van den Hauwe who was still feeling the effects of the dreadful tackle in midweek which saw Chelsea defender Darren Wood sent off.

In Leicester's team this day was Laurie Cunningham, on loan from Marseille. He had been a key member of the great West Brom team of the late 1970s under Ron Atkinson and was the first British player to be transferred to Real Madrid in 1979. Sadly, he was killed in a car crash in 1989 aged just thirty-three.

Everton took the lead through Kevin Richardson but were pegged back in the second half by goals from Gary McAllister from the penalty spot and Alan Smith. With Manchester United winning 3-1 away to Aston Villa, at the half-way stage of the season the Blues trailled the League leaders by twelve points.

It's A Grand Old Team To Play For

In the summer of 1982, Kevin Sheedy became the first player to join Everton from Liverpool since Johnny Morrissey twenty years previously. His first season at the club was hugely successful as Sheedy scored 13 goals for the Blues, earning him the Supporters' Club Player Of The Year Award.

Kevin's wand of a left-foot was seen to maximum effect in an FA Cup quarter-final tie against Ipswich Town in 1985. He curled a free-kick past goalkeeper Paul Cooper's right only for the referee to say it had to be re-taken. Unfazed, Kevin stepped up and planted the ball into the net to Cooper's left.

Also that year, it was his slide-rule pass which allowed Andy Gray and Trevor Steven to combine for the sublime third goal against Bayern Munich.

December 1985

```
P141      Retrotext      Sat 21 Dec 1985

        FOOTBALL
League Division One, Highfield Road
COVENTRY CITY        1 3   EVERTON
Gibson 60                  Lineker 50 86
                           Sharp 62


Everton Line-Up
1 Neville Southall, 2 Gary Stevens,
3 Neil Pointon, 4 Kevin Ratcliffe,
5 Pat Van Den Hauwe, 6 Adrian Heath,
7 Trevor Steven, 8 Gary Lineker,
9 Graeme Sharp, 10 Paul Bracewell,
11 Kevin Sheedy

Manager Howard Kendall Attendance 10,518
P22 W12 D4 L6 F48 A28 Pts40 Pos6th
Match Report  Results Tables Fixtures
```

```
P141      Retrotext      Thu 26 Dec 1985

        FOOTBALL
League Division One, Goodison Park
EVERTON          3 1   MANCHESTER UTD
Sharp 18 47            Stapleton 14
Lineker 41


Everton Line-Up
1 Neville Southall, 2 Gary Stevens,
3 Neil Pointon, 4 Kevin Ratcliffe,
5 Pat Van Den Hauwe, 6 Adrian Heath,
7 Trevor Steven, 8 Gary Lineker,
9 Graeme Sharp, 10 Paul Bracewell,
11 Kevin Sheedy

Manager Howard Kendall Attendance 42,550
P23 W13 D4 L6 F51 A29 Pts43 Pos5th
Match Report  Results Tables Fixtures
```

Several Everton players would be involved in the World Cup in Mexico at the end of the season and before the next game, the draw was made for the group stages of the competition.

England would face Poland, Morocco and Portugal, Scotland would have to overcome West Germany, Uruguay and Denmark, while Billy Bingham's Northern Ireland were paired with Brazil, Spain and Algeria.

It was also announced that live football would return to television screens early in 1986 after being unavailable for several months. A deal had been brokered by Everton chairman Philip Carter on behalf of the Football League with the BBC and ITV.

Howard Kendall was able to welcome back Pat van den Hauwe from injury for the trip to Highfield Road to play Coventry City, plus Kevin Sheedy from suspension. Psycho would play at centre-half with youngster Ian Marshall out injured.

Two goals from Gary Lineker and another from Graeme Sharp gave the Blues all three points and narrowed the gap with Manchester United to nine. That could be reduced even further on Boxing Day when the Blues would welcome Ron Atkinson's side to Goodison Park.

Apart from the FA Cup Final in May which denied Everton the treble, the Blues had a terrific recent record against Manchester United, including the famous 5-0 hammering last season, followed by the Milk Cup win at Old Trafford just a few days later.

That run of form had continued this season, with a 2-0 win over Ron Atkinson's side in the Charity Shield and two victories in the Screen Sport Super Cup.

Despite falling behind to a Frank Stapleton goal, the home side produced a festive feast for the bumper Boxing Day crowd and roared back with two goals from Graeme Sharp and one from Gary Lineker.

Having been seventeen points behind United just a few weeks ago, Howard Kendall's side had now reduced the arrears to six.

Other Boxing Day results also went in the Blues' favour with second-placed Liverpool losing 1-0 at Manchester City and third-placed West Ham going down by the same score at Tottenham.

Up next for the Toffees was another home game against Sheffield Wednesday, a team they beat 5-1 at Hillsborough back in September but who were having a terrific season under manager Howard Wilkinson, standing in sixth spot in the table.

It's A Grand Old Team To Play For

In January 1982, Everton signed Adrian 'Inchy' Heath from Stoke City for a club record fee of £700,000, beating the previous highest transfer when Gordon Lee brought John Gidman to Goodison Park.

The day before Heath's arrival, Everton had drawn 1-1 at Old Trafford with a very youthful team, nine of which were aged 23 or under, and with Inchy still a few days short of his 21st birthday, it was a clear sign Howard Kendall was building for the future.

Inchy paid a key role in helping the Blues reach two Wembley finals in 1984, famously latching on to Kevin Brock's back pass in the League Cup tie at Oxford United and grabbing the last-gasp winner against Southampton in the FA Cup semi-final at Highbury.

December 1985

```
P141        Retrotext      Sat 28 Dec 1985
          FOOTBALL
League Division One, Goodison Park
EVERTON           3 1  SHEFFIELD WED.
Stevens 19             Stevens 51 (og)
Lineker 24 85

Everton Line-Up
1 Neville Southall, 2 Gary Stevens,
3 Neil Pointon, 4 Kevin Ratcliffe,
5 Pat Van Den Hauwe, 6 Adrian Heath
(Alan Harper), 7 Trevor Steven,
8 Gary Lineker, 9 Graeme Sharp,
10 Paul Bracewell, 11 Kevin Sheedy

Manager Howard Kendall Attendance 41,456
P24 W14 D4 L6 F54 A30 Pts46 Pos3rd
Match Report  Results Tables Fixtures
```

```
P311 CEEFAX 311   Sat 16 Dec   15:01/11
football          SUNDAY'S DIVISION
                  ONE TEAMS       2/3
EVERTON v MANCHESTER CITY
Howard Kendall starts his new reign at
the scene of many a former triumph,
with ex-Evertonians Peter Reid and Alan
Harper both making their City debuts.

Kendall's final line-up depends on Paul
Lake's (ankle) fitness - he has not
trained all week - but fit-again Gary
Megson is back in the squad for the
first time this season.

Northern Ireland midfielder Norman
Whiteside could return after six weeks
out through suspension and an achilles
tendon injury. Colin Harvey adds Stefan
Rehn and Neil Pointon to the 13 on duty
in last Saturday's defeat at Tottenham.
Next Page Football   Cricket    Latest
```

What a momentous year 1985 had been for Everton Football Club. The Canon League trophy, the European Cup Winners' Cup and the Charity Shield had all been secured, Peter Reid and Neville Southall were named Footballer of the Year by the PFA and FWA respectively and Howard Kendall was Manager of the Year.

On top of that, in recognition of their achievements, the Blues also received the accolade of European Team of the Year.

As defending champions, the first half of the 1985-86 season had not always gone according to plan, largely due to the long-term injuries to Derek Mountfield and Peter Reid.

But, with those two due back in the New Year and the partnership of Gary Lineker and Graeme Sharp blossoming, there were plenty of reasons to be cheerful about the months ahead.

This victory was the Blues' third on the bounce, lifting them into third spot in the table, one point behind the season's surprise package Chelsea and three points adrift of Manchester United.

It also took Lineker's goal tally in League and Cup to twenty-one, with every reason to expect plenty more between now and the end of the campaign.

This is an original Ceefax page recovered from an old VHS recording.

The match a week before Christmas in 1989 was the first time long-time collaborators Colin Harvey and Howard Kendall had faced each other as managerial adversaries. It was honours-even as the game finished 0-0 in front of just 21,491 fans.

Former Blues Alan Harper, Peter Reid, Ian Bishop and Gary Megson were in the City side, together with future Blues' left-back Andy Hinchcliffe.

When Kendall rejoined Everton for a second spell in November 1990, Reid was appointed player-manager by City chairman, Peter Swales.

It's A Grand Old Team To Play For

Though a Geordie by birth, Kevin Richardson joined Everton in 1978, turning professional in 1980. He was a key member of the side Howard Kendall developed during the 80s, winning the FA Cup against Watford in 1984 and acting as a reliable stand-in during the momentous 1984-85 season when the Blues won the League title and the European Cup-Winners' Cup.

After leaving the club in September 1986 for Watford in a £250,000 deal, he eventually joined Arsenal and played in the famous game at Anfield in 1989 when the Gunners' snatched the League title from Liverpool in the dying seconds.

He also gave a man-of-the-match performance for Aston Villa in the 1994 League Cup Final when the Midlands outfit defeated Manchester United 3-1.

January 1986

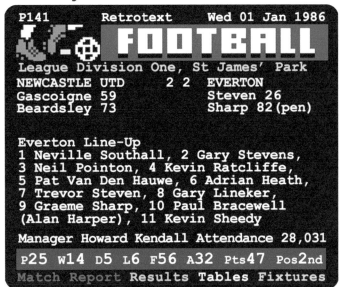

Manchester United's game at Newcastle had been postponed at the weekend due to a frozen pitch and this match was rated only 50:50 at one stage.

It was a long trek to the North East for Evertonians but those who made the journey saw a terrific first-half performance from the visitors who led at the interval through Trevor Steven.

The game swung just before the hour mark when Paul Gascoigne and Paul Bracewell tussled for a ball and the referee gave the free-kick Newcastle's way. Bracewell was incensed and was booked for dissent, as was Graeme Sharp.

Passions were aroused still further when Peter Beardsley took the free kick and Gascoigne levelled things up. The riled up Bracewell then launched himself into a clash with Billy Whitehurst, the Blues' midfielder coming off worse and having to be carried from the pitch.

He was replaced by Alan Harper but then Kevin Sheedy hobbled off and the home side took advantage of their numerical advantage to take the lead through Beardsley.

Everton's ten-men stuck to the task and when Graeme Sharp was fouled in the area, the referee gave a penalty which Sharp himself converted.

Howard Kendall was very much of the opinion that it was two points dropped at St James' Park rather than one gained and he was left to grapple with an injury crisis ahead of the FA Cup game with Exeter.

As well as Paul Bracewell and Kevin Sheedy, Trevor Steven also limped off the pitch at one stage, reducing the Blues to nine men, but he was able to hobble back on. Of the three, surprisingly, Bracewell was given the most chance of being fit for the weekend.

Ultimately, though, Bracewell was ruled out of the clash with the fourth division minnows, together with Steven, Sheedy and long-term casualty Peter Reid, meaning the entire midfield which had carried all before it the previous season was missing.

Everton dominated against their lowly opponents but a draw was on the cards until Gary Stevens broke the deadlock ten minutes from the end to set up a fourth-round tie with Blackburn or Nottingham Forest, who drew 1-1.

Elsewhere, although ineligible to play in League games due to issues around his insurance payout at the time of his retirement, Mark Higgins was named in the Manchester United team to play Rochdale in the FA Cup, a game United won 2-0.

It's A Grand Old Team To Support

Colin Harvey has supported Everton from his school days, watching the matches from the Boys' Pen.

The tremendous backing for the team in the Bayern Munich match took his mind back to the night when Everton last won the League title by beating West Brom in 1970. "The response of the crowd was unbelievable then and just as good when we beat Bayern," he said.

He is well aware of the traditional School of Science image. "In my opinion, all Everton fans want to see good footballers who work hard. Some people think the tag means pure football but you have to have both. The players have to give it a good 'go' as well."

From the match programme versus QPR, Monday 6th May 1985

EVERTON
NIL SATIS
NISI OPTIMUM
GOODISON
PARK L4

January 1986

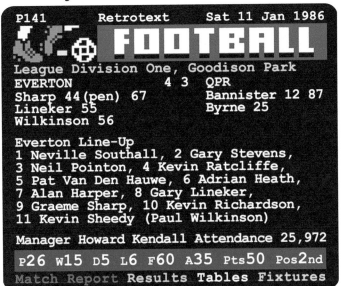

P141   Retrotext   Sat 11 Jan 1986

FOOTBALL

League Division One, Goodison Park
EVERTON   4 3 QPR
Sharp 44(pen) 67   Bannister 12 87
Lineker 55   Byrne 25
Wilkinson 56

Everton Line-Up
1 Neville Southall, 2 Gary Stevens,
3 Neil Pointon, 4 Kevin Ratcliffe,
5 Pat Van Den Hauwe, 6 Adrian Heath,
7 Alan Harper, 8 Gary Lineker,
9 Graeme Sharp, 10 Kevin Richardson,
11 Kevin Sheedy (Paul Wilkinson)

Manager Howard Kendall Attendance 25,972

P26 W15 D5 L6 F60 A35 Pts50 Pos2nd
Match Report Results Tables Fixtures

P141   Retrotext   Sat 18 Jan 1986

FOOTBALL

League Division One, St Andrews
BIRMINGHAM CITY   0 2 EVERTON
                        Lineker 36 46

Everton Line-Up
1 Neville Southall, 2 Gary Stevens,
3 Neil Pointon, 4 Kevin Ratcliffe,
5 Pat Van Den Hauwe, 6 Alan Harper,
7 Trevor Steven, 8 Gary Lineker,
9 Graeme Sharp, 10 Kevin Richardson,
11 Adrian Heath

Manager Howard Kendall Attendance 10,502

P27 W16 D5 L6 F62 A35 Pts53 Pos2nd
Match Report Results Tables Fixtures

Before the QPR game at the weekend, manager Howard Kendall and chairman Phillip Carter had flown to Zurich to meet Juventus officials about arranging a money-spinning friendly between Everton and the European Cup winners.

Boosted by the news that long-term injury casualties Derek Mountfield and Peter Reid were back in light training, the Blues aimed to gain revenge against QPR for the 3-0 defeat on their plastic pitch back in September.

Of the three walking wounded from the battle with Newcastle on New Year's Day, only Kevin Sheedy was fit enough to take his place in the line-up and he had to leave the field early with a recurrence of his groin injury.

QPR's Gary Bannister (with two) and John Byrne had scored the goals in their win at Loftus Road and both players were on the scoresheet here with barely twenty-five minutes played, leaving the Blues a mountain to climb.

Yet again, the players showed tremendous character and by midway through the second-half the game had been turned on its head. Despite Bannister pulling one back near the end, the Blues gained another valuable three points in the quest to retain their title.

After an inconsistent first half of the campaign, the Blues were beginning to generate momentum, with this victory over relegation-threatened Birmingham City making it seven games unbeaten.

In midweek, Birmingham had been knocked out of the FA Cup by non-League Altrincham, after which manager Ron Saunders resigned so Keith Leonard was in temporary charge of the home team.

Goal machine Gary Lineker was the man to increase Birmingham's misery and his brace took his tally for the season to twenty-four in all competitions.

Howard Kendall's side now stood just two points behind leaders Manchester United, though having played a game more, after Ron Atkinson's side conceded two goals in the last ten minutes to lose 3-2 at Old Trafford to Nottingham Forest.

Liverpool were third having accrued the same number of points as Everton, while surprise package Chelsea were also on fifty-three points and they had two games in hand on both Merseyside clubs.

There was more positive news on Saturday as Peter Reid came through a reserve game without any reaction to his injuries after playing the full ninety minutes in a 2-1 win over West Brom.

It's A Grand Old Team To Support

George Bailey is possibly Everton's greatest fan. He founded the Everton Supporters Club in 1950 along with the late Joe Doyle.

His Dad took him to the Crystal Palace in 1906, the day the club won the FA Cup for the first time and he was in the crowd when 'Dixie' Dean headed his record-breaking 60th League goal against Arsenal in 1928.

George recalls that the players would walk to the games with the fans, many living in the terraced houses near Goodison Park. "The great Dixie had a heart of gold. I've known people go up to him before a game and he would give them a few bob from his own pocket or a ticket for the match," he recalled.

From the Liverpool Echo, Friday 18th May 1984

EVERTON
NIL SATIS
NISI OPTIMUM
GOODISON
PARK L4

January 1986

From The Teletext Archive

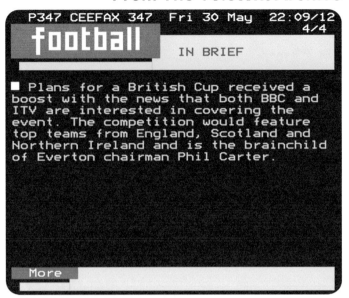

Everton had another reserve game against Derby County on the Tuesday after the West Brom game and Howard Kendall let Peter Reid decide for himself whether he was okay to turn out again and, of course, he told the boss he was.

Though Everton lost 1-0 to Derby, Reid came through the match unscathed and was now well on the way to returning to first team action after five months out.

There was more good news for Reid when he was named Merseyside Sports Personality of 1985, an accolade voted for by Liverpool Echo readers.

Several of the Blackburn team who faced the Blues were at the club when Kendall was manager, while for centre-back Glenn Keeley it was a return to the scene of his short-lived Everton career back in 1982, when he was sent off in the first half of the derby against Liverpool in which Ian Rush scored four goals in a 5-0 win.

The home side had dominated proceedings against their second division opponents and went in at half-time two goals to the good, through Pat van den Hauwe and Gary Lineker. But 'Psycho' put one into his own net just after the re-start to spark the visitors into life and the crowd were relieved when Lineker made it 3-1.

This is an original Ceefax page recovered from an old VHS recording.

At the end of the 1985-86 season, with no prospect of any European football in the 1986-87 campaign for English clubs due to the Heysel ban, Philip Carter put forward his idea for a British Cup.

Carter had just been elected as President of the Football League and the Cup concept was part of a five-point plan to revitalise football at a time when the sport was still struggling to come to terms with the effects of the Brussels and Bradford disasters, though ultimately it didn't come to fruition.

It's A Grand Old Team To Play For

Goalkeeper Jim Arnold was well-known to Howard Kendall from his time as manager at Blackburn Rovers and when he became Everton boss in May 1981, Jim was one of the first players he signed - together with a younger 'keeper called Neville Southall.

Over the next couple of seasons, the pair jostled for the number one slot, with both at times appearing to be the preferred choice. At the start of the 1983-84 campaign, Arnold was in pole position but after seven games he was replaced by Southall and never played for the first team again.

Frustrated at his lack of opportunities, Jim asked for a transfer in January 1984 which Kendall rejected. He eventually signed another deal with the club but at the end of the 1984-85 season he moved to Port Vale.

February 1986

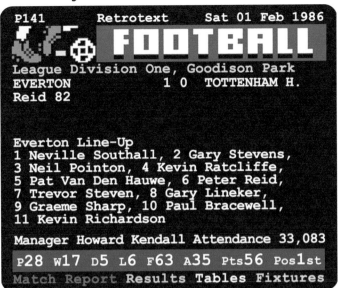

With Everton safely through to the fifth round, the draw paired them with Tottenham Hotspur or Notts County who had played out a 1-1 at Meadow Lane. In the replay, Spurs were emphatic 5-0 winners, setting up a sequence of four games against the Blues over the next few weeks - once in the FA Cup, once in the League and twice in the two-legged Screen Sport Super Cup semi-final.

With one eye on the future, there was a new signing in the form of eighteen-year-old Warren Aspinall from Wigan, then managed by ex-Blue Bryan Hamilton, for a fee of £100,000. But Aspinall would stay with Wigan until the end of the season as the club were pushing for promotion from Division Three.

Peter Reid had another chance to prove his fitness with a midweek reserve game against Hull City and though the team lost 2-0, he came through without any problems, putting him in line for a recall to the first team against Tottenham on Saturday.

When the team-sheet came through, after five months out, Reid's name was on it and the midfield maestro celebrated his return with a rare goal which put the Blues on top of the table, at least for twenty-four hours as Manchester United played West Ham on the Sunday in a live TV game.

West Ham did Everton a great favour at Upton Park by coming from a goal down to beat United 2-1, with both goals scored by future Everton players: Huyton-born Mark Ward and Tony Cottee.

The result kept the Blues one point ahead of United though having played a game more. Chelsea were still in a strong position just two points behind Howard Kendall's side having played two games less.

Liverpool's hopes had been dented on Saturday with a 2-1 defeat at Ipswich Town to leave them three points adrift of Everton after the same number of games.

A depleted squad travelled down to London in midweek for the first leg of the Screen Sport Super Cup with Kevin Ratcliffe, Paul Bracewell, Adrian Heath, Gary Lineker and Graeme Sharp missing out.

Ian Marshall came in for Ratcliffe with recent signings Darrin Coyle from Linfield and Peter Billing from South Liverpool making their debuts and Paul Wilkinson replacing Sharp up front.

Spurs largely dominated but the under-strength visitors gained a creditable goalless draw, mainly thanks to Neville Southall, with the second leg at Goodison Park still to come.

It's A Grand Old Team To Play For

With Jim Arnold keen to move on and play regular football, Howard Kendall signed England Under-21 goalkeeper Bobby Mimms from Rotherham for £150,000 as Neville Southall's understudy towards the end of the historic 1984-85 season.

Mimms made his full debut in October 1985, replacing Southall who had been sent off in a match against Chelsea, but he was then loaned out to Notts County. In March of that season, with the Blues top of the table and in an FA Cup semi-final, disaster struck when the big Welshman dislocated his ankle on international duty.

In Southall's absence, Mimms performed superbly for the rest of the campaign as Everton just missed out on a League and Cup double and he continued in goal until 'Big Nev' returned to first-team action in October 1986.

February 1986

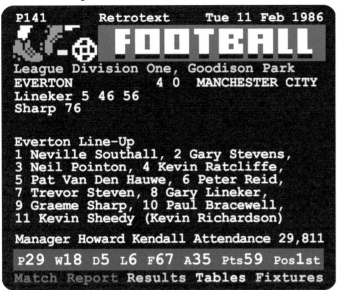

Everton's game at Watford on Saturday 8th February was called off as four inches of snow had fallen on the Vicarage Road pitch.

But the postponement gave physio John Clinkard more time to work on the walking wounded ahead of a re-arranged midweek clash with Manchester City.

Though Everton didn't play at the weekend, the club's position at the top of the table was consolidated when Liverpool and Manchester United drew 1-1 at Anfield on the Sunday.

This left the Blues ahead of United on goal difference with the same number of games played, with Kenny Dalglish's side two points back having played a game more.

Everton welcomed back Gary Lineker, Graeme Sharp, Paul Bracewell, Kevin Sheedy and Kevin Ratcliffe against City and the home side overwhelmed Billy McNeill's side, who had previously been on a good run having amassed nineteen points from a possible twenty-one.

Lineker claimed another hat-trick, taking his League total to twenty-two, and his strike partner Sharp was also on target as the Division's top scorers took their tally to sixty-seven.

The icy weather continued to play havoc with Everton's fixtures and the FA Cup fifth round clash with Tottenham due to be televised live on Sunday 16th February was called off and re-scheduled for midweek. However, with no improvement, that match also had to be moved to early March.

On the Monday, the quarter-final draw was made and the Blues knew they would be facing Luton Town or Arsenal in the last eight, after those two sides drew 2-2 at Kenilworth Road.

Kevin Sheedy had limped out of his comeback game against Manchester City and it was subsequently discovered he needed an operation on his right knee which meant he would be out of action for a few weeks.

Everton's 2-0 win at Anfield, courtesy of skipper Kevin Ratcliffe after a mistake by Bruce Grobbelaar and goal machine Gary Lineker, took the Blues eight points clear of Liverpool, though there was concern for Paul Bracewell who had to be replaced at half-time.

With both sides having just twelve games left to play, this appeared to be a decisive victory for Howard Kendall's men and they were now firm favourites to retain the title.

It's A Grand Old Team To Play For

When Alan Harper was at Liverpool, he was understudy at right back to Phil Neal and with his first-team opportunities limited he decided it was time to move on. Bob Paisley offered him a new deal but when Howard Kendall made his interest known in the summer of 1983, the life-long Reds supporter became a Blue.

Everton paid an initial £30,000 fee to Liverpool with a further £30,000 due when Harper had made 30 first-team appearances which was triggered during the 1983-84 campaign. Alan also scored against his former club when coming on as a substitute in a 1-1 draw at Goodison in March 1984.

Alan showed his versatility throughout his Everton career which ended with a transfer to Sheffield Wednesday for £275,000 in the summer of 1988.

March 1986

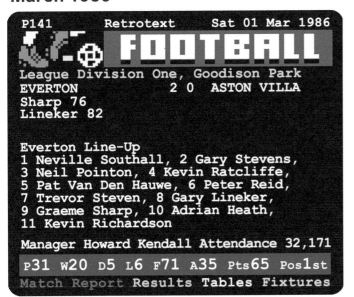

```
P141      Retrotext      Sat 01 Mar 1986
      FOOTBALL
League Division One, Goodison Park
EVERTON            2  0  ASTON VILLA
Sharp 76
Lineker 82


Everton Line-Up
1 Neville Southall, 2 Gary Stevens,
3 Neil Pointon, 4 Kevin Ratcliffe,
5 Pat Van Den Hauwe, 6 Peter Reid,
7 Trevor Steven, 8 Gary Lineker,
9 Graeme Sharp, 10 Adrian Heath,
11 Kevin Richardson

Manager Howard Kendall Attendance 32,171
P31 W20 D5 L6 F71 A35 Pts65 Pos1st
Match Report  Results  Tables  Fixtures
```

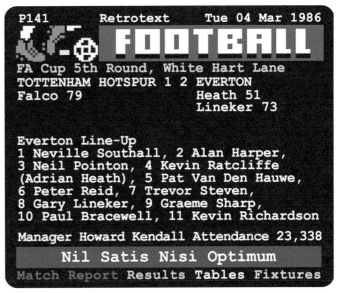

```
P141      Retrotext      Tue 04 Mar 1986
      FOOTBALL
FA Cup 5th Round, White Hart Lane
TOTTENHAM HOTSPUR 1  2  EVERTON
Falco 79                    Heath 51
                            Lineker 73


Everton Line-Up
1 Neville Southall, 2 Alan Harper,
3 Neil Pointon, 4 Kevin Ratcliffe
(Adrian Heath), 5 Pat Van Den Hauwe,
6 Peter Reid, 7 Trevor Steven,
8 Gary Lineker, 9 Graeme Sharp,
10 Paul Bracewell, 11 Kevin Richardson

Manager Howard Kendall Attendance 23,338
      Nil Satis Nisi Optimum
Match Report  Results  Tables  Fixtures
```

The derby victory over Liverpool didn't come without cost, though, with a number of players back on John Clinkard's treatment table.

Paul Bracewell had been suffering from pain in his ankle since being injured at Newcastle on New Year's Day and the decision was taken to put his foot in plaster. Howard Kendall also had to pull Peter Reid and Gary Lineker out of the England squad with knee and back injuries.

Reid and Lineker recovered sufficiently to take their place against Villa, together with Adrian Heath who had missed the last five games. Andy Gray missed out on the chance to play at Goodison again after being ruled out through suspension.

Graeme Sharp celebrated the announcement of him signing a new four-year deal with the club by breaking the deadlock with his eighteenth goal of the season and Gary Lineker secured the points shortly afterwards.

Manchester United lost 1-0 at Southampton so the Blues were six points clear of the Red Devils having played one game more.

Liverpool were eleven points behind but won 2-1 at White Hart Lane on the Sunday, Ian Rush scoring the winner in the 90th minute, to reduce the gap.

The wintry weather had caused chaos with the FA Cup ties and several fifth round matches still had to be decided with just a few days before the sixth round games were scheduled.

Paul Bracewell's foot was now out of plaster and he came back into the side but Gary Stevens missed out with a swollen knee.

His replacement Alan Harper had to switch to centre-back in the first-half as skipper Kevin Ratcliffe limped off and he performed superbly.

Adrian Heath got back on the goal trail after his injury absence while Gary Lineker was on target yet again, his thirty-second goal of the campaign.

Everton's opponents in the sixth round would be Luton Town after David Pleat's side beat Arsenal 3-0 in a second replay. It would be a re-match of the previous season's semi-final which the Blues won 2-1 after extra-time.

On the same evening, Kevin Sheedy was on the comeback trail just fifteen days after his cartilage operation in the mini derby against Liverpool.

Everton won the match 2-1 thanks to goals by Paul Wilkinson and Irish youngster Darrin Coyle.

It's A Grand Old Team To Play For

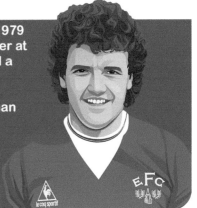

When John Bailey moved from Blackburn Rovers to Everton in the summer of 1979 the fee was settled by the first-ever football tribunal. The Blues valued the player at £200,000 but the tribunal decided the club must pay £200,000 immediately and a further £100,000 when he had played 50 games for the first team.

It was ironic that the manager playing hard ball with Everton was none other than former player and future boss, Howard Kendall!

John was a huge fan favourite during his time with the Blues and was a key member of the team which won the FA Cup in 1984 under Howard. With his first-team opportunities increasingly limited after the arrival of Pat van den Hauwe, he moved to Newcastle United in October 1985 for a fee of £100,000.

March 1986

```
P141    Retrotext    Sat 08 Mar 1986
       FOOTBALL
FA Cup 6th Round, Kenilworth Road
LUTON TOWN         2 2   EVERTON
Harford 22               Sharp 65
Stein 63                 Heath 77


Everton Line-Up
1 Neville Southall, 2 Gary Stevens,
3 Neil Pointon (Adrian Heath 64),
4 Alan Harper, 5 Pat Van Den Hauwe,
6 Peter Reid, 7 Trevor Steven,
8 Gary Lineker, 9 Graeme Sharp,
10 Paul Bracewell, 11 Kevin Richardson

Manager Howard Kendall Attendance 15,529
        Nil Satis Nisi Optimum
Match Report Results Tables Fixtures
```

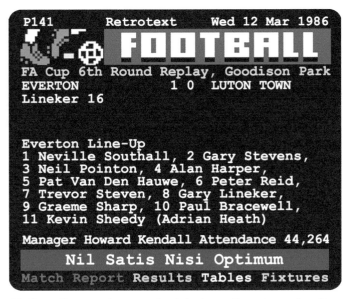

```
P141    Retrotext    Wed 12 Mar 1986
       FOOTBALL
FA Cup 6th Round Replay, Goodison Park
EVERTON            1 0   LUTON TOWN
Lineker 16


Everton Line-Up
1 Neville Southall, 2 Gary Stevens,
3 Neil Pointon, 4 Alan Harper,
5 Pat Van Den Hauwe, 6 Peter Reid,
7 Trevor Steven, 8 Gary Lineker,
9 Graeme Sharp, 10 Paul Bracewell,
11 Kevin Sheedy (Adrian Heath)

Manager Howard Kendall Attendance 44,264
        Nil Satis Nisi Optimum
Match Report Results Tables Fixtures
```

Former Everton favourite Andy King was in the Luton Town line-up for this FA Cup clash, his career having been revitalised since a move back to Kenilworth Road where his career started back in 1975.

The home side looked well on course to avenge the semi-final defeat during the last campaign when they took a 2-0 lead on their plastic pitch. But the Blues refused to accept that their tremendous run in the FA Cup, a competition they hadn't lost in for eighteen matches, was coming to an end.

Graeme Sharp pulled one back then Adrian Heath, on as a tactical substitution for left-back Neil Pointon, equalised to earn the visitors a thoroughly deserved replay at Goodison Park a few days later.

Earlier in the week, with champions Everton banned from the competition because of Heysel, the first legs of the quarter-final stage of the European Cup had been played.

The results were Bayern Munich 2 Anderlecht 1; Steaua Bucharest 1 Kuusysi 0; Aberdeen 2 Gothenburg 2; Barcelona 1 Juventus 0.

The second legs would be played in two weeks time - on the same day the Blues were playing Tottenham in the Screen Sport Super Cup.

Before the replay against Luton, the draw for the semi-final stage of the competition was made, bringing the prospect of a first all-Merseyside FA Cup Final ever closer.

Liverpool or Watford would play Southampton while West Ham or Sheffield Wednesday would be the Blues' opponents if they could knock out David Pleat's side.

Just three weeks after his cartilage operation, Kevin Sheedy was ready to return to the first team, though club captain Kevin Ratcliffe was still missing due to the injury which forced him to come off at Tottenham in the fifth round.

Gary Lineker had been scoring goals for fun all season but the one he scored in the replay must have been his best of the campaign. He showed brilliant acceleration to burst between two Luton defenders and latch on to Trevor Steven's ball over the top before smashing it into the net.

Just before half-time, Trevor Steven had the chance to make it 2-0 from the penalty spot but Les Sealey saved it.

In the other sixth round tie, Sheffield Wednesday beat West Ham 2-1 to set up a repeat of the 1966 FA Cup Final in the semi-final at Villa Park.

It's A Grand Old Team To Play For

Champions Everton beat off competition from Manchester United and Liverpool to sign Gary Lineker from Leicester City for a fee of £800,000 in June 1985, a move which led to the departure a few weeks later of fan favourite Andy Gray to Aston Villa.

Lineker scored forty goals in his one and only season with the Blues, including three hat-tricks, the last of which against Southampton came a few days after Everton had been beaten at relegation-threatened Oxford United to effectively hand the League title to Liverpool. He scored his last goal for the club in the FA Cup Final defeat by the Reds a week later, as the Blues finished the season without a trophy.

Much in demand after winning the Golden Boot for scoring six goals for England at the 1986 World Cup in Mexico, Lineker moved to Barcelona after the tournament.

March 1986

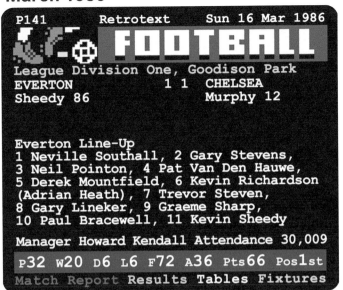

P141   Retrotext   Sun 16 Mar 1986

FOOTBALL

League Division One, Goodison Park
EVERTON   1 1   CHELSEA
Sheedy 86   Murphy 12

Everton Line-Up
1 Neville Southall, 2 Gary Stevens,
3 Neil Pointon, 4 Pat Van Den Hauwe,
5 Derek Mountfield, 6 Kevin Richardson
(Adrian Heath), 7 Trevor Steven,
8 Gary Lineker, 9 Graeme Sharp,
10 Paul Bracewell, 11 Kevin Sheedy

Manager Howard Kendall Attendance 30,009
P32 W20 D6 L6 F72 A36 Pts66 Pos1st
Match Report Results Tables Fixtures

P141   Retrotext   Wed 19 Mar 1986

FOOTBALL

Screen Sport Super Cup Semi-Final,
2nd Leg, Goodison Park
EVERTON   3 1   TOTTENHAM H.
Heath 76   aet   Falco 48
Mountfield 91   (3 1)
Sharp 112
Everton Line-Up
1 Neville Southall, 2 Peter Billing
(Pat Van Den Hauwe), 3 Neil Pointon,
4 Ian Marshall, 5 Derek Mountfield,
6 Kevin Richardson, 7 Alan Harper,
8 Adrian Heath, 9 Paul Wilkinson
(Graeme Sharp), 10 Darrin Coyle,
11 Kevin Sheedy
Manager Howard Kendall Attendance 12,008
Nil Satis Nisi Optimum
Match Report Results Tables Fixtures

Peter Reid had been a virtual passenger after twenty minutes of the replay against Luton with a muscle injury but he had to stay on the pitch as Kevin Sheedy was also struggling.

Reid was convinced that the injury was brought on by playing on the artificial surface at Kenilworth Road a few days before.

On the plus side, Derek Mountfield was fit enough to be named in the starting line up and slotted in alongside Pat van den Hauwe.

Psycho had done a terrific job at centre-half since his own comeback from injury against Coventry in December with the Blues unbeaten since then.

A special mention should also be made for Neil Pointon at left-back who had been tremendous since making his debut in the 6-1 win against Arsenal following his move from Scunthorpe.

Chelsea had already beaten Everton at Stamford Bridge and knocked the Blues out of the League Cup. This was the first time a match at Goodison had been televised live and John Hollins' side went ahead but Kevin Sheedy equalised late on.

Liverpool had won 2-1 at Southampton but Kenny Dalglish's side were still three points behind Howard Kendall's men having played a game more.

The day after the Chelsea game, Peter Reid recorded in his football diary Everton Winter, Mexico Summer: "The boss wasn't at Bellefield today and no-one knew where he had gone." Press speculation was rife that Kendall was being lined up for the manager's job at Barcelona with Terry Venables expected to leave in the summer.

Kendall returned from his mysterious absence to name a team for the Super Cup semi-final without eight first team players and the emphasis very much on youth. In came Peter Billing, Paul Wilkinson, Ian Marshall and Darrin Coyle who had all played in the first leg.

Mark Falco put the visitors ahead but Adrian Heath equalised to force extra-time, when Derek Mountfield hit the goal trail again and Graeme Sharp made the game safe.

So, the Blues were in the Final of the competition designed to fill the gap for clubs barred from Europe. But the same evening, the quarter-final second legs of the European Cup, the big prize which had been denied to the Blues, were decided.

Bayern Munich lost 3-2 to Anderlecht, Steaua Bucharest beat Finnish minnows Kuusysi, Aberdeen went out on away goals to Gothenburg and Barcelona beat Juventus 2-1 on aggregate.

If You Know Your History

In November 1990, Howard Kendall left the manager's job at Manchester City to re-join Everton, with Colin Harvey stepping down and accepting the role of coach. Peter Reid was appointed player-manager at Maine Road in charge of a side which included Everton old boys Adrian Heath, Neil Pointon, Alan Harper and Wayne Clark.

Liverpool had beaten the Blues 3-1 in a League game at Anfield the week before this FA Cup tie, but Kendall's side earned a gritty 0-0 draw in the first game to force this remarkable replay. Everton won the second replay at Goodison Park a week later courtesy of a goal from Dave Watson, by which time Ronnie Moran was in charge of Liverpool after Kenny Dalglish sensationally quit the role.

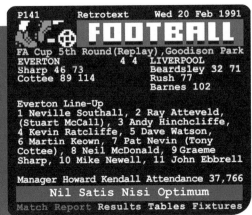

P141   Retrotext   Wed 20 Feb 1991

FOOTBALL

FA Cup 5th Round(Replay),Goodison Park
EVERTON   4 4   LIVERPOOL
Sharp 46 73   Beardsley 32 71
Cottee 89 114   Rush 77
                          Barnes 102

Everton Line-Up
1 Neville Southall, 2 Ray Atteveld,
(Stuart McCall), 3 Andy Hinchcliffe,
4 Kevin Ratcliffe, 5 Dave Watson,
6 Martin Keown, 7 Pat Nevin (Tony
Cottee), 8 Neil McDonald, 9 Graeme
Sharp, 10 Mike Newell, 11 John Ebbrell

Manager Howard Kendall Attendance 37,766
Nil Satis Nisi Optimum
Match Report Results Tables Fixtures

March 1986

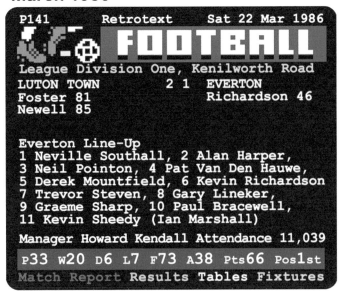

```
P141      Retrotext      Sat 22 Mar 1986
       FOOTBALL
League Division One, Kenilworth Road
LUTON TOWN       2 1       EVERTON
Foster 81                  Richardson 46
Newell 85


Everton Line-Up
1 Neville Southall, 2 Alan Harper,
3 Neil Pointon, 4 Pat Van Den Hauwe,
5 Derek Mountfield, 6 Kevin Richardson
7 Trevor Steven, 8 Gary Lineker,
9 Graeme Sharp, 10 Paul Bracewell,
11 Kevin Sheedy (Ian Marshall)
Manager Howard Kendall Attendance 11,039
P33 W20 D6 L7 F73 A38 Pts66 Pos1st
Match Report Results Tables Fixtures
```

```
P141      Retrotext      Sat 29 Mar 1986
       FOOTBALL
League Division One, Goodison Park
EVERTON          1 0       NEWCASTLE UTD
Richardson 29


Everton Line-Up
1 Bobby Mimms, 2 Gary Stevens,
3 Pat Van Den Hauwe (Adrian Heath),
4 Kevin Ratcliffe, 5 Derek Mountfield,
6 Peter Reid, 7 Trevor Steven,
8 Gary Lineker, 9 Graeme Sharp,
10 Paul Bracewell, 11 Kevin Richardson
Manager Howard Kendall Attendance 40,594
P34 W21 D6 L7 F74 A38 Pts69 Pos1st
Match Report Results Tables Fixtures
```

The day before the Luton game, the draw for the semi-finals of the European Cup was made. Favourites Barcelona would play Gothenburg of Sweden, while Anderlecht's reward for knocking out Bayern Munich was a tie against Romanian side Steaua Bucharest.

Back again on Kenilworth Road's plastic pitch, Everton suffered yet another injury blow just before half-time when Kevin Sheedy was forced off with a torn hamstring.

Kevin Richardson put the visitors ahead just after the break and the Blues looked on course for another vital three points in the bid to retain the title. But the match turned on its head in the final ten minutes with the home side scoring twice to avenge for the FA Cup defeat earlier in the month.

Liverpool moved level on points with Howard Kendall's side after their 6-0 hammering of Oxford United, though Kenny Dalglish's team had played one game more. Manchester United were three points back in third spot having played thirty-three games after a 2-2 draw in a local derby with City.

After the weekend's games, it was announced that Gary Lineker had been voted the PFA Player of the Year, succeeding team-mate Peter Reid who had received the honour the previous season.

There were no midweek domestic games due to an international break, with Wales facing the Republic of Ireland in Dublin. Neville Southall was the solitary Blue involved due to injuries to Kevin Ratcliffe, Pat van den Hauwe and Kevin Sheedy.

Wales won the match 1-0 but there was the worst possible news for Evertonians as Neville Southall had to be carried off with a dislocated ankle and would miss the rest of the season.

Rookie goalkeeper Bobby Mimms was hastily called back from his loan spell at Notts County and would have to try and fill the boots of the best 'keeper in the country as Everton sought to secure an FA Cup and League title double.

Howard Kendall did receive some good news this week, as the transfer window ended without utility player Alan Harper being tempted away. He had been operating on a weekly contract after failing to reach agreement with the club and was planning to assess his options at the end of the campaign.

Another key utility player, Kevin Richardson, scored the only goal against Newcastle which kept Everton's hopes of retaining the title on track, especially as Liverpool were held to a goalless draw at Hillsborough.

If You Know Your History

The day after Mike Walker was appointed as Everton manager on a three-and-a-half year deal, his new team were involved in an FA Cup third round tie at Bolton. Walker sat in the dugout at Burnden Park along with caretaker boss Jimmy Gabriel and coach Colin Harvey to see the Blues draw 1-1 despite having Barry Horne sent off.

After a few days working with the players, this was Walker's first proper match in charge. With Paul Rideout injured, he brought Brett Angell to the club on loan from Southend for a second time - he had spent a month at Goodison under Howard Kendall in September. It was a frantic game which could easily have finished 6-6 despite the visitors being down to ten men for much of the second half.

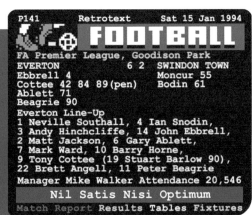

```
P141      Retrotext      Sat 15 Jan 1994
       FOOTBALL
FA Premier League, Goodison Park
EVERTON          6 2       SWINDON TOWN
Ebbrell 4                  Moncur 55
Cottee 42 84 89(pen)       Bodin 61
Ablett 71
Beagrie 90
Everton Line-Up
1 Neville Southall, 4 Ian Snodin,
3 Andy Hinchcliffe, 14 John Ebbrell,
2 Matt Jackson, 6 Gary Ablett,
7 Mark Ward, 10 Barry Horne,
9 Tony Cottee (19 Stuart Barlow 90),
22 Brett Angell, 11 Peter Beagrie
Manager Mike Walker Attendance 20,546
       Nil Satis Nisi Optimum
Match Report Results Tables Fixtures
```

March 1986

From The Teletext Archive

```
P141        Retrotext      Mon 31 Mar 1986
FOOTBALL
League Division One, Old Trafford
MANCHESTER UTD      0 0    EVERTON


Everton Line-Up
1 Bobby Mimms, 2 Gary Stevens,
3 Pat Van Den Hauwe, 4 Kevin Ratcliffe
5 Derek Mountfield, 6 Peter Reid,
7 Trevor Steven, 8 Gary Lineker
(Adrian Heath), 9 Graeme Sharp,
10 Paul Bracewell, 11 Kevin Richardson

Manager Howard Kendall Attendance 51,189

P35 W21 D7 L7 F74 A38 Pts70 Pos2nd
Match Report Results Tables Fixtures
```

```
P307 CEEFAX 307   Thu 31 Mar   20:18/48
BBC       FOOTBALL: EVERTON MADE
                    TO WAIT
Everton face a heavy fine if they
are found guilty of "poaching"
manager Mike Walker from Norwich.

A Premiership inquiry has taken
place in Manchester after the
original meeting was adjourned so
more evidence could be considered.

Everton chief executive Jim
Greenwood put his club's case with
the help of director Keith Tamlin.

Premier League secretary Mike
Foster said: "There is no 'normal'
punishment and decisions will be
conveyed in due course."

SATURDAY PREMIERSHIP TEAM NEWS ON 304
Hammam     PremTeams Prem Fixs PremTable
```

With Neville Southall out of action, Howard Kendall moved quickly to secure a back-up goalkeeper to Bobby Mimms and having been priced out of a bid to sign Andy Goram from Oldham, he secured the services of Fred Barber from Darlington.

As it was the Easter weekend, there was another full programme of games on Monday, with Everton away at Manchester United and Liverpool entertaining Manchester City.

The Blues could only manage a 0-0 draw at Old Trafford whereas Liverpool won 2-0 at Anfield with ex-Blue Steve McMahon scoring both of them. The results took the Reds to the top of the table on goal difference though Howard Kendall's side still had a game in hand.

There was another injury headache for Kendall after recently crowned PFA Player of the Year Gary Lineker limped off just after half-time, potentially jeopardising his place in the FA Cup semi-final coming up at the weekend.

Everton were still waiting to see which team they would play in the Final of the Screen Sport Super Cup, Liverpool or Norwich. But it was announced that due to fixture congestion plus a general apathy towards the competition, the Final would take place next season and no longer be at Wembley.

This is an original Ceefax page recovered from an old VHS recording.

Mike Walker was appointed Everton manager in January 1994 but Norwich City chairman Robert Chase claimed the Blues had made an illegal approach to him and demanded compensation.

In the middle of April, the Premier League panel comprising of a QC, Steve Coppell and Rick Parry, found in the Canaries' favour and fined the club a total of £125,000.

At this point in the season, Everton had only three games left to avoid relegation and a goalless draw at home to Coventry followed by a 3-0 loss at Leeds dropped them into the bottom three going into the final game of the season against Wimbledon.

The Blues came from 2-0 down to win that match 3-2 and preserve their top flight status, but after twelve games of the following campaign - with the team bottom of the table with only eight points from fourteen games - Walker was sacked.

Joe Royle was appointed manager in his place and he rejuvenated the club, taking the team to mid-table security and winning the FA Cup.

If You Know Your History

Mike Walker was appointed Everton manager in January 1994 after an impressive spell as Norwich City boss during which time he guided the Canaries to a third-place finish in the Premier League and a high profile run in the UEFA Cup where they beat Bayern Munich.

Walker's first League game in charge was a chaotic 6-2 success over fellow strugglers Swindon Town which took the Blues seven points clear of the relegation places. But only three more wins followed and before this match, his team lay in the drop zone. Somehow, Everton came back from two goals down to claim an unlikely victory and secure their place in the top flight for another season, but Walker's tenure at Goodison was short-lived and he was sacked in November.

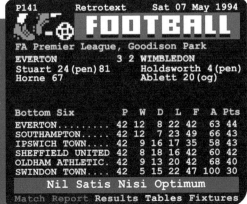

```
P141      Retrotext     Sat 07 May 1994
FOOTBALL
FA Premier League, Goodison Park
EVERTON             3 2  WIMBLEDON
Stuart 24(pen)81         Holdsworth 4(pen)
Horne 67                 Ablett 20(og)


Bottom Six          P  W  D  L  F   A Pts
EVERTON.........   42 12  8 22 42  63 44
SOUTHAMPTON......  42 12  7 23 49  66 43
IPSWICH TOWN.....  42  9 16 17 35  58 43
SHEFFIELD UNITED.  42  8 18 16 42  60 42
OLDHAM ATHLETIC..  42  9 13 20 42  68 40
SWINDON TOWN.....  42  5 15 22 47 100 30
      Nil Satis Nisi Optimum
Match Report Results Tables Fixtures
```

April 1986

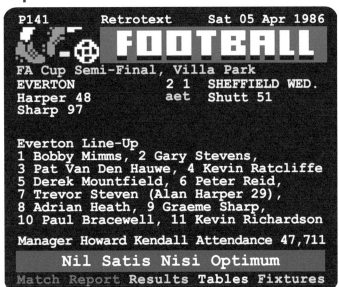

P141   Retrotext   Sat 05 Apr 1986

FOOTBALL

FA Cup Semi-Final, Villa Park
EVERTON   2   1   SHEFFIELD WED.
Harper 48   aet   Shutt 51
Sharp 97

Everton Line-Up
1 Bobby Mimms, 2 Gary Stevens,
3 Pat Van Den Hauwe, 4 Kevin Ratcliffe
5 Derek Mountfield, 6 Peter Reid,
7 Trevor Steven (Alan Harper 29),
8 Adrian Heath, 9 Graeme Sharp,
10 Paul Bracewell, 11 Kevin Richardson

Manager Howard Kendall Attendance 47,711

Nil Satis Nisi Optimum

Match Report   Results   Tables   Fixtures

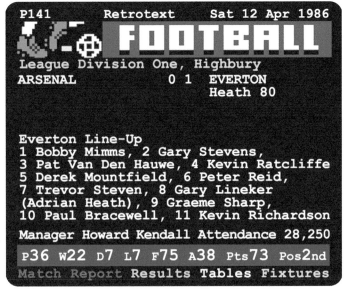

P141   Retrotext   Sat 12 Apr 1986

FOOTBALL

League Division One, Highbury
ARSENAL   0   1   EVERTON
                         Heath 80

Everton Line-Up
1 Bobby Mimms, 2 Gary Stevens,
3 Pat Van Den Hauwe, 4 Kevin Ratcliffe
5 Derek Mountfield, 6 Peter Reid,
7 Trevor Steven, 8 Gary Lineker
(Adrian Heath), 9 Graeme Sharp,
10 Paul Bracewell, 11 Kevin Richardson

Manager Howard Kendall Attendance 28,250

P36 W22 D7 L7 F75 A38 Pts73 Pos2nd

Match Report   Results   Tables   Fixtures

It had been a season of one injury problem after another and ahead of the FA Cup semi-final, Neil Pointon became the latest victim when he damaged knee ligaments in a reserve game and was ruled out for the rest of the season.

Though Everton had beaten Sheffield Wednesday 5-1 at Hillsborough and 3-1 at Goodison this season, both managers knew that in a one-off Cup match anything can happen.

The bookmakers had the Blues favourites to reach a third successive Final at odds of 5/6, with the Owls 11/4.

As expected, Gary Lineker didn't recover from the injury picked up at Old Trafford with Adrian Heath stepping in for him and with less than half-an-hour on the clock, Everton's injury hoodoo had struck again as Trevor Steven was forced off to be replaced by Alan Harper.

It was Harper who gave the Blues the lead just after half-time but almost immediately Wednesday were back in it, courtesy of Carl Shutt.

Graeme Sharp missed two great chances to win it in ninety minutes, but he volleyed home a great pass from Paul Bracewell in extra time to put Everton in the Final for third season running.

While Everton were beating Sheffield Wednesday, Liverpool advanced to the first all-Merseyside FA Cup Final with a 2-0 victory over Southampton at White Hart Lane, Ian Rush scoring both goals in extra-time.

Thoughts now turned back to the race for the title and though it had looked the winners would be Everton or Liverpool, John Lyall's West Ham were making a late charge, standing just seven points behind the top two with three games in hand.

Gary Lineker had recovered from the injury he picked up at Old Trafford, while Trevor Steven was back in the line-up after limping out of the FA Cup semi-final.

Having beaten Arsenal 6-1 at Goodison earlier in the campaign, Adrian Heath's goal ten minutes from time gave the visitors a double over the Gunners, who had endured a troubled season.

Liverpool beat Coventry City 5-0 to boost their goal difference so there was no change in the standings at the top, with both teams on seventy-three points but with Everton having a potentially crucial game in hand.

Elsewhere, West Ham defeated Oxford United 3-1 to keep alive their own title aspirations.

If You Know Your History

After Joe Royle took over as manager in November 1984 with Everton bottom of the table, the Blues went on a five-game unbeaten run with three wins and a draw. On Boxing Day they lost 4-1 at home to Sheffield Wednesday but bounced back to hammer Ipswich Town 4-1 on New Year's Eve.

In the FA Cup third round, Andy Hinchcliffe's goal against Derby County saw Royle's men into the fourth round where Matt Jackson's late strike saw off Bristol City at Ashton Gate. A stunning 5-0 success over Norwich City at Goodison then set-up a home quarter-final tie with Newcastle, settled by a Dave Watson header. In the semi-final, the Blues produced a wonderful performance to make it to Wembley.

P141   Retrotext   Sun 09 Apr 1995

FOOTBALL

FA Cup Semi-Final, Elland Road, Leeds
TOTTENHAM HOTSPUR   1   4   EVERTON
Klinsmann 64 (pen)   Jackson 35
                            Stuart 55
                          Amokachi 82 90

Everton Line-Up
1 Neville Southall, 2 Matt Jackson,
6 Gary Ablett, 18 Joe Parkinson,
5 Dave Watson, 26 David Unsworth,
17 Anders Limpar, 10 Barry Horne,
8 Graham Stuart, 15 Paul Rideout
(11 Daniel Amokachi), 3 Andy
Hinchcliffe

Manager Joe Royle   Attendance 38,226

Nil Satis Nisi Optimum

Match Report   Results   Tables   Fixtures

April 1986

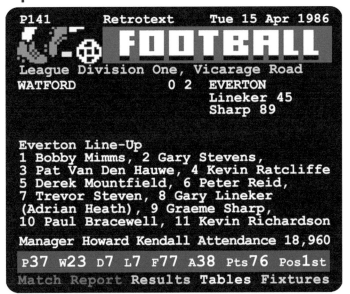

```
P141      Retrotext      Tue 15 Apr 1986
FOOTBALL
League Division One, Vicarage Road
WATFORD           0 2   EVERTON
                        Lineker 45
                        Sharp 89

Everton Line-Up
1 Bobby Mimms, 2 Gary Stevens,
3 Pat Van Den Hauwe, 4 Kevin Ratcliffe
5 Derek Mountfield, 6 Peter Reid,
7 Trevor Steven, 8 Gary Lineker
(Adrian Heath), 9 Graeme Sharp,
10 Paul Bracewell, 11 Kevin Richardson

Manager Howard Kendall Attendance 18,960

P37 w23 D7 L7 F77 A38 Pts76 Pos1st
Match Report  Results Tables Fixtures
```

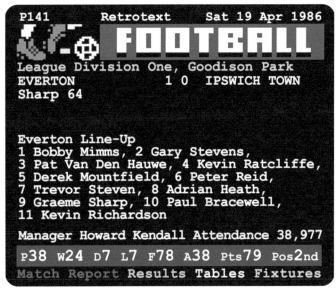

```
P141      Retrotext      Sat 19 Apr 1986
FOOTBALL
League Division One, Goodison Park
EVERTON           1 0   IPSWICH TOWN
Sharp 64

Everton Line-Up
1 Bobby Mimms, 2 Gary Stevens,
3 Pat Van Den Hauwe, 4 Kevin Ratcliffe,
5 Derek Mountfield, 6 Peter Reid,
7 Trevor Steven, 8 Adrian Heath,
9 Graeme Sharp, 10 Paul Bracewell,
11 Kevin Richardson

Manager Howard Kendall Attendance 38,977

P38 w24 D7 L7 F78 A38 Pts79 Pos2nd
Match Report  Results Tables Fixtures
```

Having already been named PFA Player of the Year by his peers, Gary Lineker was also named the Football Writers' Association Footballer of the Year, the accolade won by Neville Southall the season before. He was only the fourth player to win both awards in the same season.

Lineker had been an instant hit at Everton in his debut season, scoring thirty-three goals up to this point as the Blues chased their first-ever League and FA Cup double.

There was bad news for Paul Bracewell on the international front as, with the World Cup in Mexico just a couple of months away, he had been omitted from the England squad to play a friendly against Scotland. Gary Stevens, Peter Reid and Trevor Steven were all included, as well as Lineker.

Despite playing through the pain barrier due to the injury he picked up on New Year's Day, Bracewell had continued to perform superbly for the Blues as his midfield partner Peter Reid was always quick to acknowledge and appreciate.

At Watford, on a bog of a pitch, Lineker gave the visitors the lead just before half-time but didn't re-appear for the second period due to injury. Graeme Sharp's header near the end, his twenty-second goal of the campaign, finally secured the points.

The crucial win over Watford took Everton back to the top of the table with Liverpool facing a tricky test on Luton's plastic pitch twenty-four hours later.

But the Reds battled to a 1-0 win at Kenilworth Road to go above the Blues once more though still having played a game more.

Gary Lineker's hamstring injury at Vicarage Road kept him out of the lineup against Ipswich Town allowing Adrian Heath to make a rare start, though his contribution off the bench this season had been immense.

Ian Atkins, who had been sold to Ipswich by Howard Kendall earlier in the season, returned to Goodison Park with the visitors and they proved to be a stubborn team to breakdown.

Graeme Sharp was the player who breached their defences midway through the second half, heading home a Kevin Richardson cross for his twenty-third goal of the season.

Liverpool were away at bottom club West Brom and goals from Kenny Dalglish and Ian Rush gave them maximum points so it was 'as you were' at the top.

The Reds now had three games left and the Blues four.

It's A Grand Old Team To Play For

Daniel Amokachi rose to prominence playing for Nigeria at the 1994 World Cup and was signed by Everton boss Mike Walker for a fee of £3 million in August of that year.

When Walker was sacked in November, Amokachi played in new manager Joe Royle's first game in charge, a 2-0 win over Liverpool, but was substituted and didn't feature in the first team again until the following Spring.

By then, Royle's 'Dogs Of War' had been transformed, reaching the FA Cup semi-final where they faced hot-favourites Tottenham Hotspur. When Paul Rideout was injured, the manager told 'Amo' to warm up but before he knew it the Nigerian was on the field of play and went on to score two goals in eight minutes as the Toffees won 4-1 to book a place in the Final.

April 1986

P141   Retrotext   Sat 26 Apr 1986

FOOTBALL

League Division One, City Ground
NOTTINGHAM FOREST 0 0 EVERTON

Everton Line-Up
1 Bobby Mimms, 2 Gary Stevens,
3 Pat Van Den Hauwe, 4 Kevin Ratcliffe
5 Derek Mountfield, 6 Peter Reid,
7 Trevor Steven, 8 Gary Lineker,
9 Graeme Sharp, 10 Paul Bracewell,
11 Kevin Sheedy (Adrian Heath)
Manager Howard Kendall Attendance 30,171

P39 W24 D8 L7 F78 A38 Pts80 Pos2nd
Match Report Results Tables Fixtures

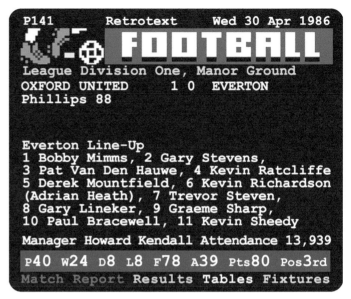

P141   Retrotext   Wed 30 Apr 1986

FOOTBALL

League Division One, Manor Ground
OXFORD UNITED   1 0   EVERTON
Phillips 88

Everton Line-Up
1 Bobby Mimms, 2 Gary Stevens,
3 Pat Van Den Hauwe, 4 Kevin Ratcliffe
5 Derek Mountfield, 6 Kevin Richardson
(Adrian Heath), 7 Trevor Steven,
8 Gary Lineker, 9 Graeme Sharp,
10 Paul Bracewell, 11 Kevin Sheedy
Manager Howard Kendall Attendance 13,939

P40 W24 D8 L8 F78 A39 Pts80 Pos3rd
Match Report Results Tables Fixtures

In the run-up to Everton's next two games, both away from home, England played Scotland at Wembley. Gary Lineker had been pulled out of the squad by Howard Kendall due to his injury, but Gary Stevens started the match with Peter Reid and Trevor Steven on the bench.

Graeme Sharp had also been withdrawn from the Scotland squad, as had Pat van den Hauwe from the Wales squad facing a friendly with Uruguay.

For England, Reid came on at half-time for the injured Ray Wilkins and was on the receiving end of a strong tackle by Graeme Souness which, by the end of the match, had caused severe bruising from his knee downwards. He was on John Clinkard's treatment table the next day with ice applied to the affected area but there was no ligament damage

Neville Southall apart, the Blues were at full strength for the game at the City Ground, with the players withdrawn from international duty all declared fit, and Kevin Sheedy also back after coming through a midweek reserve game without any issues.

As expected, it was a tough game and a draw was a fair result. But with Liverpool beating strugglers Birmingham 5-0, the Reds now had a two-point advantage at the top

After picking up a knock playing for England, Peter Reid was also in the wars at the City Ground where he injured his foot after just ten minutes. He almost came off at half-time but battled on, though he left the stadium on crutches.

This evening was to be pivotal in the destination of the League title.

There was a big setback for the Blues on the morning of the game as Reid failed a fitness test. He was running okay but when he tried a couple of block tackles with the physio there was too much pain.

With Birmingham and West Brom doomed, Oxford were one of three teams trying to stave off relegation and they made life tough for the Blues.

Gary Lineker had three good chances in the second half to score and, when fully fit, he probably would have taken them.

But he didn't and ninety seconds from time the home team scored the winner and moved out of the relegation places.

With Liverpool winning at Leicester and West Ham beating Ipswich Town at Upton Park, the Blues dropped to third in the table and the chance to retain their title looked to have gone.

If You Know Your History

When Joe Royle took over from Mike Walker in November 1994, the Blues were bottom of the table with only one win all season and just eight points from fourteen games. But in his first game in charge, Everton beat Liverpool 2-0 and with a newly-found belief and determination Royle's 'Dogs Of War' gradually moved up the table.

The improved League form was reflected in a brilliant FA Cup run which took the team to the semi-final against hot favourites Spurs at Elland Road where the Blues produced a sensational performance to win 4-1. Royle's men were once again huge underdogs in the Final against Manchester United, but Paul Rideout's goal and brilliant goalkeeping by Neville Southall enabled Dave Watson to lift the Cup.

P141   Retrotext   Sat 20 May 1995

FOOTBALL

FA Cup Final, Wembley Stadium
EVERTON   1 0   MANCHESTER UTD
Rideout 30

Everton Line-Up
1 Neville Southall, 2 Matt Jackson,
6 Gary Ablett, 18 Joe Parkinson,
5 Dave Watson, 26 David Unsworth,
17 Anders Limpar (11 Daniel Amokachi)
10 Barry Horne, 8 Graham Stuart,
15 Paul Rideout (9 Duncan Ferguson),
3 Andy Hinchcliffe
Manager Joe Royle   Attendance 79,592
Man of the Match Dave Watson
1995 FA Cup Winners
Match Report Results Tables Fixtures

April 1986

P141   Retrotext   Sat 03 May 1986
FOOTBALL
League Division One, Goodison Park
EVERTON   6 1   SOUTHAMPTON
Mountfield 9   Puckett 58
Steven 28
Lineker 29 34 63
Sharp 51
Everton Line-Up
1 Bobby Mimms, 2 Gary Stevens,
3 Pat Van Den Hauwe, 4 Kevin Ratcliffe,
5 Derek Mountfield, 6 Peter Reid,
7 Trevor Steven, 8 Gary Lineker,
9 Graeme Sharp, 10 Paul Bracewell
(Adrian Heath), 11 Kevin Sheedy
Manager Howard Kendall Attendance 33,062
P41 W25 D8 L8 F84 A40 Pts83 Pos3rd
Match Report **Results Tables Fixtures**

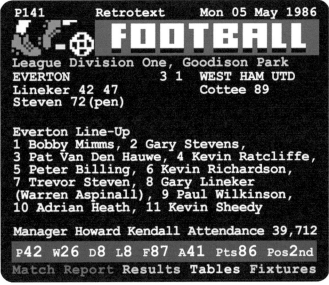

P141   Retrotext   Mon 05 May 1986
FOOTBALL
League Division One, Goodison Park
EVERTON   3 1   WEST HAM UTD
Lineker 42 47   Cottee 89
Steven 72(pen)

Everton Line-Up
1 Bobby Mimms, 2 Gary Stevens,
3 Pat Van Den Hauwe, 4 Kevin Ratcliffe,
5 Peter Billing, 6 Kevin Richardson,
7 Trevor Steven, 8 Gary Lineker
(Warren Aspinall), 9 Paul Wilkinson,
10 Adrian Heath, 11 Kevin Sheedy
Manager Howard Kendall Attendance 39,712
P42 W26 D8 L8 F87 A41 Pts86 Pos2nd
Match Report **Results Tables Fixtures**

The destination of the Division One crown was no longer in Everton's hands and all the players could do was win their last two games and hope Liverpool slipped up away at Chelsea.

Peter Reid was passed fit to play after missing out at the Manor Ground on Wednesday so, for once, the home side would be at almost full strength. Southampton on the other hand were struggling to put out a team.

Peter Shilton was injured so seventeen-year-old Keith Granger was in goal, with a sixteen-year-old at left back and a twenty-one-year-old at centre-half.

Not surprisingly, the visitors' inexperienced defence couldn't cope with what the Blues threw at them and they were four down at the break.

Gary Lineker claimed his hat-trick midway through the second half but thankfully for Southampton fans that was the end of the goalfest.

It finished 6-1 but the result was irrelevant when news came through from Stamford Bridge that Liverpool had beaten Chelsea 1-0 courtesy of a Kenny Dalglish goal.

The title was heading back to Anfield but the FA Cup Final a week later would still give the Blues the chance to win a trophy.

It had been a long, hard season for the Blues in defence of their title, hampered by long-term injuries to Derek Mountfield, Peter Reid and latterly Neville Southall, as well as shorter absences from the team for virtually every other player.

This game could at one stage have been the title decider but as it was the only reward on offer was securing second spot in the table. Everton shrugged off the disappointment of Saturday to produce a dominant display to which the Hammers simply had no answer.

Gary Lineker added two more goals to the three he scored at the weekend to take his tally in the League to thirty - the first Blues striker to reach that landmark since Bob Latchford back in 1977-78.

Trevor Steven made it 3-0 from the penalty spot before future Everton player Tony Cottee earned a consolation for the visitors at the death. So, Howard Kendall's side finished the campaign as runners-up and were left to rue the defeat at Oxford United which cost them the title.

But credit to Liverpool, who since falling eight points behind their great rivals when losing the Anfield derby 2-0 back in February had remained unbeaten in their remaining twelve League games, winning eleven of them.

It's A Grand Old Team To Play For

With Derek Mountfield a long-term injury absentee, Everton had hoped to sign Dave Watson in time for the 1986 Charity Shield match against Liverpool, but, having just penned a new three-year deal, Norwich City were reluctant to lose their club captain and demanded a £1 million fee. A compromise of £900,000 was eventually reached and Watson made his Division One debut for the Blues a week later.

The Liverpool-born player struggled to be accepted by some sections of the fans and after boos greeted his name being called in a match against Southampton in March Howard Kendall took to his programme notes to defend him. Watson eventually won the supporters over and was a key member of the team which won the League that season. Everton's fortunes declined after that but he became a stalwart of the team for over ten years, giving a man of the match performance in the 1995 FA Cup Final victory.

April 1986

```
P141      Retrotext      Sat 10 May 1986
            FOOTBALL
FA Cup Final, Wembley Stadium
LIVERPOOL          3 1   EVERTON
Rush 57 84               Lineker 28
Johnston 63


Everton Line-Up
1 Bobby Mimms, 2 Gary Stevens
(Adrian Heath), 3 Pat Van Den Hauwe,
4 Kevin Ratcliffe, 5 Derek Mountfield,
6 Peter Reid, 7 Trevor Steven,
8 Gary Lineker, 9 Graeme Sharp,
10 Paul Bracewell, 11 Kevin Sheedy
Manager Howard Kendall Attendance 98,000
          Nil Satis Nisi Optimum
Match Report Results Tables Fixtures
```

On the Tuesday before the Cup Final, Liverpool had beaten Norwich City 3-1 at Anfield (4-2 on aggregate) to secure their place in the Screen Sport Super Cup Final against Everton, which would be played in September over two legs.

The Blues should have had a penalty on twenty minutes when Steve Nicol pushed Graeme Sharp in the box but referee Alan Robinson - the same official who didn't award Everton a spot kick in the Milk Cup Final in 1984 after Alan Hansen handled the ball - waved away protests.

Howard Kendall's side took a deserved lead near the half-hour mark when Peter Reid threaded a pass through to Gary Lineker who scored at the second attempt. In the second period, there were chances for the Blues to extend the advantage as Liverpool faltered and argued amongst each other.

But, out of nowhere, the game turned on its head. Gary Stevens gave the ball away and it was fed through to Ian Rush who rounded Bobby Mimms and levelled the game up. With their tails up, five minutes later Craig Johnston made it 2-1 and with Everton chasing an equaliser, Rush struck again.

The Evertonians in the crowd were left in utter disbelief at how a game which seemed to be have been won had instead, somehow, been lost.

A few days before the Wembley showpiece, Barcelona played Steaua Bucharest in the European Cup Final held in Seville.

In the semi-finals, Terry Venables side had scraped through against Gothenburg, losing the first leg 3-0 but winning the second leg 3-0 and going through 5-4 on penalties. The Romanian side lost 1-0 to Anderlecht in their first leg, but won 3-0 in the second leg.

It was a poor final which finished 0-0 after extra time. Barcelona missed all their penalties and Steaua missed two of their four but won 2-0.

Peter Reid watched the match on TV and said: "It really brought home how much we had lost because of the Heysel disaster, because I'd have backed us to beat either of the two teams."

On the day of the Cup Final, UEFA had confirmed that no English clubs would be allowed into their competitions during the 1986-87 season, but the organisation held out hope that they may be able to do so in twelve months time.

If they had been permitted, Liverpool, as champions, would have been in the European Cup with Everton in the European Cup-Winners' Cup.

On the Sunday following the FA Cup Final, Liverpool and Everton players took a joint tour of the city on an open-top bus, but it must have been a strange experience for the Blue contingent having lost out to the Reds in both competitions.

Peter Reid missed the tour and was reprimanded by the club but, speaking to the Liverpool Echo, he was defended by his mum, who said:

"Peter was one of only two Scousers out there on the pitch. He was physically sick at losing but he was still the one who rounded up the players at Wembley to salute the fans."

With the season over, thoughts now turned to the World Cup in Mexico where Reid, Gary Stevens, Gary Lineker, Trevor Steven and Graeme Sharp would all be involved.

It's A Grand Old Team To Play For

Joe Royle became the youngest player to represent Everton when he made his debut in 1966, aged just sixteen. He became a regular in the side in 1967-68 and during the title-winning season of 1969-70 he contributed twenty-three goals.

A back injury hampered Joe in the early 1970s and he was eventually sold to Manchester City by Harry Catterick's successor, Billy Bingham.

Joe began his management career at Oldham where he had terrific success before becoming Everton boss in 1994 after the disastrous spell under Mike Walker had left the Blues bottom of the table. His first game was a 2-0 victory over Liverpool and by the end of campaign he had guided the team to mid-table security and won the FA Cup for the fifth time in the club's history.

It's A Grand Old Team To Support

As a little boy, I idolised Sir Matt Busby's Manchester United. But that was before I had ever stepped into Goodison Park. And, believe me, once I had done that there was no other club for me but Everton.

It is difficult to define just what puts the Goodison club a cut above every other... even United. There is something intangible in the air that casts you under its spell and never releases you.

I could have joined United or Liverpool. I went to see Matt Busby and Bill Shankly, both great men and great managers. But as soon as I stepped inside Goodison Park and met manager Harry Catterick, I knew deep down that Everton was the club I had to join.
From Royle Flush by Joe Royle (Pelham Books, 1969)

EVERTON
NIL SATIS
NISI OPTIMUM
GOODISON
PARK L4

Four: 1986-1987
EVERTON FC*

 HOWARD KENDALL - MANAGER
 COLIN HARVEY - COACH
 MICK HEATON - COACH
 JOHN CLINKARD - PHYSIO
 ADRIAN HEATH

 ALAN HARPER
 BOBBY MIMMS
 DAVE WATSON
 DEREK MOUNTFIELD
 GARY STEVENS

 GRAEME SHARP
 IAN MARSHALL
 KEVIN LANGLEY
 KEVIN RATCLIFFE
 KEVIN RICHARDSON

 KEVIN SHEEDY
 NEIL ADAMS
 NEIL POINTON
 NEVILLE SOUTHALL
 PAT VAN DEN HAUWE

 PAUL BRACEWELL
 PAUL POWER
 PAUL WILKINSON
 PETER REID
 TREVOR STEVEN

*as at the start of the season

August 1986

```
P141    Retrotext      Sat 16 Aug 1986
⚽ FOOTBALL
FA Charity Shield, Wembley Stadium
EVERTON          1 1   LIVERPOOL
Heath 80               Rush 87


Everton Line-Up
1 Bobby Mimms, 2 Alan Harper,
3 Paul Power, 4 Kevin Ratcliffe,
5 Ian Marshall, 6 Kevin Langley,
7 Trevor Steven, 8 Adrian Heath,
9 Graeme Sharp, 10 Kevin Richardson,
11 Kevin Sheedy (Neil Adams)
(Paul Wilkinson)

Manager Howard Kendall Attendance 88,231
    Nil Satis Nisi Optimum
Match Report Results Tables Fixtures
```

```
P141    Retrotext      Sat 23 Aug 1986
⚽ FOOTBALL
League Division One, Goodison Park
EVERTON          2 0   NOTT'M FOREST
Sheedy 27 65


Everton Line-Up
1 Bobby Mimms, 2 Alan Harper,
3 Paul Power, 4 Kevin Ratcliffe,
5 Dave Watson, 6 Kevin Langley,
7 Trevor Steven, 8 Adrian Heath,
9 Graeme Sharp, 10 Kevin Richardson,
(Paul Wilkinson), 11 Kevin Sheedy

Manager Howard Kendall Attendance 35,198
  P1 W1 D0 L0 F2 A0 Pts3 Pos5th
Match Report Results Tables Fixtures
```

During the summer, Barcelona did come calling but not for Howard Kendall, as Terry Venables had opted to stay with the club. Instead, it was forty-goal striker Gary Lineker who was lured away in a £2.8 million deal agreed before the start of the World Cup, where he had been top scorer with six goals.

With the likelihood of more first-team football following Lineker's departure, Adrian Heath signed a new four-year-deal, while Peter Reid put pen-to-paper on a two-year contract.

Reid was carrying an injury he picked up in Mexico which required a month's rest while Paul Bracewell was still troubled by the foot injury he sustained on New Year's Day and Derek Mountfield was continuing to have issues with his knee following his cartilage operation.

All three were ruled out of the Charity Shield, together with Neville Southall, Gary Stevens, Pat van den Hauwe and Neil Pointon.

New signings were 22-year-old midfielder Kevin Langley from Wigan for £120,000, Paul Power, a £65,000 acquisition from Manchester City and England under-21 midfielder Neil Adams from Stoke for £150,000.

This was the first occasion on which the Charity Shield match was broadcast live on television.

In the build-up to the Charity Shield, the Blues had gone on a pre-season tour of Holland and Germany and due to the extensive number of first-teamers absent through injury, there were plenty of opportunities for the summer purchases to stake their claims.

Howard Kendall was very pleased with their contributions and they would often be called upon in the first few weeks of the season as the club's injury issues persisted.

Derek Mountfield was one of those who was out which prompted Kendall to move into the transfer market, targeting Norwich's centre-half, Dave Watson.

The Blues initially offered £600,000 but the East Anglian outfit wanted a million and a compromise figure of £900,000 was agreed.

Watson made his debut in this season-opener, alongside two players who were still on the transfer list after refusing to sign new deals, Alan Harper and Kevin Richardson. Though the transfer window had closed, both could leave the club at short-notice being out-of-contract.

Kevin Sheedy made a great start to the new campaign, scoring twice as the Blues beat Brian Clough's lively Nottingham Forest side.

It's A Grand Old Team To Support

In January 1991, I was working on my first paper, the Surrey Herald. Our local team, Woking, having shocked West Brom in the FA Cup, had drawn Everton at Goodison in the 4th round. My job was to get some quotes from Howard Kendall but my hero gave me nothing: "Not even thought about it," was probably his strongest quote. So rather than risk ridicule, I made them up. "Taking nothing for granted," was the gist!

After the game, I had another chance to impress the great HK and in the post-match press conference I asked if he'd enjoyed the occasion or was there too much pressure to win the damn thing? "What damn thing? This is the FA Cup!" he said. He didn't add "You idiot!" but he might as well have done and I retreated to the corner of the room...

Rob Sloman, Director *Everton, Howard's Way*

EVERTON NIL SATIS NISI OPTIMUM GOODISON PARK L4

August 1986

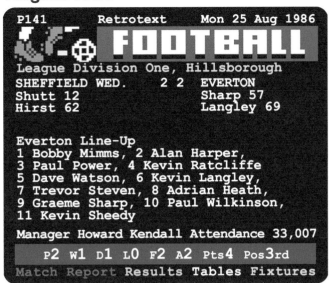

P141   Retrotext   Mon 25 Aug 1986

FOOTBALL

League Division One, Hillsborough
SHEFFIELD WED.   2 2   EVERTON
Shutt 12   Sharp 57
Hirst 62   Langley 69

Everton Line-Up
1 Bobby Mimms, 2 Alan Harper,
3 Paul Power, 4 Kevin Ratcliffe
5 Dave Watson, 6 Kevin Langley,
7 Trevor Steven, 8 Adrian Heath,
9 Graeme Sharp, 10 Paul Wilkinson,
11 Kevin Sheedy

Manager Howard Kendall Attendance 33,007

P2 W1 D1 L0 F2 A2 Pts4 Pos3rd

Match Report **Results Tables Fixtures**

P141   Retrotext   Sat 30 Aug 1986

FOOTBALL

League Division One, Highfield Road
COVENTRY CITY   1 1   EVERTON
Pickering 23   Marshall 78

Everton Line-Up
1 Bobby Mimms, 2 Alan Harper,
3 Paul Power, 4 Kevin Ratcliffe
5 Dave Watson, 6 Kevin Langley
(Ian Marshall), 7 Trevor Steven,
8 Adrian Heath, 9 Graeme Sharp,
10 Neil Adams, 11 Kevin Sheedy

Manager Howard Kendall Attendance 13,662

P3 W1 D2 L0 F5 A3 Pts5 Pos6th

Match Report **Results Tables Fixtures**

In this Bank Holiday Monday clash, Sheffield Wednesday were seeking to avenge their FA Cup semi-final loss to the Blues back in April.

It was Wednesday's scorer that day, Carl Shutt, who put the home side ahead but that was cancelled out by Graeme Sharp in the second-half.

Substitute David Hirst scored with his first touch of the ball to put Howard Wilkinson's side ahead again, before Kevin Langley crowned an excellent display by levelling things up.

There was more injury woe for Kendall to deal with as Gary Stevens would be out longer than expected with a stomach muscle strain which required rest. This prompted the manager to enquire about the availablity of Manchester United full-back Mike Duxbury but he was rebuffed.

It was clearly going to be a challenging early season for the Toffees with no imminent return for Neville Southall, Derek Mountfield, Neil Pointon, Pat van den Hauwe, Peter Reid and Paul Bracewell, with the midfield duo both in plaster after operations.

To make matters worse, free agent Kevin Richardson had agreed terms with Watford and would be leaving the Blues in his search for regular first-team football for a fee of £225,000.

Howard Kendall handed another of his summer signings, Neil Adams, a League debut at Highfield Road and he showed up well on his first start.

But it was Coventry who went ahead through Nick Pickering and the visitors could have been further behind at half-time with the new central defensive partnership of Dave Watson and Kevin Ratcliffe looking a little vulnerable.

In the second half, Howard Kendall took off Kevin Langley, thrusting young defender Ian Marshall into the fray and he demonstrated his eye for goal by firing home the equaliser.

Over in Spain, Gary Lineker scored two goals on his League debut for Barcelona and in an interview with France Football magazine expanded on his reasons for leaving Everton.

"English footballers desperately miss the European competitions. For our clubs and players that ban is a serious blow and it puts them in a kind of obligatory prison."

On the international front, Dave Watson and Trevor Steven were in Bobby Robson's England squad but Graeme Sharp was omitted from new Scotland boss Andy Roxburgh's squad.

If You Know Your History

Joe Royle's impact as Everton manager after taking over from Mike Walker was sensational, winning the FA Cup and Charity Shield and guiding the Blues into a first European campaign since the Heysel ban on English clubs was introduced in 1985.

In the first round of the European Cup-Winners' Cup, the Blues beat Icelandic minnows KR Reykjavik 6-3 on aggregate to set up a second round tie with Feyenoord. Everton dominated the first-leg but it finished 0-0 and the Dutch side won the second leg 1-0 to go through.

The team shrugged off the disappointment of elimination by going on a six game unbeaten League run including this win over Liverpool.

P141   Retrotext   Sat 18 Nov 1995

FOOTBALL

FA Premier League, Anfield
LIVERPOOL   1 2   EVERTON
Fowler 88   Kanchelskis
                53 68

Everton Line-Up
1 Neville Southall, 2 Matt Jackson,
6 Gary Ablett (26 David Unsworth 21),
14 John Ebbrell, 5 Dave Watson,
21 Craig Short, 17 Andrei Kanchelskis,
18 Joe Parkinson, 8 Graham Stuart,
15 Paul Rideout, 17 Anders Limpar

Manager Joe Royle   Attendance 40,818

Nil Satis Nisi Optimum

Match Report **Results Tables Fixtures**

September 1986

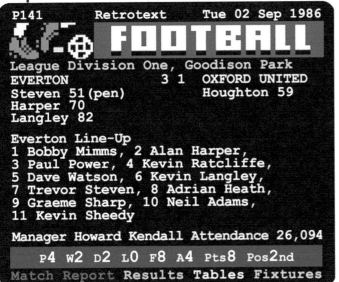

```
P141      Retrotext      Tue 02 Sep 1986
[FOOTBALL logo]
League Division One, Goodison Park
EVERTON            3 1   OXFORD UNITED
Steven 51(pen)           Houghton 59
Harper 70
Langley 82

Everton Line-Up
1 Bobby Mimms, 2 Alan Harper,
3 Paul Power, 4 Kevin Ratcliffe,
5 Dave Watson, 6 Kevin Langley,
7 Trevor Steven, 8 Adrian Heath,
9 Graeme Sharp, 10 Neil Adams,
11 Kevin Sheedy

Manager Howard Kendall Attendance 26,094

P4 W2 D2 L0 F8 A4 Pts8 Pos2nd
Match Report Results Tables Fixtures
```

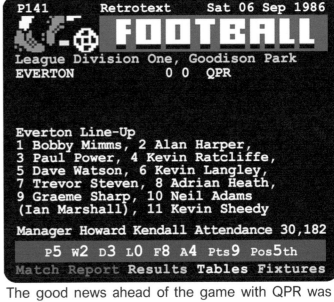

```
P141      Retrotext      Sat 06 Sep 1986
[FOOTBALL logo]
League Division One, Goodison Park
EVERTON            0 0   QPR

Everton Line-Up
1 Bobby Mimms, 2 Alan Harper,
3 Paul Power, 4 Kevin Ratcliffe,
5 Dave Watson, 6 Kevin Langley,
7 Trevor Steven, 8 Adrian Heath,
9 Graeme Sharp, 10 Neil Adams
(Ian Marshall), 11 Kevin Sheedy

Manager Howard Kendall Attendance 30,182

P5 W2 D3 L0 F8 A4 Pts9 Pos5th
Match Report Results Tables Fixtures
```

The games were coming thick and fast, stretching Everton's reduced playing resources to the limit.

Next up was an Oxford United side which had done so much damage to the Blues' title hopes on the last day of April.

After a fairly even first half, Trevor Steven put the Blues ahead from the penalty spot but Ray Houghton levelled for the visitors. Alan Harper then underlined his importance to the team by making it 2-1 and Kevin Langley grabbed his second goal in four League games.

In the draw for the second round of the League Cup, now sponsored by Littlewoods, the Blues were drawn against Newport County with the first leg at Goodison Park.

After losing Kevin Richardson to Watford, and in the midst of an unprecedented injury crisis, Howard Kendall was desperate not to lose the versatile Alan Harper and before the next game it was announced that the Liverpool-born player had signed a new deal.

Meanwhile, ex-Everton skipper Mark Higgins, who was forced to retire with a pelvic injury a year earlier but had battled back to fitness with Manchester United, was attracting interest from Wigan Athletic, where his father was once player-manager.

The good news ahead of the game with QPR was that Gary Bannister would not be playing due to suspension. The season before, Bannister had scored all three goals at Loftus Road as the Blues were battered 3-0 and grabbed two more in the 4-3 defeat at Goodison back in January.

There were two new names in the QPR line up; Sammy Lee, who had signed from Liverpool during the summer, plus future England goalkeeper David Seaman who had moved from Birmingham for £250,000.

The two youngsters in Everton's midfield. Kevin Langley and Neil Adams, again acquitted themselves well but it was a game of few chances with a point apiece a fair result.

On the injury front, Peter Reid and Paul Bracewell were due to have their plaster casts removed in the coming days, while Derek Mountfield would be taking part in a reserve game against Oldham during the week.

It was also revealed that legendary England goalkeeper Gordon Banks would provide regular coaching sessions for the 'keepers at the club including Fred Barber and Mike Stowell as well as the injured Neville Southall and current first-choice stopper Bobby Mimms.

It's A Grand Old Team To Play For

After a protracted wrangle with Manchester United, Andrei Kanchelskis finally signed for Everton on 25th August 1995 for a fee of £5 million and made his debut in a 2-0 win over Southampton at Goodison Park the following day.

His first season at the club was nothing short of sensational. He contributed sixteen goals, including a double against Liverpool at Anfield in November and a brilliant hat-trick against Sheffield Wednesday in the penultimate match of the 1995-96 campaign as the Blues just missed out on securing a UEFA Cup place.

The flying winger failed to hit the same heights during the following season and he was transferred to Fiorentina in a deal worth £8 million at the end of January 1997, just a few days after the Blues lost an FA Cup tie to Bradford City.

September 1986

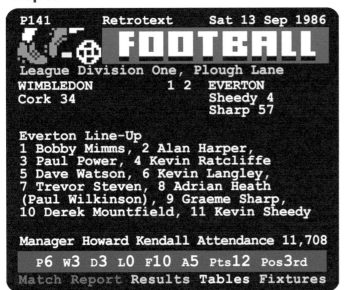

```
P141      Retrotext      Sat 13 Sep 1986
          FOOTBALL
League Division One, Plough Lane
WIMBLEDON         1 2    EVERTON
Cork 34                  Sheedy 4
                         Sharp 57

Everton Line-Up
1 Bobby Mimms, 2 Alan Harper,
3 Paul Power, 4 Kevin Ratcliffe
5 Dave Watson, 6 Kevin Langley,
7 Trevor Steven, 8 Adrian Heath
(Paul Wilkinson), 9 Graeme Sharp,
10 Derek Mountfield, 11 Kevin Sheedy

Manager Howard Kendall Attendance 11,708
P6 W3 D3 L0 F10 A5 Pts12 Pos3rd
Match Report Results Tables Fixtures
```

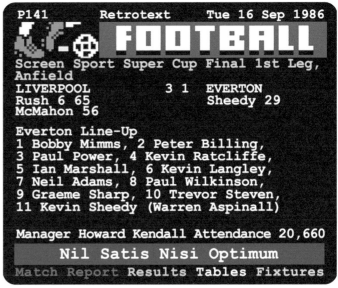

```
P141      Retrotext      Tue 16 Sep 1986
          FOOTBALL
Screen Sport Super Cup Final 1st Leg,
Anfield
LIVERPOOL         3 1    EVERTON
Rush 6 65                Sheedy 29
McMahon 56

Everton Line-Up
1 Bobby Mimms, 2 Peter Billing,
3 Paul Power, 4 Kevin Ratcliffe,
5 Ian Marshall, 6 Kevin Langley,
7 Neil Adams, 8 Paul Wilkinson,
9 Graeme Sharp, 10 Trevor Steven,
11 Kevin Sheedy (Warren Aspinall)

Manager Howard Kendall Attendance 20,660
Nil Satis Nisi Optimum
Match Report Results Tables Fixtures
```

After losing their first-ever game in the top flight, newly-promoted Wimbledon had made a terrific start to the season, winning four games on the bounce and earning their manager, Dave Bassett, the Manager of the Month award for August.

The Dons stood proudly on top of the table with twelve points from five games, three points ahead of the Blues going into this match. It had been a remarkable rise for the club which was playing in Division Four as recently as season 1980-81.

Everton had been boosted during the week by the news that Derek Mountfield had come through a reserve match against Oldham without any reaction to his injury and he was added to the squad which travelled down to Plough Lane.

On a very wet day in London, Everton's opening goal came after a slip by a Wimbledon defender which allowed Trevor Steven to skip clear then pull the ball back for Kevin Sheedy to convert.

Alan Cork pounced on a defensive lapse to equalise for the home side before Graeme Sharp headed a Sheedy free-kick into the net.

The Blues were now the only unbeaten team in Division One but there was more injury woe as Derek Mountfield picked up a groin strain.

The Final of this much-maligned competition had been held over from the previous season due to difficulty in scheduling it but apathy from fans meant there was to be no renewal this season.

With Derek Mountfield ruled out, Howard Kendall had sought permission from the Football League to play new signing Dave Watson, who had turned out for Norwich City during the previous campaign. Kendall argued that as the Final was being staged in a new season, Watson should be eligible, but the authorities disagreed.

As well as Mountfield, Adrian Heath and Alan Harper were also out after picking up knocks at Plough Lane.

Ian Marshall passed a late fitness test to take his place in defence, while 21-year-old Peter Billing, a signing from non-League club South Liverpool back in January who had played in both legs of the semi-final against Spurs, came in at right-back.

Ian Rush put the Reds ahead but Kevin Sheedy smashed in the equaliser before hobbling off near half-time. The second period was a much more one-sided affair with ex-Blue Steve McMahon making it 2-1 and then Rush again ensuring Everton had it all to do in the second leg.

If You Know Your History

Manager Joe Royle left Everton on transfer deadline day in March 1997 after a dispute with chairman Peter Johnson over incoming transfers. Long-serving captain Dave Watson took on the role of caretaker boss until the end of the season when the Blues finished in fifteenth spot, two points above the relegation zone.

Sky television pundit and former fan favourite Andy Gray was in pole position to take on the manager's role but when he surprisingly pulled out, Howard Kendall was appointed by Johnson for his third spell as boss, with Adrian Heath as his assistant. After a poor season for the Blues, this point against Coventry and a defeat for Bolton at Chelsea meant Everton survived the drop on goal difference.

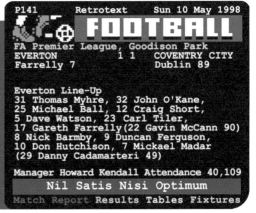

```
P141      Retrotext      Sun 10 May 1998
          FOOTBALL
FA Premier League, Goodison Park
EVERTON           1 1    COVENTRY CITY
Farrelly 7               Dublin 89

Everton Line-Up
31 Thomas Myhre, 32 John O'Kane,
25 Michael Ball, 12 Craig Short,
5 Dave Watson, 23 Carl Tiler,
17 Gareth Farrelly(22 Gavin McCann 90)
8 Nick Barmby, 9 Duncan Ferguson,
10 Don Hutchison, 7 Mickael Madar
(29 Danny Cadamarteri 49)
Manager Howard Kendall Attendance 40,109
Nil Satis Nisi Optimum
Match Report Results Tables Fixtures
```

September 1986

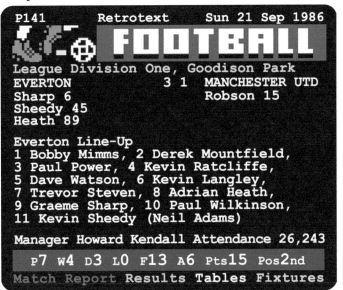

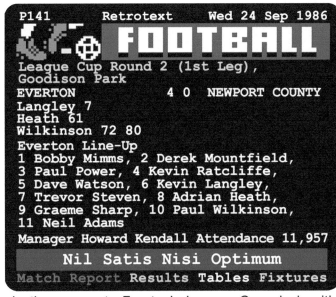

Manchester United had made a poor start to the season and after four games stood bottom of the Division One table with just one point. A 5-1 win at Old Trafford the week before had eased the pressure on manager Ron Atkinson but the Red Devils then suffered a midweek defeat at Watford.

Howard Kendall was able to welcome back Derek Mountfield and Adrian Heath from injury as well as Dave Watson who had been ineligible for the midweek Super Cup game. Kevin Sheedy had recovered from the knock he picked up against Liverpool but Alan Harper was still out.

Apart from the 1985 FA Cup Final, Everton had dominated recent meetings with United and that excellent record was extended in this televised match.

Graeme Sharp put the home side ahead with a towering header from Paul Power's cross, but Bryan Robson equalised for the visitors. Kevin Sheedy restored the Blues' advantage on the stroke of half-time, unusually with his right foot, his fifth goal of the campaign.

Adrian Heath had not scored since signing his new contract after Gary Lineker left, but he put that straight near the end to maintain the team's unbeaten start to the season.

In the run-up to Everton's League Cup clash with Newport County, it was announced that Luton Town had been thrown out of the competition with their tie awarded to their opponents, Cardiff City.

After the destruction caused by Millwall fans at Kenilworth Road in May 1985, Luton had introduced a members-only scheme which barred visiting fans, but League Cup rules stated that twenty-five percent of tickets ahould be allocated to away supporters.

When Luton refused to allow this, the League felt they had no choice but to act as they did, though talks between the club and Football League President Philip Carter, Everton's chairman, were ongoing to try and resolve the matter.

On the evening before, third division Fulham had been battered 10-0 by Liverpool and Newport, who stood two places above the London outfit in the table, were determined such a hammering would not happen to them.

Kevin Langley gave the home side the lead in an uneventful first-half and Adrian Heath made it 2-0 just after the hour mark. Paul Wilkinson's two goals then doubled the scoreline to leave the Welsh side with a mountain to climb in the second leg at Somerton Park.

It's A Grand Old Team To Support

The Old Lady gracefully holding her head and shoulders high above the terraced houses as I got closer to her for my first visit back in the mid-80s was a wondrous vision to behold. My Dad's family were all Reds but because of his work in the forces we were always moving around so opportunities to visit were limited. However, the blues called out to me.

Visiting Goodison Park for the first time was a dream come true as it was for my children too - I certainly wasn't losing them to "that lot" across Stanley Park! The players' names and numbers from the 84/85 team come quicker to me now than any song lyrics. Everton is in your blood, its touch incessant. Progression is a necessary part of life but leaving the proud Old Lady is going to be heart-breaking.
Daniel Wood (@footballint80s @when_football_was_better)

EVERTON NIL SATIS NISI OPTIMUM GOODISON PARK L4

September 1986

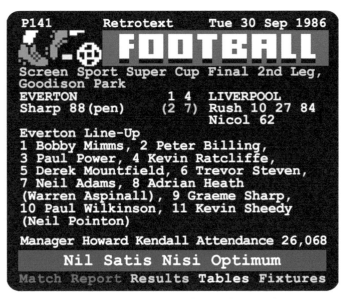

Everton put their unbeaten League record on the line at White Hart Lane, a ground where they had won on their last three visits.

Unfortunately, that record never looked like being extended as Tottenham ran out convincing winners with Clive Allen notching up two more goals to take his tally for the season to ten - and Spurs had only scored thirteen in total.

Though it was the Blues' first defeat of the season and they dropped to third in the table, with so many first-team players out through injury it had been a sterling effort from the squad to attain the position they had, establishing a strong foundation from which to approach the rest of the season.

In Europe, the prospects of the ban on English clubs being lifted in the near future seemed to be dwindling.

After an incident on a North Sea ferry where Manchester United and West Ham fans were involved in a mass brawl, England fans fought with Swedish fans at a recent friendly in Stockholm.

President of UEFA, Jacques George said: "Our conditions for changing our ruling on the ban was that the behaviour of English fans must improve. I regret to say this has not been the case."

Ahead of the second leg of the Super Cup Final, Neil Pointon was back in contention having been out of action since the previous season with a broken ankle.

In front of a healthy crowd and with a deficit to claw back, Everton made a very positive start and had decent chances to reduce the arrears.

But once Ian Rush fired home after just ten minutes the writing was on the wall and the Welsh striker, who had agreed to join Juventus at the end of the season, made it 2-0 at the break.

In the second half, Trevor Steven missed a penalty before Steve Nicol made it 3-0. With the game petering out, Rush secured his hat-trick and Graeme Sharp scored a consolation goal for the home side.

Rush's total in Merseyside derbies now stood at sixteen, just three behind Dixie Dean's record with two League matches and, as it turned out, a League Cup tie still to play before his transfer to Italy.

Howard Kendall was not best pleased with the display of his players and cancelled their planned day off so they could watch the match again and discuss what went wrong.

If You Know Your History

Everton began the 1999-2000 season slowly, with a draw and two defeats from the opening three games. But four wins in the next five League games meant the Blues were in seventh spot in the table coming into this match, three points ahead of Liverpool.

The visitors made a dream start when Kevin Campbell put them ahead and should have added to the tally as Gerard Houllier's side struggled to make a breakthrough. The match exploded with sixteen minutes left after a tussle between Sandor Westerveld and Francis Jeffers saw both players dismissed and a youthful Steven Gerrard suffered the same fate after a high tackle on Campbell in the dying minutes of the match.

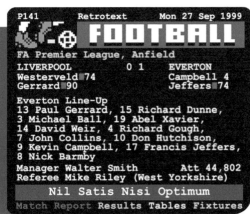

October 1986

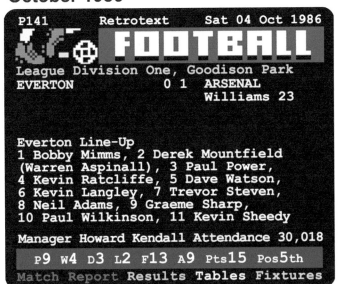

```
P141    Retrotext    Sat 04 Oct 1986
██ FOOTBALL
League Division One, Goodison Park
EVERTON          0 1   ARSENAL
                       Williams 23


Everton Line-Up
1 Bobby Mimms, 2 Derek Mountfield
(Warren Aspinall), 3 Paul Power,
4 Kevin Ratcliffe, 5 Dave Watson,
6 Kevin Langley, 7 Trevor Steven,
8 Neil Adams, 9 Graeme Sharp,
10 Paul Wilkinson, 11 Kevin Sheedy

Manager Howard Kendall Attendance 30,018

 P9 W4 D3 L2 F13 A9 Pts15 Pos5th
Match Report  Results Tables Fixtures
```

```
P141    Retrotext    Tue 07 Oct 1986
██ FOOTBALL
League Cup Round 2 (2nd Leg),
Somerton Park
NEWPORT COUNTY  1 5  EVERTON
Carter 2        (1 9) Wilkinson 3 42 87
                      Sharp 20
                      Mullen 29(og)
Everton Line-Up
1 Bobby Mimms, 2 Alan Harper,
3 Paul Power (Neil Pointon),
4 Kevin Ratcliffe, 5 Dave Watson,
6 Kevin Langley, 7 Neil Adams
(Warren Aspinall), 8 Trevor Steven,
9 Graeme Sharp, 10 Paul Wilkinson
11 Kevin Sheedy
Manager Howard Kendall  Attendance 7,172
      Nil Satis Nisi Optimum
Match Report  Results Tables Fixtures
```

Adrian Heath picked up an ankle injury during the first-half of the Super Cup clash with Liverpool and hadn't recovered sufficiently to take his place in the line-up against the Gunners.

Looking to bounce back from two successive defeats, Everton started well but fell behind to a Steve Williams goal direct from a corner-kick.

With time running out, Howard Kendall took off defender Derek Mountfield and gave young striker Warren Aspinall his opportunity but the equaliser eluded the home side.

Ahead of the midweek League Cup match with Newport, the Liverpool Echo gave a rundown on the club's walking wounded:

"Neville Southall, recovering from a dislocated ankle, is back in training. Gary Stevens (stomach muscle) might be able to start light training in a week's time, although he won't be allowed to do any work until he is completely pain-free.

Peter Reid, who suffered a stress fracture above his ankle, is in light training and is hoping to step up his work-rate soon.

Paul Bracewell, who had two pieces of floating cartilage removed from his foot, is walking again and should be training within a fortnight."

After three successive losses, the Blues travelled to Somerton Park to defend the 4-0 lead established in the first leg and hoping to get back on the winning trail.

Howard Kendall was able to welcome back Alan Harper after the invaluable utility player had missed the last six games with a thigh injury. He would slot in at right back.

The third division side shocked their illustrious visitors by taking a second minute lead but before the home crowd had stopped celebrating, Paul Wilkinson had equalised. Graeme Sharp made it 2-1 and then Newport's player-manager Jimmy Mullen headed the ball into his own net.

Shortly before the break, Wilkinson was on the mark again and he claimed his first hat-trick in senior football three minutes from time to complete a resounding 9-1 aggregate victory.

In the draw for the third round, Everton were handed yet another tie with Sheffield Wednesday with the Blues having home advantage.

The following evening in the Central League, the reserves were also banging the goals in with a 7-0 victory over Middlesbrough, with the young striker signed from Wigan, Warren Aspinall, scoring five.

It's A Grand Old Team To Play For

Kevin Campbell was signed by Everton boss Walter Smith in March 1999, initially on loan from Turkish side Trabzonspor. When he joined, the Blues were in a relegation scrap, but Kevin scored nine goals in eight games - including a hat-trick in a 6-0 thrashing of West Ham - and the team gradually climbed the table.

Kevin's transfer was made permanent during the summer and in September that year he famously scored the goal which gave Everton a rare victory at Anfield.

During his time at Everton, Kevin was made club captain, a testament to his impact both on and off the field. He joined West Brom in January 2005 and was instrumental in keeping the Baggies in the Premier League, the first team to do so after being bottom of the table at Christmas.

October 1986

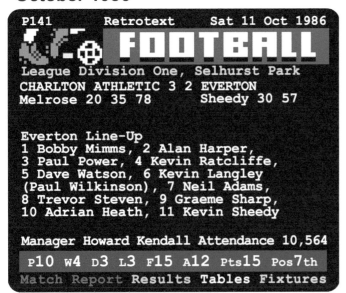

P141   Retrotext   Sat 11 Oct 1986

FOOTBALL

League Division One, Selhurst Park
CHARLTON ATHLETIC 3 2 EVERTON
Melrose 20 35 78   Sheedy 30 57

Everton Line-Up
1 Bobby Mimms, 2 Alan Harper,
3 Paul Power, 4 Kevin Ratcliffe,
5 Dave Watson, 6 Kevin Langley
(Paul Wilkinson), 7 Neil Adams,
8 Trevor Steven, 9 Graeme Sharp,
10 Adrian Heath, 11 Kevin Sheedy

Manager Howard Kendall Attendance 10,564

P10 W4 D3 L3 F15 A12 Pts15 Pos7th
Match Report Results Tables Fixtures

P141   Retrotext   Sat 18 Oct 1986

FOOTBALL

League Division One, The Dell
SOUTHAMPTON   0 2   EVERTON
                    Steven 79(pen)
                    Wilkinson 82

Everton Line-Up
1 Bobby Mimms, 2 Alan Harper,
3 Paul Power, 4 Kevin Ratcliffe,
5 Dave Watson (Warren Aspinall),
6 Derek Mountfield, 7 Trevor Steven,
8 Adrian Heath, 9 Graeme Sharp,
10 Paul Wilkinson, 11 Kevin Langley

Manager Howard Kendall Attendance 18,009

P11 W5 D3 L3 F17 A12 Pts18 Pos6th
Match Report Results Tables Fixtures

Adrian Heath was added to the squad travelling down to London for the meeting with Charlton Athletic and he would come straight back into the team after missing two games at the expense of midweek hat-trick hero Paul Wilkinson.

Under manager Lennie Lawrence, Charlton had been promoted to the top flight for the first time since the 1950s but were one of the favourites to drop back down again and coming into this fixture had yet to win a home match, though they had beaten Manchester United 1-0 at Old Trafford and Chelsea 1-0 at Stamford Bridge.

The home side were also struggling to find the back of the net and so far this campaign had only scored more than one goal once, in a 3-2 defeat at Oxford.

The visitors found themselves a goal down after twenty minutes when Jim Melrose scored but Kevin Sheedy's trusty left foot brought the Blues level. Melrose then lobbed Bobby Mimms to restore Charlton's advantage at the break.

Howard Kendall's side came out for the second period with all guns blazing and Sheedy's left foot again did the business. But it was Scottish striker Melrose who would have the final say by grabbing his hat-trick, condemning Everton to a third successive League defeat.

Kevin Sheedy's reward for his brilliant early season form, which had brought him seven goals, was a recall to Jack Charlton's Republic of Ireland team for the European Championship qualifier against Scotland.

Graeme Sharp was back in the Scotland team for that one, while Dave Watson would be lining up for England at Wembley against Northern Ireland.

Neville Southall, meanwhile, stepped up his comeback with a game for the reserves against Hull alongside several other first-teamers. The match attracted a bumper 1,600 crowd to Goodison Park and the Blues won 1-0.

It was planned for Southall to turn out for the A team at the weekend, a fixture in which Peter Reid would begin his comeback following three months out with a stress fracture of the shin.

It was announced this week that another great Everton goalkeeper, Ted Sagar, had died aged seventy-six. He was in goal for the 1933 FA Cup Final and made 495 appearances for the Blues.

Sheedy missed the game with Southampton after picking up an injury in midweek but the Blues bounced back from three straight League defeats to record their third win on the spin at The Dell.

If You Know Your History

Walter Smith had enjoyed a trophy-laden career as manager of Glasgow Rangers and he joined Everton in the summer of 1998 after Howard Kendall left. His four seasons with the Blues were hampered by financial restrictions with the club finishing in the lower half of the table and he was sacked after a heavy FA Cup loss at Middlesbrough.

David Moyes succeeded Smith in March 2002 with Everton once again flirting with relegation. He guided the club to safety and over the next few years developed a team generally capable of holding its own in the higher echelons of the Premier League, finishing fourth in 2004-05 and qualifying for the Champions League playoff round, as well as reaching the FA Cup Final in 2009.

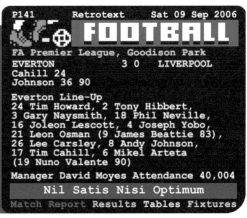

P141   Retrotext   Sat 09 Sep 2006

FOOTBALL

FA Premier League, Goodison Park
EVERTON   3 0   LIVERPOOL
Cahill 24
Johnson 36 90

Everton Line-Up
24 Tim Howard, 2 Tony Hibbert,
3 Gary Naysmith, 18 Phil Neville,
16 Joleon Lescott, 4 Joseph Yobo,
21 Leon Osman (9 James Beattie 83),
26 Lee Carsley, 8 Andy Johnson,
17 Tim Cahill, 6 Mikel Arteta
(19 Nuno Valente 90)

Manager David Moyes Attendance 40,004
Nil Satis Nisi Optimum
Match Report Results Tables Fixtures

October 1986

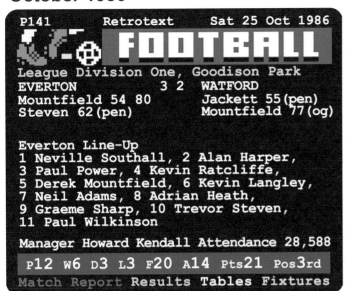

P141 Retrotext Sat 25 Oct 1986

FOOTBALL

League Division One, Goodison Park
EVERTON   3 2 WATFORD
Mountfield 54 80   Jackett 55 (pen)
Steven 62 (pen)   Mountfield 77 (og)

Everton Line-Up
1 Neville Southall, 2 Alan Harper,
3 Paul Power, 4 Kevin Ratcliffe,
5 Derek Mountfield, 6 Kevin Langley,
7 Neil Adams, 8 Adrian Heath,
9 Graeme Sharp, 10 Trevor Steven,
11 Paul Wilkinson

Manager Howard Kendall Attendance 28,588

P12 W6 D3 L3 F20 A14 Pts21 Pos3rd
Match Report Results Tables Fixtures

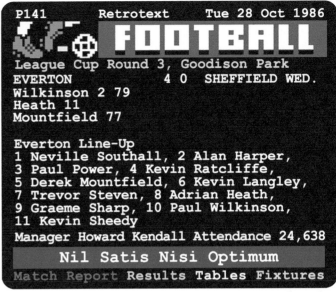

P141 Retrotext Tue 28 Oct 1986

FOOTBALL

League Cup Round 3, Goodison Park
EVERTON   4 0 SHEFFIELD WED.
Wilkinson 2 79
Heath 11
Mountfield 77

Everton Line-Up
1 Neville Southall, 2 Alan Harper,
3 Paul Power, 4 Kevin Ratcliffe,
5 Derek Mountfield, 6 Kevin Langley,
7 Trevor Steven, 8 Adrian Heath,
9 Graeme Sharp, 10 Paul Wilkinson,
11 Kevin Sheedy

Manager Howard Kendall Attendance 24,638

Nil Satis Nisi Optimum
Match Report Results Tables Fixtures

On the injury front for the Blues, after the outstanding win over Southampton at the weekend, it seemed to be one step forward, one step back, as had been the case for most of the campaign.

Neville Southall and Peter Reid both came through unscathed in the A team game with Manchester City and were now scheduled in the Central League mini-derby at Anfield. Pat van den Hauwe was also on the comeback trail having not played at all this season due to a blood disorder.

But Dave Watson was the victim of the latest injury hoodoo, expected to be absent for a month after being substituted at The Dell due to a hamstring strain.

In the mini-Derby, Southall came through unscathed but Reid was substituted just after half-time suffering from cramp though there was no reaction from the shin injury which had kept him out since the World Cup. Everton won the game 2-1.

Neville Southall made his long-awaited return to the first team for the game with Watford, a fixture which had been a goal-fest in recent years and this was one was no different.

Five goals were scored, three by Derek Mountfield, who also gave away a penalty, and the victory moved the Blues up to third in the table.

After making twenty-seven appearances for the Blues since Neville Southall was injured, goalkeeper Bobby Mimms was angry at being dropped to make way for the big Welshman and requested a transfer.

Neville Southall retained his place for the League Cup tie against Sheffield Wednesday, with top scorer Kevin Sheedy returning to the line-up after missing two games.

Paul Wilkinson clearly revelled in the newly-named Littlewoods Cup for, after scoring five in the previous round against Newport County, he notched a double against Wednesday, the first inside two minutes.

When Adrian Heath made it 2-0 after just eleven minutes with a fantastic volley it was effectively game over and Derek Mountfield showed he had rediscovered his scoring boots when he was on target in the second half.

After the draw was made for the third round, Everton would have to make the long journey to East Anglia to face Norwich City.

Under manager Ken Brown, the Canaries were having a terrific season and lay second in the Division One table, one point ahead of the Blues.

It's A Grand Old Team To Play For

Tim Cahill came to prominence during his days at Millwall, helping the club to reach the FA Cup Final against Manchester United in 2004. In the summer of that year, Everton manager David Moyes signed him for £2 million and he would later say it was one of the best transfer deals he made during his time at the club. During his eight seasons with the Blues, Cahill made 278 appearances and scored 68 goals before moving to MLS side New York Red Bulls at the end of the 2011-12 campaign.

Cahill is also arguably the best Australian international of all-time, having played and scored for his country at three consecutive World Cups (2006, 2010 and 2014) including a superb left foot volley in 2014 against the Netherlands which was voted one of the goals of the tournament. He helped the Aussies qualify for another World Cup in 2018, where he played once, and retired later that year.

November 1986

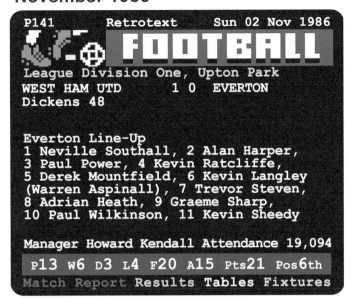

```
P141        Retrotext      Sun 02 Nov 1986
   FOOTBALL
League Division One, Upton Park
WEST HAM UTD      1 0    EVERTON
Dickens 48


Everton Line-Up
1 Neville Southall, 2 Alan Harper,
3 Paul Power, 4 Kevin Ratcliffe,
5 Derek Mountfield, 6 Kevin Langley
(Warren Aspinall), 7 Trevor Steven,
8 Adrian Heath, 9 Graeme Sharp,
10 Paul Wilkinson, 11 Kevin Sheedy

Manager Howard Kendall Attendance 19,094
P13 W6 D3 L4 F20 A15 Pts21 Pos6th
Match Report  Results Tables Fixtures
```

```
P141        Retrotext      Sat 08 Nov 1986
   FOOTBALL
League Division One, Goodison Park
EVERTON           2 2    CHELSEA
Steven 26(pen)           Jones 44
Sheedy 66                Pates 87


Everton Line-Up
1 Neville Southall, 2 Alan Harper,
3 Paul Power, 4 Kevin Ratcliffe,
5 Derek Mountfield, 6 Kevin Langley,
7 Trevor Steven, 8 Adrian Heath,
9 Graeme Sharp, 10 Paul Wilkinson,
11 Kevin Sheedy

Manager Howard Kendall Attendance 29,748
P14 W6 D4 L4 F22 A17 Pts22 Pos8th
Match Report  Results Tables Fixtures
```

With Dave Watson out injured, this match was an opportunity for Derek Mountfield to re-establish himself in his favoured position on the day he celebrated his twenty-fourth birthday.

Broadcast live on television, the game proved to be something of a low-key affair with very few chances and it was ultimately settled by a header from Hammers' midfielder Alan Dickens.

It was Everton's fourth defeat in six League games and saw them drop to sixth in the table, though still only five points adrift of leaders Nottingham Forest.

As Liverpool won the double last season, if it were not for the Heysel ban preventing English clubs playing in UEFA competitions, the Blues would have been involved in the European Cup-Winners' Cup and this week saw the second legs of the second round being played out.

Wrexham drew 0-0 with Real Zaragoza in the first leg and the return match at the Racecourse Ground finished 2-2 after extra-time, eliminating the Welsh side on the away goals rule.

Favourites to lift the trophy were Ajax, a team managed by Johan Cruyff and with Frank Rijkaard and Marco van Basten in their ranks. They beat Greek side Olympiakos 4-0 at home and drew 1-1 away to book their place in the quarter-finals.

After a disastrous start to the season which saw Manchester United sitting in the relegation places, Ron Atkinson was sacked this week, less than eighteen months after leading his side to that FA Cup Final victory over Everton.

The press speculated as to who might succeed Big Ron at Old Trafford, with Howard Kendall and Brian Clough reputedly amongst the front runners, but it was Aberdeen boss Alex Ferguson who was appointed to the role.

Another under pressure manager was John Hollins, whose Chelsea side were struggling near the bottom of the table after performing brilliantly the season before and being involved in the title race before fading to finish sixth.

Chelsea had proved difficult opponents for the Blues during that campaign, including knocking Howard Kendall's side out of the League Cup.

It was a similar story this time around despite Everton taking the lead through a Trevor Steven penalty. The visitors equalised on the stroke of half-time but Kevin Sheedy blasted the home side in front midway through the second period.

When Chelsea's Kevin McAllister was sent off, it appeared the points were secure but defender Colin Pates shocked the Blues at the death.

If You Know Your History

Everton's road to Wembley in 2009 began at Moss Rose, where the Blues defeated Macclesfield 1-0 thanks to a Leon Osman goal just before half-time. The fourth round draw paired David Moyes' side with Rafa Benitez's Liverpool and after a 1-1 draw at Anfield, Steven Gerrard equalising after Joleon Lescott put the visitors ahead, the replay went Everton's way courtesy of Dan Gosling's famous strike.

Aston Villa were the opponents in the fifth round with the Blues winning 3-1 to book a place in the quarter-finals, where they faced Middlesbrough at Goodison, coming from a goal down to go through 2-1 with Marouane Fellaini and Louis Saha on target. In the Final, after taking an early lead, Everton lost 2-1 to Chelsea.

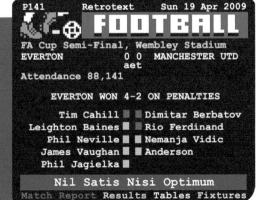

```
P141        Retrotext      Sun 19 Apr 2009
   FOOTBALL
FA Cup Semi-Final, Wembley Stadium
EVERTON          0 0    MANCHESTER UTD
                   aet
Attendance 88,141

        EVERTON WON 4-2 ON PENALTIES

    Tim Cahill ■   ■ Dimitar Berbatov
  Leighton Baines ■   ■ Rio Ferdinand
    Phil Neville ■   ■ Nemanja Vidic
  James Vaughan ■   ■ Anderson
    Phil Jagielka ■
        Nil Satis Nisi Optimum
Match Report  Results Tables Fixtures
```

November 1986

P141   Retrotext   Sat 15 Nov 1986

FOOTBALL

League Division One, Filbert Street
LEICESTER CITY   0 2   EVERTON
                         Heath 23
                         Sheedy 66

Everton Line-Up
1 Neville Southall, 2 Alan Harper,
3 Paul Power, 4 Kevin Ratcliffe,
5 Derek Mountfield, 6 Kevin Langley,
7 Trevor Steven (Warren Aspinall),
8 Adrian Heath, 9 Graeme Sharp,
10 Neil Adams, 11 Kevin Sheedy

Manager Howard Kendall Attendance 13,450

P15 W7 D4 L4 F24 A17 Pts25 Pos7th
Match Report Results Tables Fixtures

P141   Retrotext   Wed 19 Nov 1986

FOOTBALL

League Cup Round 4, Carrow Road
NORWICH CITY   1 4   EVERTON
Barham 31   Sheedy 21
                       Sharp 36
                       Steven 78 (pen)
                       Heath 84

Everton Line-Up
1 Neville Southall, 2 Alan Harper,
3 Paul Power, 4 Kevin Ratcliffe,
5 Derek Mountfield, 6 Kevin Langley,
7 Trevor Steven, 8 Adrian Heath,
9 Graeme Sharp, 10 Neil Adams,
11 Kevin Sheedy
Manager Howard Kendall Attendance 17,988

Nil Satis Nisi Optimum
Match Report Results Tables Fixtures

Though undoubtedly it was two points dropped for the Blues against Chelsea, pushing them down to the lowest position in the table all season, eighth, they were still only four points behind new League leaders, Liverpool.

On the injury front, Dave Watson played in a reserve game against Blackburn without suffering any ill-effects while Pat van den Hauwe had started light training after overcoming his blood disorder.

Leicester had done the double over Everton during the previous campaign, winning 3-1 at Filbert Street on the opening day of the season and beating the Blues 2-1 at Goodison.

But, since then, boss Gordon Milne had been made general manager with former Blue Bryan Hamilton recruited as team manager.

Hamilton is most remembered by Evertonians as the player whose 'goal' referee Clive Thomas controversially disallowed in the 1977 FA Cup semi-final against Liverpool.

Howard Kendall pushed Adrian Heath up front to partner Graeme Sharp and the moved paid off with Inchy opening the scoring. The visitors then needed Neville Southall to keep Leicester out before Kevin Sheedy sealed the points..

Trevor Steven had limped off near the end of the clash at Filbert Street and Kevin Ratcliffe needed stitches for a cut on his chin but both were expected to be in the line-up at Carrow Road for a tough-looking League Cup tie.

After coming through a reserve game successfully, ex-Norwich captain Dave Watson was added to the party which travelled to East Anglia, together with long-term injury victim Neil Pointon.

The Canaries were above Everton in the League table but they had no answer on the night to a storming performance from the Blues and, in particular, Kevin Sheedy. The Irish international opened the scoring to take his tally to the season to ten, more than he recorded in the whole of the previous campaign.

Graeme Sharp scored his first League goal from open play since September and Adrian Heath was again on target, while Trevor Steven converted a penalty which Inchy had earned. The four goals took the team's tally over four games in the competition to a remarkable seventeen

In the draw for the fifth round, Everton were paired with Liverpool, who beat Coventry City 3-1 in a replay at Anfield, all three goals being penalties scored by Jan Molby.

It's A Grand Old Team To Play For

Phil Jagielka joined Everton from Sheffield United for a transfer fee of £4 million in 2007 and served the club with distinction for twelve years, becoming club captain in 2013 following Phil Neville's retirement.

He scored the winning penalty for the Blues in the shootout at the end of the FA Cup semi-final against Manchester United in 2009, but less than a week later he suffered the agony of a ruptured anterior cruciate ligament which ruled him out of the Final against Chelsea. Jagielka scored nineteen goals for the club, his most spectacular being against Liverpool in September 2014, , a 30-yard, injury-time half-volley equaliser at the Kop end of Anfield. With first-team opportunities increasingly limited under manager Marco Silva, he left Everton to re-join the Blades in the summer of 2019 after 386 appearances for the Blues.

November 1986

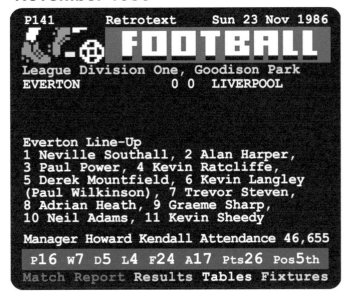

Since beating Liverpool at Anfield back in February in what appeared at the time to be a decisive victory in the title race, Everton had played their rivals from across the park four times without winning.

Kenny Dalglish's side came out on top in the FA Cup Final, the Charity Shield encounter finished all-square and in the two-legged Super Cup Final the Blues were hammered 7-2 on aggregate, with Ian Rush scoring eight goals altogether.

This match was broadcast live on television but was not the most entertaining of games though there were two major talking points which occurred within the space of a couple of minutes midway through the first-half.

First, that man again, Ian Rush, turned Derek Mountfield and put the ball in the back of net only for referee George Courtney to disallow the 'goal' for a foul. Then, Adrian Heath was upended in the area by Mark Lawrenson but referee Courtney waved away appeals for a penalty.

In the TV studio, Jimmy Hill felt the referee was right with the Rush decision but wrong not to award a penalty. Recently retired West Ham and England star Trevor Brooking, though, believed the referee had got it wrong on both counts.

Kevin Langley had done a terrific job since the start of the season as the Blues battled an enormous injury crisis. He had made the step up from playing for third division Wigan Athletic seamlessly and played in every League game so far in the season.

But Howard Kendall felt in the goalless draw with Liverpool that his form was dipping and so opted to leave the midfielder out of the side for the trip to Maine Road.

He was replaced with ex-City player Paul Power allowing Neil Pointon to return at left-back after his long absence.

Having taken a fifth minute lead through Adrian Heath, the visitors dominated the first-half but were pegged back before the break against the run of play.

After weathering a City barrage early in the second period, the Blues went ahead through Power but the player did not celebrate the goal back on his old stomping ground.

Chances at both ends followed before Inchy secured the points with his fourth goal in four games.

The victory moved Everton into fourth place in the table, five points behind new leaders Arsenal, who beat Aston Villa 4-0 at Villa Park.

If You Know Your History

Everton made a poor start to the 2010-11 season and at the end of September were bottom of the table with 3 points from 6 games. The Blues were unbeaten in October, though, registering three wins and a draw, including this victory over Roy Hodgson's Liverpool.

The Blues finished the campaign in a solid seventh spot but there was to be disappointment in the FA Cup. In the fourth round, after a 1-1 draw at Goodison with Carlo Ancelotti's Chelsea, Leighton Baines struck a superb freekick in the dying seconds of the replay at Stamford Bridge to force a penalty shootout which the Blues won 4-3. Sadly, in the next round, Everton slumped to a shock 1-0 home defeat by Championship side Reading to exit the competition.

December 1986

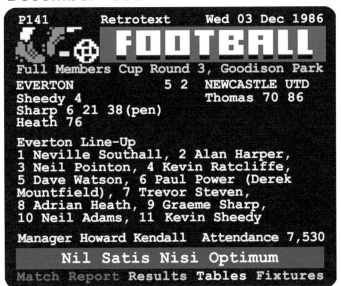

P141	Retrotext	Wed 03 Dec 1986

FOOTBALL

Full Members Cup Round 3, Goodison Park
EVERTON   5 2   NEWCASTLE UTD
Sheedy 4   Thomas 70 86
Sharp 6 21 38(pen)
Heath 76

Everton Line-Up
1 Neville Southall, 2 Alan Harper,
3 Neil Pointon, 4 Kevin Ratcliffe,
5 Dave Watson, 6 Paul Power (Derek
Mountfield), 7 Trevor Steven,
8 Adrian Heath, 9 Graeme Sharp,
10 Neil Adams, 11 Kevin Sheedy

Manager Howard Kendall Attendance 7,530

Nil Satis Nisi Optimum

Match Report Results Tables Fixtures

P141	Retrotext	Sat 06 Dec 1986

FOOTBALL

League Division One, Goodison Park
EVERTON   4 0   NORWICH CITY
Power 18
Steven 28(pen)
Pointon 78
Heath 89
Everton Line-Up
1 Neville Southall, 2 Gary Stevens,
3 Neil Pointon, 4 Kevin Ratcliffe,
5 Dave Watson, 6 Paul Power,
7 Trevor Steven, 8 Adrian Heath,
9 Graeme Sharp (Paul Wilkinson),
10 Alan Harper, 11 Kevin Sheedy
Manager Howard Kendall Attendance 26,755

P18 w9 D5 L4 F31 A18 Pts32 Pos3rd

Match Report Results Tables Fixtures

In the programme for this match, there was a very helpful section for Everton fans entitled 'Introducing The Full Members' Cup'.

The name of the competition derived from the fact that it was open to Full Members of the Football League, those from the First and Second Divisions. The Associate Members (from the Third and Fourth Divisions) competed for the Freight Rover Trophy.

The competition had started the previous season but excluded the six clubs that would have been playing in Europe if the Heysel ban was not in place as those took part in the Screen Sport Super Cup.

A crowd of over 68,000 watched the final at Wembley, where Chelsea beat Manchester City 5-4 in a thrilling encounter. Recent Blues' purchase Paul Power was captain of City that day, as he had been in the famous 1981 FA Cup Final won by the wonder goal of Tottenham's Ricky Villa.

The first round was solely for Second Division clubs who were joined in the second round by seven First Division teams. The winners of those ties advanced to this third round stage where they were joined by the highest-placed teams in the top division who had accepted the invitation to take part.

As convincing winners on the night, the Blues would now meet Charlton Athletic in the quarter-final.

The attendance at Goodison on Wednesday was the lowest-ever for a first-team match at the ground but the hardy souls who braved the rain were treated to a superb display by the Blues, crowned off by Graeme Sharp's first hat-trick for the club.

Though Derek Mountfield had performed well in his absence, Dave Watson was restored to the side against Newcastle and he retained his place for the weekend game against Norwich.

Also in the line-up and making his first appearance of the season was Gary Stevens, who had been involved in a reserve game at Newcastle United on Thursday evening together with Peter Reid. Howard Kendall travelled to St James' Park to watch the match, which the Blues won 2-1.

Paul Power had been pushed into midfield against his old club Manchester City the week before, scoring one of the goals, and he hit the back of the net once more. Trevor Steven made it 2-0 from the penalty spot before Neil Pointon scored his first goal for the club since his move from Scunthorpe.

The fourth goal was a gem, with Kevin Sheedy scooping the ball over the visitors' defence and Adrian Heath smashing it home on the volley.

If You Know Your History

After David Moyes left Everton to follow in the footsteps of Sir Alex Ferguson at Old Trafford at the end of the 2012-13 season, chairman Bill Kenwright appointed Roberto Martinez as the new Blues' boss. Martinez had just won the FA Cup with Wigan and, on the road to Wembley, the Latics had beaten Everton 3-0 at Goodison in the quarter-finals.

The Spaniard's attacking brand of football made the Blues attractive to watch and in his first season the club finished fifth, qualifying for the Europa League. But in the next two campaigns the team's form became inconsistent and, despite reaching the semi-finals of both the FA Cup and League Cup, Martinez was sacked in May 2016.

P141	Retrotext	Sat 23 Nov 2013

FOOTBALL

FA Premier League, Goodison Park
EVERTON   3 3   LIVERPOOL
Mirallas 8   Coutinho 5
Lukaku 72 82   Suarez 19
              Sturridge 89
Everton Line-Up
24 Tim Howard, 23 Seamus Coleman,
3 Leighton Baines(10 Gerard Deulofeu)
18 Gareth Barry, 15 Sylvain Distin,
6 Phil Jagielka, 20 Ross Barkley,
16 James McCarthy, 17 Romelu Lukaku,
11 Kevin Mirallas(21 Leon Osman),
22 Steven Pienaar(26 John Stones)
Manager Roberto Martinez
Attendance 39,576

Nil Satis Nisi Optimum

Match Report Results Tables Fixtures

December 1986

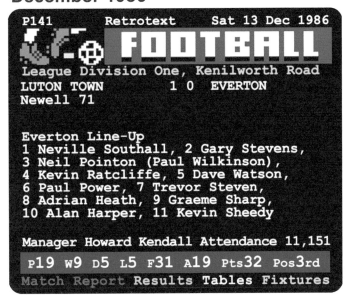

```
P141    Retrotext    Sat 13 Dec 1986
FOOTBALL
League Division One, Kenilworth Road
LUTON TOWN        1  0   EVERTON
Newell 71


Everton Line-Up
1 Neville Southall, 2 Gary Stevens,
3 Neil Pointon (Paul Wilkinson),
4 Kevin Ratcliffe, 5 Dave Watson,
6 Paul Power, 7 Trevor Steven,
8 Adrian Heath, 9 Graeme Sharp,
10 Alan Harper, 11 Kevin Sheedy

Manager Howard Kendall Attendance 11,151
P19 W9 D5 L5 F31 A19 Pts32 Pos3rd
Match Report  Results Tables Fixtures
```

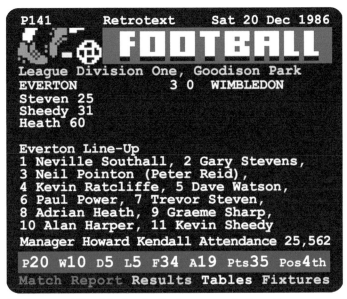

```
P141    Retrotext    Sat 20 Dec 1986
FOOTBALL
League Division One, Goodison Park
EVERTON          3  0   WIMBLEDON
Steven 25
Sheedy 31
Heath 60

Everton Line-Up
1 Neville Southall, 2 Gary Stevens,
3 Neil Pointon (Peter Reid),
4 Kevin Ratcliffe, 5 Dave Watson,
6 Paul Power, 7 Trevor Steven,
8 Adrian Heath, 9 Graeme Sharp,
10 Alan Harper, 11 Kevin Sheedy
Manager Howard Kendall Attendance 25,562
P20 W10 D5 L5 F34 A19 Pts35 Pos4th
Match Report  Results Tables Fixtures
```

On the Monday after the Norwich game, the draw was made for the third round of the FA Cup with Everton aiming to make it to the Final for the fourth year in a row. The Blues were given a home tie with Southampton, reviving memories of the dramatic semi-final win in this competition in 1984.

Holders Liverpool were drawn away to Luton Town, who had been permitted to take part in the FA Cup despite their ban on away supporters which had caused them to be barred from the League Cup.

In the run-up to Everton's game at the weekend on the dreaded plastic pitch at Kenilworth Road, fans were told in no uncertain terms not to waste their time and money travelling south as they would not be permitted into the ground.

Howard Kendall believed that it was the defeat at Luton on the run-in to the title last season which cost his side the championship, more so than the loss to Oxford United. But there was more disappointment for the Blues as the home side took all the points courtesy of scouser Mike Newell, who would sign for Everton in 1989.

It was the first defeat in eight matches for Kendall's men but they would now embark on a brilliant run which would see them win seven games on the bounce.

This was Wimbledon's first game at Goodison since they were hammered 8-0 in a League Cup tie in 1978 when they were in the bottom tier of English football. Bob Latchford scored five that night, with Martin Dobson grabbing a hat-trick.

Before it, Howard Kendall had agreed that unsettled goalkeeper Bobby Mimms could join Sunderland on a month's loan but with the proviso he could be recalled immediately if Neville Southall picked up an injury. Mike Stowell would take his place for the reserve matches.

On the injury front, Paul Bracewell suffered a setback on his road to recovery from the injury to the top of his foot which occurred on the first day of the year as surgery was required to release a tendon restricting his movement.

His midfield partner, Peter Reid, was closing in on his return after another successful reserve outing and playing for an England XI to mark the re-opening of Bradford's Valley Parade ground following the devastating fire in May 1985.

The midfield maestro was named on the bench and made his comeback after six months out with the Blues leading 3-0, receiving a tremendous ovation from the Goodison Park faithful.

It's A Grand Old Team To Support

I became a Blue on 28th April 1962, but things could have been different as the week beforehand my dad and I couldn't get into Anfield. The next Saturday, my dad made sure we had tickets for Everton versus Cardiff at Goodison Park. Harry Catterick's team won 8-3 and Alex Young became my hero.

I've seen League title wins in 1963, 1970, 1985 and 1987, FA Cups in 1966, 1984 and 1995 as well as European glory in Rotterdam. I feel so sorry for fans who are used to mediocrity and can only dream about a bright future. Right now our club is a mess, but I'll never give up on it.
Elton Welsby, Broadcaster

EVERTON
NIL SATIS
NISI OPTIMUM
GOODISON
PARK L4

December 1986

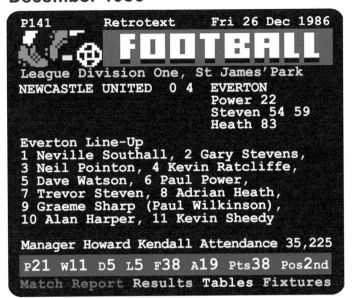

```
P141        Retrotext      Fri 26 Dec 1986
       FOOTBALL
League Division One, St James' Park
NEWCASTLE UNITED  0  4  EVERTON
                       Power 22
                       Steven 54 59
                       Heath 83

Everton Line-Up
1 Neville Southall, 2 Gary Stevens,
3 Neil Pointon, 4 Kevin Ratcliffe,
5 Dave Watson, 6 Paul Power,
7 Trevor Steven, 8 Adrian Heath,
9 Graeme Sharp (Paul Wilkinson),
10 Alan Harper, 11 Kevin Sheedy

Manager Howard Kendall Attendance 35,225
P21 W11 D5 L5 F38 A19 Pts38 Pos2nd
Match Report  Results Tables Fixtures
```

```
P141        Retrotext      Sun 28 Dec 1986
       FOOTBALL
League Division One, Goodison Park
EVERTON         5  1  LEICESTER CITY
Heath 15 74           Moran 81
Wilkinson 21
O'Neill 47(og)
Sheedy 87
Everton Line-Up
1 Neville Southall, 2 Gary Stevens,
3 Neil Pointon, 4 Kevin Ratcliffe,
5 Dave Watson, 6 Paul Power
(Warren Aspinall), 7 Trevor Steven,
8 Adrian Heath, 9 Paul Wilkinson,
10 Alan Harper, 11 Kevin Sheedy
Manager Howard Kendall Attendance 39,748
P22 W12 D5 L5 F43 A20 Pts41 Pos2nd
Match Report  Results Tables Fixtures
```

As the crucial festive period approached, when all Division One teams would play four games in little over a week, there was bad news for Peter Reid. He had reported stiffness in both thighs after his cameo appearance against Wimbledon and would not be risked against Newcastle United on Boxing Day.

Before the Christmas games, Everton stood fourth in the table, six points behind leaders Arsenal with twenty games played.

The Blues had battered the Magpies in the Full Members' Cup three weeks earlier but it was expected to be a much stiffer task in front of a full house at St James' Park.

After withstanding an early Geordie barrage, Paul Power continued his goalscoring run midway through the first half. In the second period, the home side again knocked on the door for ten minutes or so before two goals from Trevor Steven in the space of five minutes turned the match in the visitors' favour.

Adrian Heath rounded off a superb display from the team with his sixth strike in six games.

Howard Kendall was naturally delighted with the performance and singled out Trevor Steven and Kevin Sheedy who, he said, were playing as well as they had ever done for the club.

Leicester City had done Everton a favour on Boxing Day by holding League leaders Arsenal to a 1-1 draw, reducing the gap between the Blues and the Gunners to four points.

There was one enforced change for the home team, with Graeme Sharp missing out due to suspension, giving Paul Wilkinson an opportunity to shine.

Having played on the Friday, several teams were back in action on the Saturday but the Blues had an extra day to rest and they produced another sensational performance with Trevor Steven and Kevin Sheedy again exceptional.

Adrian Heath added two more goals to his ever-growing tally as the home side made it nine goals in two Christmas crackers. Inchy was named by Howard Kendall as his man of the match, with a special mention for Dave Watson who he felt had played his best game for the club.

Leicester manager Bryan Hamilton was full of praise for the victors, saying: "Everton are the best team we have played. It was men against boys. They were fantastic, different class."

Bookmakers William Hill had certainly been impressed with the Blues, making them 15/8 favourites to regain the League title.

If You Know Your History

In February 2016, Farhad Moshiri became Everton's new majority shareholder and when Roberto Martinez left the club at the end of the season, he made Southampton boss Ronald Koeman his number one target for the vacant manager's job.

Koeman enjoyed a solid first season in charge with the highlights being this victory over Pep Guardiola's Manchester City and a 6-3 thrashing of Bournemouth, Romelu Lukaku scoring four, as the Blues finished seventh. But the following campaign unravelled quickly and following a 5-2 home defeat by Arsenal, Koeman was sacked with David Unsworth installed as caretaker boss until Sam Allardyce was appointed at the end of November 2017.

```
P141        Retrotext      Sun 15 Jan 2017
       FOOTBALL
FA Premier League, Goodison Park
EVERTON         4  0  MAN CITY
Lukaku 34
Mirallas 47
Davies 79
Lookman 90+4
Everton Line-Up
1 Joel, 23 Seamus Coleman, 3 Leighton
Baines, 30 Mason Holgate, 25 Ramiro
Funes Mori, 5 Ashley Williams, 26 Tom
Davies, 18 Gareth Barry (16 James
McCarthy), 10 Romelu Lukaku,
8 Ross Barkley (31 Ademola Lookman),
11 Kevin Mirallas (2 Morgan Schneiderlin)
Manager Ronald Koeman Attendance 39,588
        Nil Satis Nisi Optimum
Match Report  Results Tables Fixtures
```

January 1987

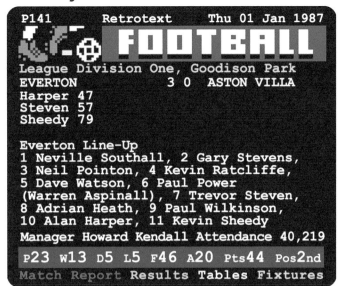

```
P141       Retrotext      Thu 01 Jan 1987
        FOOTBALL
League Division One, Goodison Park
EVERTON            3  0   ASTON VILLA
Harper 47
Steven 57
Sheedy 79

Everton Line-Up
1 Neville Southall, 2 Gary Stevens,
3 Neil Pointon, 4 Kevin Ratcliffe,
5 Dave Watson, 6 Paul Power
(Warren Aspinall), 7 Trevor Steven,
8 Adrian Heath, 9 Paul Wilkinson,
10 Alan Harper, 11 Kevin Sheedy
Manager Howard Kendall Attendance 40,219
P23 W13 D5 L5 F46 A20 Pts44 Pos2nd
Match Report Results Tables Fixtures
```

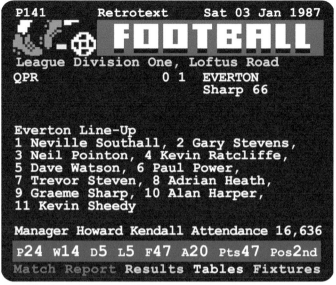

```
P141       Retrotext      Sat 03 Jan 1987
        FOOTBALL
League Division One, Loftus Road
QPR                0  1   EVERTON
                             Sharp 66

Everton Line-Up
1 Neville Southall, 2 Gary Stevens,
3 Neil Pointon, 4 Kevin Ratcliffe,
5 Dave Watson, 6 Paul Power,
7 Trevor Steven, 8 Adrian Heath,
9 Graeme Sharp, 10 Alan Harper,
11 Kevin Sheedy

Manager Howard Kendall Attendance 16,636
P24 W14 D5 L5 F47 A20 Pts47 Pos2nd
Match Report Results Tables Fixtures
```

Everton had scored an incredible twenty-one goals in their five matches during December and no less than twelve in their final three League games of 1986. The Blues kicked off 1987 in similar fashion with this emphatic victory over an Aston Villa side including Andy Gray, his first game back at Goodison since his shock transfer in 1985.

Alan Harper's speculative strike was deflected in just after half-time and ten minutes later Trevor Steven showed superb awareness to nip in between dithering defenders and slam home.

But the third goal was a thing of beauty, Steven fed Adrian Heath whose inch(y)-perfect cross was met on the volley by Kevin Sheedy's imperious left foot, taking his tally for the season to fourteen.

Inevitably, given the hectic nature of the holiday fixtures, the players picked up niggles and Howard Kendall recalled Bobby Mimms from his loan at Sunderland with doubts over Neville Southall's availability for the game at Loftus Road two days later. Paul Power was the other big doubt having been substituted in the New Year's Day match.

The Blues had taken maximum points from their three games over Christmas and New Year but they now faced a match on QPR's plastic pitch, a surface they had yet to win on.

Neville Southall and Paul Power both passed late fitness tests so the only change from the Villa game for the clash at Loftus Road was Graeme Sharp replacing Paul Wilkinson after serving a two-match suspension for accumulated bookings.

In a tight game, it was Sharp who produced a moment of brilliance midway through the second half to secure all three points for the visitors. The Scottish striker picked up the ball thirty yards out, danced through two tackles and picked his spot, a superb solo effort.

Everton were the only team in the top flight over the four-game holiday period to collect maximum points and this win reduced the gap with Arsenal at the top to a single point. But on Sunday, the Gunners beat north London rivals Tottenham at White Hart Lane in a televised match to increase that back to four.

Howard Kendall was always looking at players who he felt would improve his squad and he announced the signing of Ian Snodin from Leeds United for a fee of £840,000.

Snodin's former manager, Leeds legend Eddie Gray, described him as the most promising young player in English football. It was something of a coup for Kendall as the England Under-21 star had been offered better personal terms by Liverpool.

It's A Grand Old Team To Support

My Dad was a passionate season ticket holder in the Gwladys Street so when he took me, aged 9, to my first match on his birthday in 1965 I was immediately smitten, especially by the hat-trick from Fred Pickering who became my first hero. I recall fondly the 1970 team and going on the pitch after they clinched the League title. Ball and Harvey were brilliant to watch but my hero was always Howard Kendall. He had everything - tenacious yet cultured, the perfect midfielder.

When my Dad died, I was compelled to go to Goodison to support the Blues on his behalf and, like most, will miss the place, but I'm also desperate for the club to restore its reputation and its rightful place at the top of English football. As another Croxteth lad once said: Once a Blue, Always a Blue!! Cliff Woof, NewmarketRacingClub.com

EVERTON
NIL SATIS
NISI OPTIMUM
GOODISON
PARK L4

January 1987

```
P141      Retrotext      Sat 10 Jan 1987
      FOOTBALL
FA Cup 3rd Round, Goodison Park
EVERTON          2  1    SOUTHAMPTON
Sharp 36 67               Hobson 62


Everton Line-Up
1 Neville Southall, 2 Gary Stevens,
3 Neil Pointon, 4 Kevin Ratcliffe,
5 Dave Watson, 6 Paul Power,
7 Trevor Steven, 8 Adrian Heath,
9 Graeme Sharp, 10  Alan Harper,
11 Kevin Sheedy

Manager Howard Kendall Attendance 32,320
       Nil Satis Nisi Optimum
Match Report  Results Tables Fixtures
```

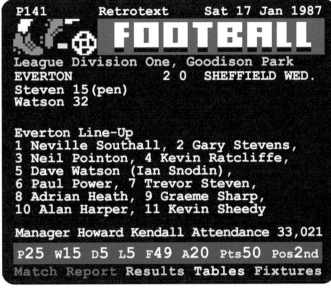

```
P141      Retrotext      Sat 17 Jan 1987
      FOOTBALL
League Division One, Goodison Park
EVERTON          2  0    SHEFFIELD WED.
Steven 15(pen)
Watson 32

Everton Line-Up
1 Neville Southall, 2 Gary Stevens,
3 Neil Pointon, 4 Kevin Ratcliffe,
5 Dave Watson (Ian Snodin),
6 Paul Power, 7 Trevor Steven,
8 Adrian Heath, 9 Graeme Sharp,
10 Alan Harper, 11 Kevin Sheedy

Manager Howard Kendall Attendance 33,021
P25 W15 D5 L5 F49 A20 Pts50 Pos2nd
Match Report  Results Tables Fixtures
```

New signing Ian Snodin was ineligible for this FA Cup third round tie with Southampton, which inevitably brought back memories of the dramatic 1984 semi-final with the Saints at Highbury.

As the Blues embarked on what fans hoped would be a record fourth successive appearance in the Final, in his programme notes Howard Kendall, who had been named the Manager of the Month for December, was in a reflective mood:

"When we came away from Wembley last May, no-one could have guessed that three members of that team would not play a full League game by the time this season's competition got under way. Pat van den Hauwe is now back in full training and Peter Reid was able to do some light ball work this week, but we are having to take things carefully with Paul Bracewell at the moment."

Southampton lined up with five at the back and proved difficult to break down. But Graeme Sharp was full of confidence after his wonderful solo goal at QPR and he broke the deadlock after seizing on indecision in the visitors' defence.

Gordon Hobson levelled the match up but five minutes later Kevin Sheedy's pinpoint cross was headed into the Gwladys Street net by Sharp, his third goal in two games.

In Monday afternoon's fourth round draw, the Blues were paired with the winners of the Oldham Athletic versus Bradford City replay which had finished 1-1 on Saturday. It was Bradford who came out on top in that match, winning 5-1, to set up a tricky tie for the Blues at the newly re-opened Valley Parade ground.

Over a year after he was first injured, Paul Bracewell was no closer to a return to action and the club sent him to a London clinic where it was decided he needed a further operation.

Wintry weather meant that Sheffield Wednesday travelled early to Merseyside and stayed overnight rather than making the journey on Saturday. Glynn Snodin was in Wednesday's team but his brother Ian had to settle for a place on Everton's bench.

A handball in the area by Wednesday centre-forward Lee Chapman gave Trevor Steven the chance to put the Blues ahead from the spot and he took it. Just after the half-hour mark, Dave Watson scored his first goal for the club, a header at the Park End of the ground, but he had to be replaced at half-time by new boy Snodin.

Arsenal drew 0-0 at home to Coventry on the Sunday so the gap between the top two was now down to two points.

It's A Grand Old Team To Play For

Kirkby-born Leighton Baines was on Everton's books as a youngster but found his first taste of League action at Wigan Athletic, where he made his debut as a seventeen-year-old in 2002. He became an integral part of the side manager Paul Jewell took from Division Two to the Premier League and in the summer of 2007, he joined Everton for a fee of five million pounds.

Baines struck up a brilliant left-wing partnership with Steven Pienaar and throughout his career regularly contributed goals as well as assists. He played every game of the 2010-11 and 2012-13 campaigns, scoring seven times in each and being voted by supporters as the Player of the Season. In 2012 and 2013, Baines was also named in the PFA Premier League Team of the Year. He retired in the summer of 2020 after making 420 appearances and scoring 39 goals.

January 1987

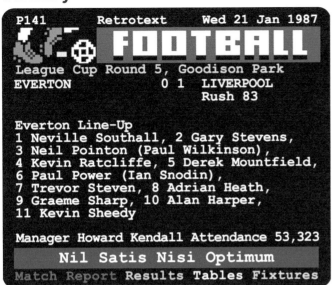

```
P141      Retrotext      Wed 21 Jan 1987
     FOOTBALL
League Cup Round 5, Goodison Park
EVERTON            0 1   LIVERPOOL
                         Rush 83

Everton Line-Up
1 Neville Southall, 2 Gary Stevens,
3 Neil Pointon (Paul Wilkinson),
4 Kevin Ratcliffe, 5 Derek Mountfield,
6 Paul Power (Ian Snodin),
7 Trevor Steven, 8 Adrian Heath,
9 Graeme Sharp, 10 Alan Harper,
11 Kevin Sheedy

Manager Howard Kendall Attendance 53,323
     Nil Satis Nisi Optimum
Match Report Results Tables Fixtures
```

```
P141      Retrotext      Sun 25 Jan 1987
     FOOTBALL
League Division One, City Ground
NOTT'M FOREST      1 0   EVERTON
Webb 25

Everton Line-Up
1 Neville Southall, 2 Gary Stevens,
3 Paul Power (Neil Pointon),
4 Kevin Ratcliffe, 5 Derek Mountfield,
6 Ian Snodin, 7 Trevor Steven,
8 Adrian Heath, 9 Paul Wilkinson,
10 Alan Harper, 11 Kevin Sheedy

Manager Howard Kendall Attendance 17,009
P26 W15 D5 L6 F49 A21 Pts50 Pos2nd
Match Report Results Tables Fixtures
```

The Blues had won seven games on the bounce and coming into yet another game against Liverpool, the players were confident of progressing to the semi-finals of the League Cup.

Dave Watson was ruled out of the line-up after being forced to leave the field on Saturday with a knee injury, but that gave a rare opportunity in this season for crowd favourite Derek Mountfield to make a start.

The first major talking point of the match was a tackle by Gary Stevens on Jim Beglin which resulted in a broken leg for the Liverpool defender.

The incident ignited strong passions on both sides, with the Reds adamant that Stevens had gone over the top.

But when tempers had calmed down after the match, it was agreed that Stevens was not the type of player to intentionally injure an opponent and he himself was sick at the extent of Beglin's injury.

In a match of few chances, Ian Rush was once again the scourge of Everton with a clinical finish just when the match looked to be heading for a replay. In five matches against their fierce local rivals this season, the Blues had now drawn two and lost three.

Dave Watson's name was again missing from the team sheet for the televised clash with Nottingham Forest as the knee injury he picked up against Sheffield Wednesday was responding more slowly to treatment than expected.

The injured Graeme Sharp was replaced by Paul Wilkinson and Ian Snodin came in for his full debut, with Paul Power moving to left-back from the midfield role where he had performed brilliantly.

Peter Reid and Pat van den Hauwe had both successfully completed a ninety-minute run-out for the reserves on Thursday evening, but Howard Kendall deemed they were not quite ready for a return to the first team.

The visitors failed to take their chances, most notably when Adrian Heath hit the post and Derek Mountfield missed with a free header, and it was Neil Webb's strike which ultimately condemned the Blues to a first League defeat since mid-December.

Fortunately, leaders Arsenal had been beaten 2-0 by Manchester United on Saturday so the gap between the top two remained at two points.

However, Liverpool had triumphed over Newcastle United by the same scoreline and now stood just two points back from the Blues in third spot.

If You Know Your History

Having served the club with distinction in two spells as a player, between 1994 and 1998 then 2000 to 2006, Duncan Ferguson was given the role of caretaker manager in December 2019 after Marco Silva was sacked following a 5-2 hammering by Liverpool at Anfield.

This was his first game in the hotseat when he was up against future Blues boss Frank Lampard and, as well as the victory, it is fondly remembered for Ferguson's celebration after the third goal, when he danced down the touchline and embraced one of the ballboys.

The big Scot was unbeaten in his four games in charge and became assistant to Carlo Ancelotti when he was appointed later that month.

```
P141      Retrotext      Sat 07 Dec 2019
     FOOTBALL
FA Premier League, Goodison Park
EVERTON            3 1   CHELSEA
Richarlison 5            Kovacic 52
Calvert-Lewin 49 84

Everton Line-Up
1 Jordan Pickford, 19 Djibril Sidibé,
5 Michael Keane, 2 Mason Holgate,
12 Lucas Digne (Leighton Baines 82),
11 Theo Walcott (Bernard 86),
18 Morgan Schneiderlin, 10 Gylfi
Sigurdsson, 17 Alex Iwobi, 9 Dominic
Calvert-Lewin, 7 Richarlison
(Tom Davies 71)
Manager Duncan Ferguson    Att 39,114
     Nil Satis Nisi Optimum
Match Report Results Tables Fixtures
```

January 1987

```
P141      Retrotext      Sat 31 Jan 1987
          FOOTBALL
FA Cup 4th Round, Valley Parade
BRADFORD CITY     0  1   EVERTON
                           Snodin 51


Everton Line-Up
1 Neville Southall, 2 Gary Stevens,
3 Pat Van Den Hauwe, 4 Kevin Ratcliffe
5 Dave Watson, 6 Peter Reid,
7 Trevor Steven, 8 Adrian Heath,
9 Paul Wilkinson, 10 Ian Snodin,
11 Paul Power

Manager Howard Kendall Attendance 15,519
       Nil Satis Nisi Optimum
Match Report Results Tables Fixtures
```

From The Teletext Archive

```
P303 CEEFAX 303  Tue 26 Dec  18:18/19
                                    3/5
BBC     FOOTBALL: PREMIERSHIP
                  REVIEW
EVERTON 4-0 MIDDLESBROUGH
Boro crashed to their heaviest defeat
of the season as Graeme Stuart struck
either side of the break for Everton.

Defender Craig Short opened the scoring
on 10 minutes with a powerful header
from Anders Limpar's cross - his first
goal since arriving at Goodison Park.

Nevill Southall did well to save a Neil
Cox header before Stuart steered in the
second following a defensive mistake by
Middlesbrough's Jamie Pollock.

Stuart pounced on a Gary Walsh error
for 3-0 and Andrei Kancheslkis finished
well to complete the rout.

PremTeams  PremTable  Prem Res Round-up
```

Just when it appeared that there was light at the end of the injury tunnel, with long-term absentees Peter Reid and Pat van den Hauwe in contention for the FA Cup tie at Bradford, came the news that leading scorer Kevin Sheedy required surgery on his knee and would be out for six weeks.

Peter Reid had played at Valley Parade just before Christmas for Bobby Robson's England XI in a match commemorating the re-opening of the ground following the dreadful fire in May 1985.

He was delighted to be given the nod to start, along with 'Psycho Pat' and Dave Watson, but Graeme Sharp was sidelined once again.

The match was given the go-ahead but the pitch was rock hard and the home side, roared on by a full house, adapted better to it.

However, it was the visitors who got the winner just after the break, Ian Snodin heading home Adrian Heath's cross, his first goal for the club, to set up a fifth round tie at Plough Lane against Wimbledon.

With Dave Watson being restored to the starting line-up at his expense, Derek Mountfield expressed his frustration at being left out of the team by asking for a transfer but Howard Kendall rejected his request.

This is an original Ceefax page recovered from an old VHS recording.

A thumping 4-0 win for Joe Royle's side on Boxing Day in 1995 against Bryan Robson's Middlesbrough. It was a much-improved performance by the Blues after they lost 2-1 at Coventry a few days before and they completed their Christmas schedule of matches with a 2-0 win at home to Leeds despite having Dave Watson sent off after eighteen minutes.

Everton continued to improve in the second-half of the season, eventually finishing in sixth spot and just being pipped for a UEFA Cup place by Arsenal.

It's A Grand Old Team To Play For

Duncan Ferguson joined Everton on loan in October 1994 with the Blues rock-bottom of the Premier League having accrued just three points from eight games.

When manager Mike Walker was sacked the following month, Joe Royle was appointed boss and in his first game in charge Everton beat Liverpool 2-0 with Ferguson scoring his first goal for the club, a towering header from a pinpoint Andy Hinchcliffe corner.

With Duncan's initial loan spell due to run out on December 28th and rumours that Leeds and Arsenal were waiting to step in, discussions over his permanent signing between Everton chairman Peter Johnson and his Rangers counterpart David Murray dragged on. Eventually, a £4 million fee was agreed and the signing made permanent with Duncan following his manager and other great names in wearing the famous Number 9 shirt.

February 1987

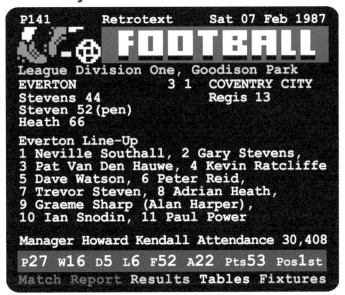

P141   Retrotext   Sat 07 Feb 1987

FOOTBALL

League Division One, Goodison Park
EVERTON   3   1   COVENTRY CITY
Stevens 44   Regis 13
Steven 52(pen)
Heath 66

Everton Line-Up
1 Neville Southall, 2 Gary Stevens,
3 Pat Van Den Hauwe, 4 Kevin Ratcliffe
5 Dave Watson, 6 Peter Reid,
7 Trevor Steven, 8 Adrian Heath,
9 Graeme Sharp (Alan Harper),
10 Ian Snodin, 11 Paul Power

Manager Howard Kendall Attendance 30,408

P27 w16 D5 L6 F52 A22 Pts53 Pos1st

Match Report Results Tables Fixtures

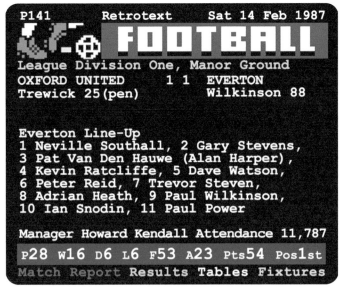

P141   Retrotext   Sat 14 Feb 1987

FOOTBALL

League Division One, Manor Ground
OXFORD UNITED   1   1   EVERTON
Trewick 25(pen)   Wilkinson 88

Everton Line-Up
1 Neville Southall, 2 Gary Stevens,
3 Pat Van Den Hauwe (Alan Harper),
4 Kevin Ratcliffe, 5 Dave Watson,
6 Peter Reid, 7 Trevor Steven,
8 Adrian Heath, 9 Paul Wilkinson,
10 Ian Snodin, 11 Paul Power

Manager Howard Kendall Attendance 11,787

P28 w16 D6 L6 F53 A23 Pts54 Pos1st

Match Report Results Tables Fixtures

Everton chairman Philip Carter, who was also President of the Football League, was seeking to work with UEFA to end the indefinite ban imposed on English clubs after the Heysel disaster.

But Carter told the Liverpool Echo: "It's not just a question of going back, we must have safeguards. We would have to be convinced that if we were re-admitted, the standard and condition of the stadia we played in were suitable and acceptable."

Though Liverpool fans instigated the mayhem which led to thirty-nine deaths, many people believed the stadium's crumbling infrastructure, in conjunction with poor segregation and inadequate policing, also played a part in the tragedy.

With League leaders Arsenal involved in a Littlewoods Cup semi-final against Tottenham on Sunday, Everton would have the opportunity to go top of the Division One table for the first time this season with victory over Coventry City.

Graeme Sharp returned to the starting line-up but the Blues fell behind early on.

Gary Stevens' deflected shot levelled the game up and Trevor Steven put the home side ahead from the penalty spot before a terrific header from Adrian Heath secured all three points and top spot.

Ahead of the weekend game with Oxford United, Everton travelled to France to play a prestige friendly against French Cup holders, Bordeaux. The match was aimed at building bridges in Europe after the Heysel disaster in anticipation of English clubs once again being permitted to play there.

Bordeaux, French champions in 1984 and 1985 and quarter-finalists in this season's European Cup-Winners' Cup, took the lead but a deflected Adrian Heath shot and a cracking twenty-five yard effort from Ian Snodin gave Howard Kendall's side an impressive victory.

Visits to the Manor Ground evoked bitter-sweet memories for Evertonians. There was the high-point of January 1984 when Inchy's goal gave Everton's revival even more momentum, and the low-point of April 1986 when a relegation threatened Oxford earned a shock win which dealt a mortal blow to the Blues' title hopes.

Paul Wilkinson had impressed Howard Kendall in midweek when up against Bordeaux's French international defender Patrick Battiston. He came into the starting line-up in place of the injured Graeme Sharp. The Blues trailed for most of the match but it was Wilkinson who seized his moment to score a deserved equaliser near the end.

It's A Grand Old Team To Support

It's pushing it to call me a "massive Evertonian", but that's how I, a latecomer to the Blues family, was once described in *The Evertonian* when talking horseracing with defender Alan Stubbs. While I was too chuffed to be embarrassed, Mark Sharman, a BBC colleague who'd got me hooked on a visit to Goodison around 2002, and whose support really is colossal, still splutters at the memory.

My special moment came in 2009, in the Cup replay against Liverpool when experiencing Goodison in ecstasy after Dan Gosling scored the goal that TV viewers missed because of the infamous tic tac advert - "the City's all ours" still rings in my ears today.
Cornelius Lysaght, Broadcaster

EVERTON NIL SATIS NISI OPTIMUM GOODISON PARK L4

February 1987

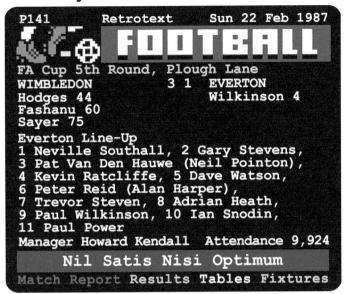

```
P141    Retrotext    Sun 22 Feb 1987
FOOTBALL
FA Cup 5th Round, Plough Lane
WIMBLEDON          3 1   EVERTON
Hodges 44                Wilkinson 4
Fashanu 60
Sayer 75
Everton Line-Up
1 Neville Southall, 2 Gary Stevens,
3 Pat Van Den Hauwe (Neil Pointon),
4 Kevin Ratcliffe, 5 Dave Watson,
6 Peter Reid (Alan Harper),
7 Trevor Steven, 8 Adrian Heath,
9 Paul Wilkinson, 10 Ian Snodin,
11 Paul Power
Manager Howard Kendall  Attendance 9,924
       Nil Satis Nisi Optimum
Match Report  Results Tables Fixtures
```

```
P141    Retrotext    Sat 28 Feb 1987
FOOTBALL
League Division One, Old Trafford
MANCHESTER UTD     0 0   EVERTON

Everton Line-Up
1 Neville Southall, 2 Gary Stevens,
3 Pat Van Den Hauwe,4 Kevin Ratcliffe,
5 Dave Watson, 6 Peter Reid
(Paul Wilkinson), 7 Trevor Steven,
8 Alan Harper, 9 Adrian Heath,
10 Ian Snodin, 11 Paul Power

Manager Howard Kendall Attendance 47,421
P29 W16 D7 L6 F53 A23 Pts55 Pos1st
Match Report  Results Tables Fixtures
```

In May 1981, when Howard Kendall succeeded Gordon Lee as Everton manager, Wimbledon earned promotion from the bottom tier of the Football League to Division Three.

In less than six years, the Dons, under the astute management of Dave Bassett, achieved the remarkable feat of reaching the top tier of the football pyramid, Division One.

In fact, after four games of the current season, the team from Plough Lane stood proudly on top of the table, until they were knocked off their perch after a 2-1 win by Everton. The Blues also came out on top when the teams met at Goodison Park in December, winning 3-0, the first of seven straight wins.

So, in front of the nation live on BBC television, Howard Kendall's team were firm favourites to win this tie and continue the pursuit of a record-breaking fourth consecutive appearance in an FA Cup Final.

Paul Wilkinson put the visitors ahead but the home side were awarded a penalty on the stroke of half-time and though Neville Southall saved the spot kick, the ball fell to Glynn Hodges who made it 1-1. The Blues were largely overpowered by the direct play of Bassett's boys in the second period and it was they who booked their place in the quarter-final.

On the transfer front, Aston Villa signed Warren Aspinall from Everton for a fee of £200,000 which could rise to £300,000. Aspinall had not made the anticipated first-team breakthrough with the Blues after joining from Wigan for £120,000.

With concern growing over the extent of Graeme Sharp's achilles injury, there was speculation that Howard Kendall would move for Birmingham striker Wayne Clarke, who had scored sixteen goals in twenty-four League games, to bolster the club's attack in the final third of the season.

There was good news in midweek for the Blues as Arsenal could only draw their game in hand on the League leaders at Oxford United, so Howard Kendall's side retained their place at the summit on goal difference.

Paul Wilkinson was surprisingly left on the bench at Old Trafford, with Kendall pairing Adrian Heath with Trevor Steven up front and bringing in Alan Harper. In a match of few chances, a draw was a fair result, but it allowed Liverpool to pull level on points with the Blues.

Arsenal were involved in the second leg of the Littlewoods Cup semi-final with Tottenham on Sunday, which they won 2-1 to make it 2-2 on aggregate, forcing a replay.

It's A Grand Old Team To Support

My favourite memory from Goodison was of a game that I went to with my dear departed Dad and fellow jockey, Sam Hitchcott, also a passionate Evertonian. Sam was driving but was done for speeding halfway up! The mood turned dramatically, though, when we got to Goodison as it always did!!

My good friend, Alan Stubbs, had left us tickets and he then proceeded to score a blockbuster from a free kick, a real rarity!! He nearly took the net off and I recall we celebrated long into the night in the Winslow!! Speeding ticket apart, it was just about the perfect day!! I will definitely miss Goodison Park but I am looking forward to a bright new era at Bramley Moore Dock.

Martin Dwyer, Derby-winning ex-jockey and Racing TV presenter

EVERTON
NIL SATIS
NISI OPTIMUM
GOODISON
PARK L4

March 1987

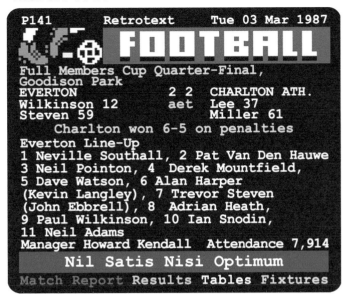

```
P141      Retrotext      Tue 03 Mar 1987
          FOOTBALL
Full Members Cup Quarter-Final,
Goodison Park
EVERTON          2 2   CHARLTON ATH.
Wilkinson 12     aet   Lee 37
Steven 59              Miller 61
        Charlton won 6-5 on penalties
Everton Line-Up
1 Neville Southall, 2 Pat Van Den Hauwe
3 Neil Pointon, 4 Derek Mountfield,
5 Dave Watson, 6 Alan Harper
(Kevin Langley), 7 Trevor Steven
(John Ebbrell), 8 Adrian Heath,
9 Paul Wilkinson, 10 Ian Snodin,
11 Neil Adams
Manager Howard Kendall  Attendance 7,914
        Nil Satis Nisi Optimum
Match Report Results Tables Fixtures
```

```
P141      Retrotext      Sun 08 Mar 1987
          FOOTBALL
League Division One, Vicarage Road
WATFORD          2 1   EVERTON
Blissett 67            Heath 36
Falco 85

Everton Line-Up
1 Neville Southall, 2 Gary Stevens,
3 Pat Van Den Hauwe (Paul Wilkinson),
4 Kevin Ratcliffe, 5 Dave Watson,
6 Peter Reid, 7 Trevor Steven,
8 Adrian Heath, 9 Wayne Clark,
10 Ian Snodin, 11 Paul Power

Manager Howard Kendall Attendance 14,035
P30 w16 D7 L7 F54 A25 Pts55 Pos2nd
Match Report Results Tables Fixtures
```

At the start of the week, Howard Kendall announced that Paul Bracewell would play no part in the club's title run-in. After a couple of operations had still not resolved the issues with his ankle, it was decided only a further period of complete rest could end the player's frustration at not having played since last year's FA Cup Final.

The quarter-final of the Full Members' Cup did not entice many fans to Goodison Park where a number of fringe players were given the opportunity to shine. Derek Mountfield played alongside the player keeping him out of first-team action, Dave Watson, while Neil Pointon was also handed a rare start.

The Blues were twice ahead and twice pegged back by the visitors resulting in an extra thirty minutes and then penalties. Neville Southall captained the side for the evening and not only did he save one of the penalties, he also scored one!

Neil Pointon was the unfortunate player to miss his penalty at the sudden death stage which allowed Charlton the chance to go through and they took it.

The rumours surrounding the interest in Wayne Clarke proved to be accurate as the Birmingham striker joined the club, together with his team-mate Stuart Storer, for a joint fee of £300,000.

After the Charlton game, Neville Southall complained of a sore knee so Howard Kendall recalled Bobby Mimms from his loan spell at Blackburn Rovers as a precaution.

Paul Wilkinson had become increasingly frustrated at not being able to claim a regular starting berth for Everton and was looking to move on after the Blues signed Wayne Clark.

Charlton had offered £300,000 for the striker, but he turned that opportunity down in anticipation of other clubs coming in for him.

For the televised game at Watford, who had Kevin Richardson in their line-up, Wilkinson again dropped down to the bench so Clark could make his debut. The title chasers led at the interval after Adrian Heath nodded home a Paul Power pull-back but the home side were the dominant force in the second-half.

Luther Blisset equalised and Mark Falco completed the comeback, a result which made it five games without a win for the Blues.

Arsenal had been beaten 1-0 at Chelsea on Saturday but Liverpool won 2-0 at home to Luton giving Kenny Dalglish's side a three-point advantage at the top of the table.

If You Know Your History

Marco Silva succeeded Sam Allardyce as Everton manager in the summer of 2018 and had an encouraging first season which featured a 4-0 win at Goodison Park over Manchester United. The second campaign was more difficult and a 5-2 defeat at Anfield in December 2019 saw Silva replaced by caretaker boss, Duncan Ferguson.

Managerial royalty in the form of Carlo Ancelotti then took the reins at Goodison and he steered the Blues through the COVID lockdown before being tempted back to Real Madrid. For reasons best known to Farhad Moshiri, ex-Liverpool boss Rafa Benitez was then made manager, lasting until January 2022 before being replaced by Frank Lampard who managed to help the Blues avoid relegation - just!

```
P141      Retrotext      Thu 19 May 2022
          FOOTBALL
FA Premier League, Goodison Park
EVERTON          3 2   CRYSTAL PALACE
Keane 54               Mateta 21
Richarlison 75         Ayew 36
Calvert-Lewin 85
Everton Line-Up
1 Jordan Pickford, 23 Seamus Coleman,
5 Michael Keane, 4 Mason Holgate,
17 Alex Iwobi, 16 Abdoulaye Doucouré,
21 André Gomes (Dele Alli 45),
19 Vitalii Mykolenko, 24 Anthony
Gordon (Demarai Gray 61),
7 Richarlison (Jonjoe Kenny 90+1),
9 Dominic Calvert-Lewin
Manager Frank Lampard Attendance 38,987
        Nil Satis Nisi Optimum
Match Report Results Tables Fixtures
```

March 1987

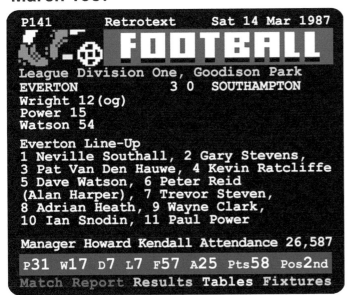

P141   Retrotext   Sat 14 Mar 1987

FOOTBALL

League Division One, Goodison Park
EVERTON   3 0   SOUTHAMPTON
Wright 12 (og)
Power 15
Watson 54

Everton Line-Up
1 Neville Southall, 2 Gary Stevens,
3 Pat Van Den Hauwe, 4 Kevin Ratcliffe
5 Dave Watson, 6 Peter Reid
(Alan Harper), 7 Trevor Steven,
8 Adrian Heath, 9 Wayne Clark,
10 Ian Snodin, 11 Paul Power

Manager Howard Kendall Attendance 26,587

P31 w17 D7 L7 F57 A25 Pts58 Pos2nd
Match Report Results Tables Fixtures

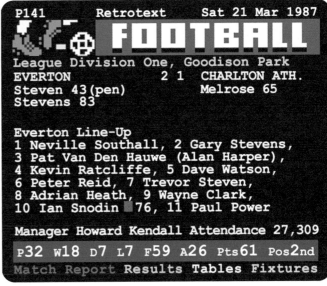

P141   Retrotext   Sat 21 Mar 1987

FOOTBALL

League Division One, Goodison Park
EVERTON   2 1   CHARLTON ATH.
Steven 43 (pen)   Melrose 65
Stevens 83

Everton Line-Up
1 Neville Southall, 2 Gary Stevens,
3 Pat Van Den Hauwe (Alan Harper),
4 Kevin Ratcliffe, 5 Dave Watson,
6 Peter Reid, 7 Trevor Steven,
8 Adrian Heath, 9 Wayne Clark,
10 Ian Snodin 76, 11 Paul Power

Manager Howard Kendall Attendance 27,309

P32 w18 D7 L7 F59 A26 Pts61 Pos2nd
Match Report Results Tables Fixtures

While Everton had a clear week before their next game against Southampton, title rivals Arsenal and Liverpool were meeting each other at Highbury in what was a dress rehearsal for the Littlewoods Cup Final in April.

Not surprisingly, it was Ian Rush who turned out to be the match winner with his 31st goal of the season. The result took Liverpool seven points clear of the Gunners and six points ahead of Everton, though they had played one game more.

But whichever team came out on top in the title race, they would not be able to compete in the European Cup, or any other UEFA competition, as the organisation's president Jacques George revealed that a committee had voted 8-3 against a return for English clubs next season.

Neville Southall was passed fit to play against the Saints but there was bad news for Graeme Sharp who would be out for three more weeks after having a minor operation.

The Blues got off to a great start when Mark Wright headed into his own net and with just fifteen minutes on the clock a shot from Paul Power somehow squirmed past Peter Shilton. Dave Watson made it 3-0 early in the second half and the home side were back to winning ways.

In his programme notes for this match, Howard Kendall addressed the issue of how a section of supporters were treating Dave Watson for coming into the team at the expense of fan favourite Derek Mountfield, particularly when his name was announced before the previous home game.

The manager said: "It cannot help Dave Watson if he feels he is not wanted here. I suppose the same people who voiced their dissatisfaction before the Southampton game were among those cheering when he scored.

If we are going to have a chance of winning the League, we have to do it together - players AND supporters."

Talking about the rivalry to the Liverpool Echo, Derek Mountfield said: "We are both professionals. Before every game I wish him all the best because we both believe it's an honour to play for Everton. That's the way it should be."

Liverpool had beaten QPR 2-1 in midweek to stand nine points ahead of the Blues coming into this match but having played two games more.

These three points against Charlton reduced the gap to six points and with the Reds losing at Tottenham on Sunday, that's how it stayed.

It's A Grand Old Team To Play For

Famously signed from Sligo Rovers for only £60,000 in January 2009, Seamus Coleman has enjoyed an amazing career both with Everton and the Republic Of Ireland. During his early days with the club, he was loaned out to Blackpool and, under manager Ian Holloway, helped the Seasiders gain promotion to the Premier League at the end of the 2009-10 season.

When back at Goodison, Coleman established himself as a key member of the team, scoring six goals during the 2013-14 campaign and being voted the club's Player of the Season as well as being named in the PFA's Premier League Team of the Year. He was made captain of his country in 2016 and became Everton's skipper in 2019 after Phil Jagielka's departure. In turbulent times for the Blues, he continues to be a shining light for the fans on and off the pitch.

March 1987

From The Teletext Archive

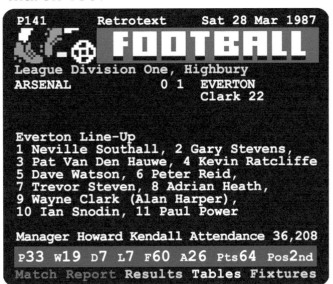

Ian Snodin's sending off against Charlton, for fighting with Andy Peake, who was also dismissed, meant he would miss games against Chelsea and West Ham.

Paul Wilkinson's two years at Everton came to end when he signed for Brian Clough's Nottingham Forest for a fee of £275,000. Howard Kendall sanctioned the move after receiving positive news on Graeme Sharp's injury situation.

The manager also cited the emergence of a young John Ebbrell for the reserves as the reason for allowing Kevin Langley to join Manchester City on loan until the end of the season, made permanent during the summer for a fee of £150,000.

A tight game at Highbury was settled midway through the first-half when goalkeeper John Lukic made a hash of a clearance which went straight to Wayne Clark thirty-five yards out. Clark showed supreme skill to lob the 'keeper and watch as the ball nestled in the back of the net. This defeat effectively killed off Arsenal's title challenge.

There was more good news for the Blues as there was a huge shock at Anfield, where Wimbledon had beaten Liverpool 2-1. The gap between the two Merseyside giants was now only three points but, crucially, Everton had two games in hand.

This is an original Ceefax page recovered from an old VHS recording.

It featured the team news on Christmas Day, 1998, for Everton's Boxing Day clash with Derby County which ended in a disappointing 0-0 draw that left both clubs in mid-table.

Walter Smith was now manager of Everton after being brought in by chairman Peter Johnson to replace Howard Kendall, whose third spell in charge at the club ended with the Blues only avoiding relegation on goal difference after a 1-1 draw with Coventry City on the last day of the season in May.

It's A Grand Old Team To Support

Fate decreed that I was born into a blue family, both sides, and resulted in an early baptism of attending matches. I have witnessed times good and bad, many players of both these iterations, yet can honestly state that my unswerving commitment has never been in question. Logically, this defies explanation but mine, our, relationship with this club is not logical, it is an emotional connection. One of enduring love.

Goodison Park has represented the touchstone of this link. Memories of family, friends, of some of the best times of my life, are coexistent with this building. Leaving it will break my heart but, as I replaced my family members, others will ultimately replace me and, hopefully, carry this club to a brighter future.

David Fehily

EVERTON
NIL SATIS
NISI OPTIMUM
GOODISON
PARK L4

April 1987

P141   Retrotext   Sat 04 Apr 1987
FOOTBALL
League Division One, Stamford Bridge
CHELSEA   1 2   EVERTON
Dixon 72   McLaughlin 23(og)
                             Harper 77

Everton Line-Up
1 Neville Southall, 2 Gary Stevens,
3 Paul Power, 4 Kevin Ratcliffe
5 Dave Watson, 6 Peter Reid,
7 Trevor Steven, 8 Adrian Heath,
9 Wayne Clark, 10 Alan Harper,
11 Kevin Sheedy (Neil Pointon)

Manager Howard Kendall Attendance 21,914

P34 W20 D7 L7 F62 A27 Pts67 Pos1st
Match Report Results Tables Fixtures

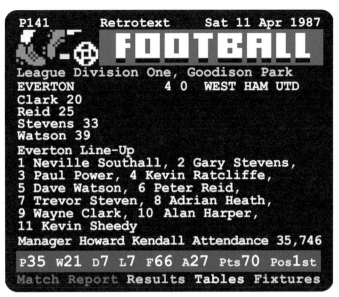

P141   Retrotext   Sat 11 Apr 1987
FOOTBALL
League Division One, Goodison Park
EVERTON   4 0   WEST HAM UTD
Clark 20
Reid 25
Stevens 33
Watson 39
Everton Line-Up
1 Neville Southall, 2 Gary Stevens,
3 Paul Power, 4 Kevin Ratcliffe,
5 Dave Watson, 6 Peter Reid,
7 Trevor Steven, 8 Adrian Heath,
9 Wayne Clark, 10 Alan Harper,
11 Kevin Sheedy
Manager Howard Kendall Attendance 35,746

P35 W21 D7 L7 F66 A27 Pts70 Pos1st
Match Report Results Tables Fixtures

In Grand National week, after the weekend's results, the bookmakers had slashed Everton's odds winning the title with Corals pricing the Blues and Liverpool as joint favourites at 10/11.

Kenny Dalglish's side would not be in League action as they faced Arsenal in the Littlewoods Cup Final on the Sunday.

During the week, Kevin Ratcliffe was on international duty with Wales and in celebrating his thirty-ninth cap, he equalled the record held by Alan Ball who notched up the same number during his career with the Blues. Pat van den Hauwe also played for Wales and picked up a knock which would rule him out at the weekend.

Alan Harper replaced the suspended Ian Snodin and Howard Kendall was able to welcome Kevin Sheedy back into the starting line-up after the Irish international confirmed his fitness after a ten-game absence with a couple of outings in the reserves. Paul Power moved to left-back in the absence of van den Hauwe.

The visitors took the lead through an own goal but Kerry Dixon equalised. Alan Harper then scored the most valuable goal of his Everton career, rifling home from twenty-five yards to take the Blues back to the top of the table.

Having lost top spot in Division One to Everton on the Saturday, Liverpool's miserable weekend was complete when they lost the Littlewoods Cup Final to Arsenal on the Sunday.

David Pleat's Tottenham Hotspur side could not be ruled out of the title race as they were in a sensational run of form. Back in December, Spurs were tenth in the table but they now stood third, still ten points behind the Blues but with two games in hand.

John Lyall's West Ham side included former Arsenal star Liam Brady, who returned to this country in March after playing his football in Italy for the previous six years.

But the Hammers were blown away by possibly Everton's best performance of the season as they scored four goals without reply in a one-side first-half. Wayne Clark started the ball rolling with his first goal on home soil, before Peter Reid and Gary Stevens fired in two spectacular strikes and Dave Watson got in on the act, too.

There was more good news after the match as Liverpool had been beaten 2-1 at Carrow Road by Norwich City. Howard Kendall's side now had a three point advantage at the top and still had a game in hand.

It's A Grand Old Team To Support

As a 10-year-old, I used to wash cars and cut privets and while I was doing the garden of a neighbour of ours, Mrs McKee, she asked if I wanted to go and watch Everton. She was a cleaner at Bellefield and had two tickets to see the reserves. Being the only Evertonian in a family of Reds (5 brothers and my father), I went on my own to watch the likes of Ronnie Goodlass coming through the ranks.

I progressed to going to first team games and my hero then and still today was Bob Latchford. In a period when we never won anything, Big Bob brought us something to cling on to and his 30 goals remains one of my most memorable moments. I've had so many fantastic times watching and working for Everton and I'm not sure how I'll cope when the last game at Goodison comes. Alan Myers, Broadcaster

EVERTON
NIL SATIS
NISI OPTIMUM
GOODISON
PARK L4

April 1987

```
P141        Retrotext       Sat 18 Apr 1987
      FOOTBALL
League Division One, Villa Park
ASTON VILLA        0  1    EVERTON
                           Sheedy 53


Everton Line-Up
1 Neville Southall, 2 Gary Stevens,
3 Paul Power, 4 Kevin Ratcliffe
5 Dave Watson, 6 Peter Reid,
7 Trevor Steven, 8 Adrian Heath,
9 Wayne Clark,  10 Ian Snodin,
11 Kevin Sheedy (Alan Harper)

Manager Howard Kendall Attendance 31,218

P36 W22 D7 L7 F67 A27 Pts73 Pos1st
Match Report Results Tables Fixtures
```

```
P141        Retrotext       Mon 20 Apr 1987
      FOOTBALL
League Division One, Goodison Park
EVERTON          3  0    NEWCASTLE UTD
Clark 48 81 89


Everton Line-Up
1 Neville Southall, 2 Gary Stevens,
3 Neil Pointon, 4 Kevin Ratcliffe,
5 Dave Watson, 6 Alan Harper,
7 Trevor Steven, 8 Adrian Heath,
9 Wayne Clark, 10 Ian Snodin,
11 Paul Power

Manager Howard Kendall Attendance 43,587
        Nil Satis Nisi Optimum
Match Report Results Tables Fixtures
```

Graeme Sharp and Pat van den Hauwe appeared in a strong reserve side, also featuring Ian Snodin and Derek Mountfield, against Newcastle United in midweek, aiming to prove their fitness for the clash with Aston Villa at the weekend.

However, Howard Kendall elected not to introduce the injured stars for the match at Villa Park, but he did put Ian Snodin back into starting line-up after his two-match suspension, with Alan Harper dropping down to the substitute's bench.

Andy Gray was in the home side's line-up, as was recent signing from the Blues, Warren Aspinall.

But neither player had much influence on the match which was settled by a sweet left-foot volley from Kevin Sheedy, to the delight of thousands of away fans inside the ground.

With Liverpool getting back to winning ways after a 3-0 victory over Nottingham Forest, there was no change between the top two.

Tottenham remained in third after narrowly beating Charlton, but after a midweek draw with Manchester City they were now nine points behind Everton with only one game in hand, though they had reached the FA Cup Final after beating Watford 4-1 in the semi-final.

On Easter Monday, there was a full fixture list in Division One. As well as Everton's home game with Newcastle, closest rivals Liverpool had a short trip down the motorway to play old foes Manchester United and outsiders for the title, Tottenham, faced a London derby at West Ham.

Peter Reid and Kevin Sheedy hadn't recovered from the knocks they had received on Saturday so Alan Harper took on the number six shirt with Paul Power replacing Sheedy and Neil Pointon filling the left-back position.

Newcastle had been bottom of the table at the beginning of March but they had been in great form since and coming into this game were clear of the relegation zone. Roared on by a sizeable number of Geordies in the big holiday crowd, the Magpies frustrated the home side in the first-half.

But just after the interval, Wayne Clark made the breakthrough, nodding in a cross from Paul Power. He slotted home his second eight minutes from time and, after good work from Power again, he headed home for his hat-trick near the end.

When news came through that Liverpool had lost at Old Trafford, it meant the Blues were now six points clear of the defending champions and could reclaim the title at Anfield on Saturday.

If You Know Your History

A run of eight defeats in nine games either side of the 2022 World Cup, including two dreadful displays at Bournemouth within the space of three days, saw Frank Lampard's tenure at Goodison Park curtailed and, in January 2023, Sean Dyche was appointed manager.

In his first game, Everton shocked Premier League leaders Arsenal but a 4-1 home defeat by Newcastle United at the end of April dropped the Blues into the relegation places. A sensational 5-1 win at high-flying Brighton lifted the gloom but going into the last match Everton were still one of three teams who could drop down to the Championship. Abdoulaye Doucouré smashed home the only goal of the game to keep Everton up but it was all too close for comfort.

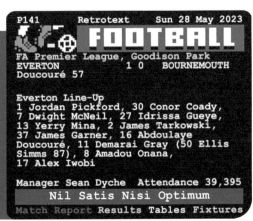

```
P141      Retrotext      Sun 28 May 2023
      FOOTBALL
FA Premier League, Goodison Park
EVERTON          1  0    BOURNEMOUTH
Doucouré 57

Everton Line-Up
1 Jordan Pickford, 30 Conor Coady,
7 Dwight McNeil, 27 Idrissa Gueye,
13 Yerry Mina, 2 James Tarkowski,
37 James Garner, 16 Abdoulaye
Doucouré, 11 Demarai Gray (50 Ellis
Simms 87), 8 Amadou Onana,
17 Alex Iwobi

Manager Sean Dyche  Attendance 39,395
        Nil Satis Nisi Optimum
Match Report Results Tables Fixtures
```

April 1987

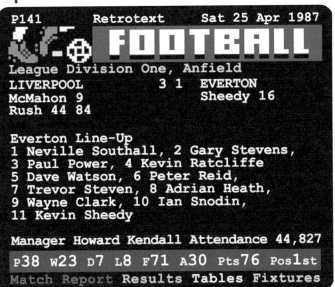

```
P141        Retrotext      Sat 25 Apr 1987
        FOOTBALL
League Division One, Anfield
LIVERPOOL          3  1  EVERTON
McMahon 9                 Sheedy 16
Rush 44 84

Everton Line-Up
1 Neville Southall, 2 Gary Stevens,
3 Paul Power, 4 Kevin Ratcliffe
5 Dave Watson, 6 Peter Reid,
7 Trevor Steven, 8 Adrian Heath,
9 Wayne Clark, 10 Ian Snodin,
11 Kevin Sheedy

Manager Howard Kendall Attendance 44,827

P38 W23 D7 L8 F71 A30 Pts76 Pos1st
Match Report Results Tables Fixtures
```

```
P300 CJEFAX 1 300 Sat 25 Dec 19:14/26
BBC CEEFAX
Football
KENWRIGHT CLINCHES EVERTON TAKEOVER 308

Football
ROBSON SET FOR NEW MAGPIES CONTRACT 309

   CRICKET LATEST      -------------------
Michael Vaughan and Alan Mullally rulid
out of third Test through injury     341
--------------------------------------------
ALL THE LATEST SPORT HEADLINES: SEE 301
Football   302 Golf/Tenn 330 Crickjt 340
M/Sport    360 Lettetu    356 Genjtal 380
BBC Sport  358 Comps 357/359 REGIONS 390

 Niws     101 Wjathet 400 TV/Radio   600
 Travel   430 Lottety 555 A-Z index  199
Headlinjs  Football Reg Sport Main Minu
```

Ahead of the Liverpool clash, Bobby Robson announced his England squad for a European Championship match in Turkey and it included four Everton players; Gary Stevens, Dave Watson, Trevor Steven and, for the first time since the World Cup, Peter Reid.

Both Reid and Kevin Sheedy recovered from the slight injuries received in the Aston Villa game to start against Liverpool, with Paul Power replacing Neil Pointon at left-back.

Everton old boy Steve McMahon gave the home side an early lead but Kevin Sheedy smashed in a free kick at the Kop end to level things up. Right on half-time, Ian Rush restored Liverpool's advantage and though the Blues had chances to equalise, the final goal was again scored by the Welshman.

Rush's double took him level with Dixie Dean as the all-time leading scorers in derby matches and he had netted nine times in six meetings between the two sides this season alone.

So, with Liverpool now only three points adrift of the Blues, the title race entered May, with Everton entertaining Manchester City and Liverpool travelling to Coventry, who would surely have one eye on their impending FA Cup Final clash with Tottenham.

This is an original Ceefax page recovered from an old VHS recording. The corruption is caused by the retrieval process.

On Christmas Day 1999, this was the headline confirming that Bill Kenwright had purchased Peter Johnson's majority shareholding in Everton to end months of uncertainty during a long, drawn-out takeover saga.

Writing in the Liverpool Echo as the twentieth century drew to a close, Charles Lambert, 'The Man On The Inside For Sport' commented on Kenwright's purchase:

"He has taken on a tough job and mere passion won't be enough. Many astute men have come unstuck when they've taken on a football club. It's a time for hard work, high ambition, wise investment, clear communication and a good helping of fortune.

May the new Millennium bring Bill and the Blues all of the above - and success will surely follow."

It's A Grand Old Team To Play For

Having started his career at Rennes, Everton manager Carlo Ancelotti signed Abdoulaye Doucouré from Watford in September 2020 for a fee around £20 million. He was one of a number of arrivals at that time, with Director of Football Marcel Brands also bringing in Brazil's Allan and Colombia's James Rodriguez.

After falling out with boss Frank Lampard, it appeared Doucouré may be forced out of the club, but the appointment of Sean Dyche in January 2023 was a turning point in his time at Everton and he became a key player in the battle against relegation. He was on target twice in the brilliant 5-1 win at Brighton before scoring his most important goal, a superb 20-yard volley on the last day of the 2022-23 season against Bournemouth which secured Premier League survival for the Blues.

May 1987

```
P141      Retrotext      Sat 02 May 1987
       FOOTBALL
League Division One, Goodison Park
EVERTON           0 0   MANCHESTER CITY


Everton Line-Up
1 Neville Southall, 2 Gary Stevens,
3 Pat Van Den Hauwe, 4 Kevin Ratcliffe
5 Dave Watson, 6 Peter Reid
(Alan Harper), 7 Trevor Steven,
8 Adrian Heath, 9 Wayne Clark,
10 Ian Snodin, 11 Paul Power

Manager Howard Kendall Attendance 37,548
P39 W23 D8 L8 F71 A30 Pts77 Pos1st
Match Report Results Tables Fixtures
```

```
P141      Retrotext      Mon 04 May 1987
       FOOTBALL
League Division One, Carrow Road
NORWICH CITY      0 1   EVERTON
                       Van Den Hauwe 1

Everton Line-Up
1 Neville Southall, 2 Gary Stevens,
3 Pat Van Den Hauwe, 4 Kevin Ratcliffe
5 Dave Watson, 6 Peter Reid,
7 Trevor Steven, 8 Adrian Heath,
9 Graeme Sharp, 10 Ian Snodin,
11 Paul Power

Manager Howard Kendall Attendance 22,278
P40 W24 D8 L8 F72 A30 Pts80 Pos1st
Match Report Results Tables Fixtures
```

Everton had good and bad news on the injury front as they approached the May Bank Holiday double bill of matches which would decide the destination of the Division One title.

Pat van den Hauwe was fit enough to return at left-back so Paul Power filled in for Kevin Sheedy whose knee injury picked up against Liverpool looked to have ended his season. Peter Reid had to pull out of the England squad in midweek but had recovered sufficiently to start.

Graeme Sharp had successfully come through ninety minutes of a Central League game against Blackburn but with Wayne Clark in such good form, Howard Kendall opted not to rush him back.

Kevin Langley, who had been so impressive for the Blues at the start of the season and had played enough games to qualify for a medal if Everton won the title, was in the Manchester City line-up.

It proved to be a frustrating afternoon for the Goodison faithful, with Peter Reid being forced off after just twenty-five minutes and the Blues struggling to break City down.

But when news of Liverpool's 1-0 defeat at Coventry City came through, it suddenly seemed like a point gained rather than two points lost.

Everton were now four points clear of their fierce rivals who only had two games left to play. A win at Carrow Road on Monday would see the title return to Goodison Park no matter what the result at Anfield where Liverpool hosted Watford.

But Norwich would be no soft touch as under manager Ken Brown they had enjoyed a great season, standing in sixth spot in the table, and a last day win at Highbury would see them finish fifth.

The eight thousand travelling Evertonians enjoyed the perfect start to the match when left-back Pat van den Hauwe smashed a loose ball with his right foot high into the net with less than a minute gone.

After that, there were few chances and the defence stood firm with Dave Watson having a fine game on his return to his old club.

The tension built up as the minutes ticked by until the final whistle blew to confirm the Blues as champions for the second time under Howard Kendall and the ninth time in the club's history.

Unlike in 1984-85 when the line-up featured the same players week-in, week-out, twenty-three players were used by Howard Kendall during this campaign due to injuries, with poor Paul Bracewell not able to take part a single match.

If You Know Your History

After winning four League games on the bounce in December, the last of which was at Turf Moor against Burnley, Everton then went thirteen matches without a win until the same opponents came to Goodison Park in April and the Blues returned to winning ways.

Though that 1-0 victory eased relegation fears, a 6-0 hammering at Chelsea in the next game had Evertonians once again wondering if the last season at Goodison Park would be in the Championship. Three home games in the space of a week would surely decide the club's fate and after a 2-0 win over Nottingham Forest, this superb display against Liverpool was followed by a narrow success over Brentford to confirm Premier League survival with games to spare.

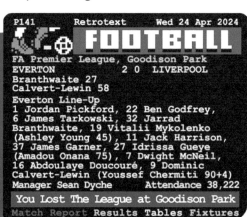

```
P141      Retrotext      Wed 24 Apr 2024
       FOOTBALL
FA Premier League, Goodison Park
EVERTON           2 0   LIVERPOOL
Branthwaite 27
Calvert-Lewin 58
Everton Line-Up
1 Jordan Pickford, 22 Ben Godfrey,
6 James Tarkowski, 32 Jarrad
Branthwaite, 19 Vitalii Mykolenko
(Ashley Young 45), 11 Jack Harrison,
37 James Garner, 27 Idrissa Gueye
(Amadou Onana 75), 7 Dwight McNeil,
16 Abdoulaye Doucouré, 9 Dominic
Calvert-Lewin (Youssef Chermiti 90+4)
Manager Sean Dyche      Attendance 38,222
You Lost The League at Goodison Park
Match Report Results Tables Fixtures
```

May 1987

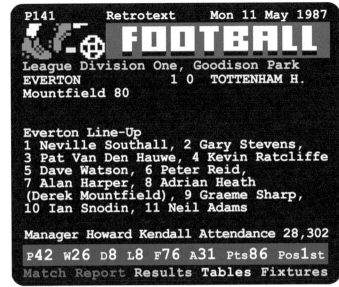

When Canon began sponsoring the Football League at the start of the 1983-84 season, they commissioned their own trophy to be presented to the champions instead of the traditional trophy which had first been used in 1891, when Everton won the title.

The Today newspaper were the new sponsors in 1986-87 and they too commissioned their own trophy but when it was revealed there was a backlash against it, with some commenting it looked like a large paperweight.

A compromise was reached and it was agreed that Everton would be presented with both trophies.

Three players had been involved in every game of this title-winning campaign, Kevin Ratcliffe, Trevor Steven and Paul Power, but the veteran Power was missing on this day after a knee operation was brought forward with the title having been secured.

The Blues were one down at the interval but turned it around in the second period through two penalties despatched by Trevor Steven and a Graeme Sharp strike.

The celebrations began at full-time with England boss Bobby Robson presenting the Today trophy and Football League president and Everton chairman, Philip Carter, presenting the original.

In this final match of the season, visitors Tottenham fielded a weakened team ahead of their FA Cup Final appearance against Coventry City at the weekend. With the Spurs' keeper Tony Parkes in inspired form, Howard Kendall replaced Adrian Heath with Derek Mountfield and the move paid off when the crowd favourite scored the only goal.

Everton were worthy winners of the Division One title, having scored the most goals and conceded the least, amassing nine more points than nearest pursuers, Liverpool.

But, of course, due to the continuing ban on English clubs in UEFA competitions, once again there would be no place for the Blues in the European Cup.

Had the ban not been in place, Everton would have competed in this season's European Cup-Winners' Cup. The Final was played two days after this match between Lokomotiv Leipzig, who won a semi-final penalty shoot-out with Bordeaux, the team Everton beat in a friendly back in February, and Ajax.

Ajax lifted the trophy after winning 1-0, Marco van Basten the scorer, and it was yet another reminder of how much Howard Kendall's team had missed out because of Heysel.

It's A Grand Old Team To Play For

Dominic Calvert-Lewin was signed by Everton manager Ronald Koeman from his home-town club Sheffield United in August 2016 for a transfer fee of £1.5 million.

He scored his first goal for the club in a 4-0 win over Hull City later that season and gradually established himself as the first-choice centre forward, particularly when Carlo Ancelotti was appointed Blues' boss in December 2019, with his goal-scoring form during the 2020-2021 season leading to an England call-up.

He famously scored a superb diving header against Crystal Palace in May 2022 as the Blues came from 2-0 down to win 3-2 and preserve their Premier League status while another towering header in a 2-0 win over Liverpool in April 2024 eased relegation fears once more.

Though Evertonians didn't know it then, this second title win in three seasons marked the end of the most successful period in the club's history.

Ahead of the club's summer tour of Australia and New Zealand, Howard Kendall received his fully deserved second Manager of the Year award and it was expected that upon his return he would sign a new and improved four-year contract.

However, ambitious Spanish side Athletic Bilbao approached Kendall with a lucrative deal which the forty-one-year-old decided to accept. Almost immediately, Colin Harvey was offered the position of Everton manager by chairman Philip Carter.

In Harvey's first match in charge, the Charity Shield at Wembley, Everton beat the FA Cup holders Coventry 1-0 thanks to a Wayne Clark goal. In the 1987-88 season, the Blues reached the semi-finals of the League Cup, losing 4-1 on aggregate to Arsenal, and finished a respectable fourth in the Division One table.

The summer of 1988 saw Gary Stevens moving to Glasgow Rangers for £1.25 million, Derek Mountfield to Aston Villa for £450,000 and Alan Harper to Sheffield Wednesday for £275,000, while Paul Power retired. In November, Adrian Heath went to Espanyol for £600,000 and Peter Reid joined QPR on a free transfer in February 1989.

Replacing them were Tony Cottee, a £2.2 million signing from West Ham, Pat Nevin from Chelsea for £925,000, Stuart McCall from Bradford City for £850,000 and Neil McDonald from Newcastle United for £525,000.

Perhaps not surprisingly given the high turnover of players, the Blues struggled in the League and finished the 1988-89 campaign in eighth spot, though they did reach the FA Cup Final where they lost in agonising fashion to Liverpool again.

Everton finished the 1989-90 season in a solid sixth spot but twenty points behind champions Liverpool. Having gone toe-to-toe with their great rivals in the middle of the decade, at the end of the 1980s the Blues looked to be slipping as far behind the Reds as they were at the start.

After a largely trouble-free Italia 90, English clubs were finally re-admitted to UEFA competitions, with the exception of Liverpool who had to serve an additional year so missed out on European Cup participation.

In Division One, the 1990-91 campaign had begun poorly for Everton, with only one win from the first ten games leaving them third from bottom of the table. At the end of October, Colin Harvey was sacked and Howard Kendall returned to Goodison Park.

But Everton's time as a dominant force in English football was over and it has not been regained since.

If You Know Your History

For Evertonians, season 2023-2024 will probably be remembered as the most tempestuous in the club's history. Sadly, fans had become accustomed to the stress of relegation fights, but the added off-the-field issues of points deductions and ownership uncertainty fuelled the levels of anxiety.

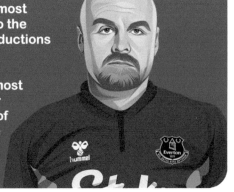

Against this scenario, Sean Dyche, his backroom staff, the players and, most importantly, the supporters, stuck together and withstood all the Premier League could throw at them, ending the campaign fourteen points clear of the relegation places even with an eight point penalty. Those efforts have ensured that the final season at Goodison Park, which coincides with the 40th anniversary of the greatest one in Everton's history, will be played out, fittingly, in the top flight of English football.

ACKNOWLEDGEMENTS

To assist my increasingly hazy recollections of the glorious 1980s era, compiling this book has involved watching various YouTube videos and reading through dozens and dozens of Everton programmes from that time plus numerous newspaper articles. These are available online at https://www.britishnewspaperarchive.co.uk/

The match data for the Retrotext pages has been mainly sourced from the English National Football Archive (ENFA) database and cross-checked with print and digital sources where possible. When there have been some discrepancies, e.g. goal times and attendances, I have generally used the ENFA statistics at https://enfa.co.uk/

The original teletext pages featured on various pages have been recovered from television programmes recorded on videotape as the teletext code, although not visible when watching a recording, was embedded on the tape. Find out more about the project to recover these pages at https://teletextarchaeologist.org/

The teletext pages, information and graphics are copyright of the respective broadcasters. The recovered data is courtesy of the respective recoverers. The rendered graphics are copyright of Jason Robertson and the The Teletext Archive.

Peter Reid's book *Everton Winter, Mexican Summer* (published by Queen Anne Press) provided a fascinating insight into the Blues' ultimately frustrating 1985-86 season which started with him being out of action for four months and ended with a World Cup quarter-final defeat against Diego Maradona's Argentina.

Special thanks to Didik Iskandar for creating the illustrations of the legendary players and managers, as well as my daughters - Hannah, Olivia and Eve - for their proof-reading; if you spot any errors now, it's down to them!